Asia and Europe in Globalization

Social Sciences in Asia

Edited by

Vineeta Sinha

Associate Editor

Syed Farid Alatas

Advisory Board

CHAN KWOK-BUN

VOLUME 8

Asia and Europe in Globalization

Continents, Regions and Nations

Edited by

Göran Therborn
Habibul Haque Khondker

BRILL
LEIDEN · BOSTON
2006

This book is printed on acid-free paper.

Library of Congress Cataloging-in-Publication Data

Asia and Europe in globalization: continents, regions, and nations / edited by Göran Therborn and Habibul Haque Khondker.
    p. cm. — (Social sciences in Asia ISSN 1567-2794 ; v. 8)
  Includes bibliographical references and indexes.
  ISBN-13: 978-90-04-15350-9
  ISBN-10: 90-04-15350-0 (pbk. : alk. paper)
  1. Globalization—Asia. 2. Globalization—Europe. 3. Asia—Social conditions—21st century. 4. Asia—Economic conditions—21st century. 5. Asia—Social policy. 6. Asia—Economic policy. 7. East and West. I. Therborn, Göran, 1941-II. Khondker, Habibul Haque.

HN652.5.A75   2006
303.48'250-409—dc22

2006047582

ISSN 1567-2794
ISBN-13: 978 90 04 15350 9
ISBN-10: 90 04 15350 0

PRINTED IN THE NETHERLANDS

CONTENTS

Religions and Other World Values

Continents and Regions of the World

NOTES ON AUTHORS

Chang Kyung-Sup, a professor of sociology at Seoul National University, is currently working on "developmental liberalism" in South Korea and "ruralism" in China. His work on East Asian development and social change has appeared in *World Development, Journal of Development Studies, Economy and Society, Rationality and Society*, among others.

Arif Dirlik is Knight Professor of History and Anthropology at the University of Oregon (retired), and a Visiting Professor at the China Center for Comparative Politics and Economics. His latest publications are *Marxism in the Chinese Revolution* (Rowman & Littlefield, 2005), *Global Modernity: Modernity in the Age of Global Capitalism* (Paradigm Press, 2006), and an edited volume, *Pedagogies of the Global* (Paradigm Press, 2006).

Ronald Findlay is Ragnar Nurkse Professor of Economics at Columbia University. His recent publications include among others *Eli Heckscher, International Trade, and Economic History* (edited with Rolf G.H. Henriksson, Håkan Lindgren and Mats Lundahl) (2006) and *Factor Proportions, Trade, and Growth* (2005).

Elisabeth Gerle is an ordained Lutheran clergywoman and Principal of the Pastoral Institute of the Swedish Church. She has a doctorate in Ethics from Princeton and is a researcher at the Raoul Wallenberg Institute of Human Rights and Humanitarian Law at Lund University, Sweden.

Jan Hjärpe is Professor of Islamology at the University of Lund, Sweden, and has worked for the Swedish Foreign Office. He is a Fellow of the Swedish Academy of Humanities and of Academia Europea.

Habibul Haque Khondker is a Professor in the Department of Social and Behavioral Sciences at Zayed University, Abu Dhabi, UAE. Previously, he taught at the National University of Singapore. His research interests and publications are on globalization theories, democracy, famine, science and gender issues.

Kim Kyong-Dong, Professor Emeritus of Seoul National University and Member of the National Academy of Sciences, Korea, is currently Visiting Professor at the KDI School of Public Policy and Management. He obtained his BA from Seoul National University, MA from the University of Michigan, and PhD from Cornell, all in sociology. He taught at NC State University at Raleigh, Duke University, and l'Ecole des Hautes Etudes en Sciences Sociales in Paris, and was a Fellow of the Woodrow Wilson International Center for Scholars in Washington, DC. He served as President of Korean Sociological Association and is Board Chair of the Korean Association for Information Society. He has published internationally in the fields of modernization, development, industrial relations, and was awarded major cultural prizes for scholarly achievements.

Le Thi Quy is the Director of the Research Center for Gender and Development and Professor at the Hanoi University of Social Science and Development. Thi Quy is involved in the Advisory Task Force of the Asian Pacific Forum of Women, Law and Development in Chiangmai, Thailand. Among the many tasks she administers in her advocacy for women's rights and gender equality are conducting research on gender issues, facilitating gender sensitivity training and discussion in universities and offices in major cities in Vietnam and contributing to local magazines.

Lee On-Jook is Professor of Sociology in the College of Education, Seoul National University. She holds a BA and MA in sociology, an MA in Human Development and Family Studies from Cornell University, and PhD in sociology from Duke University. She was a Visiting Professor at John Hopkins University and Free University of Berlin, Germany. She also served in the Policy Advisory Committee of the Ministry of Unification and Presidential Council for Democratic and Peaceful Unification. She has published in the fields of North Korean society, women, family, and migration.

Mats Lundahl is Professor of Development Economics at the Stockholm School of Economics. He has worked extensively on development problems in Latin America, Africa and Asia. Among his publications are *Peasants and Poverty: A Study of Haiti* (1979), *Unequal Treatment: A Study in the Neo-Classical Theory of Discrimination* (1984), *Politics or Markets? Essays on Haitian Underdevelopment* (1992), *Peasants and Religion: A Socioeconomic Study of Dios Olivorio and the Palma Sola Movement in the Dominican Republic* (2000), and *Knut Wicksell on Poverty: 'No Place Is Too Exalted for the Preaching of These Doctrines'* (2005). Lundahl has visited Mongolia on three occasions, mainly as a consultant for the Swedish International Development Cooperation Agency (Sida).

Kjell Å Modéer, Professor of Legal History and Holder of the Torsten and Ragnar Söderberg Foundations' Professorship in Memory of Samuel Pufendorf at the Faculty of Law, Lund University, Sweden. His main research interests and publications are in the fields of comparative legal cultures, European legal history and law and religion.

Goran Therborn is Director of the Swedish Collegium for Advanced Study in the Social Sciences, and Professor of Sociology at Cambridge University. In 2006 he was elected to the Chair of Sociology at Cambridge University. He is the author of *European Modernity and Beyond: The Trajectory of European Societies 1945–2000* (London, Sage, 1995), and *Globalizations and Modernities: Experiences and Perspectives of Europe and Latin America* (Stockholm, FRN, 1999). His latest books are *Between Sex and Power: Family in the World, 1900–2000* (Routledge, 2004) and *Inequalities of the World* (Verso, 2006).

Wang Gungwu is the Director of East Asia Institute, National University of Singapore. He was formerly Professor of Far Eastern History at Australian National University and Director of its Research School of Pacific Studies. He was Vice-Chancellor of the University of Hong Kong, 1986–1995. Among his books are *The Nanhai Trade: The Early History of Chinese Trade in the South China Sea* (1958 and 1998); *The Structure of Power in North China during the Five Dynasties* (1963); *China and the World since 1949* (1977); *Community and Nation* (1981 and 1993); *Dongnanya yu Huaren* [Southeast Asia and the Chinese] (1987); *The Chineseness of China* (1991); *The Chinese Way: China's Position in International Relations* (1995). He also edited *Changing Identities of Southeast Asian Chinese since World War II* (with Jennifer Cushman) (1988); *Global History and Migrations* (1997); *Xianggang shi xinbian* [Hong Kong History: New Perspectives] (1997); *China's Political Economy* (with John Wong) (1998) and *The Chinese Diaspora* (1998) (with Wang Ling-chin). His recent publications include, *Anglo-Chinese Encounters since 1880: War, Trade, Science and Governance.* (Cambridge, 2002); *The Iraq War and its Consequences* (edited with Irwin Abrams) (World Scientific, 2003); and *Nation-Building: Five Southeast Asian Histories* (edited) (ISEAS, 2005).

Yu Keping is Professor and Director of the China Center for Comparative Politics and Economics (CCCPE), and also Professor and Director, Center for Chinese Government Innovations, Beijing University. His major fields include Political Philosophy, Comparative Politics, Globalization, Civil Society, Governance and Politics in China. Among his many books are *Democracy and Top* (2006); *Chinese Rural Governance in the Past and Nowadays* (2004); *Globalization and Sovereignty* (2004); *Politics and Political Science* (2003); *Incremental Democracy and Good Governance in China* (2003); *Globalization and China's Political Development* (2003); *The Emerging of Civil Society and Its Significance to Governance* (and others, 2002); *Politics of Public Good or Politics of Rights* (1999); *China's Political System Nowadays* (1998).

SURFACE TENSIONS AND DEEP STRUCTURES

Wang Gungwu

In large parts of Asia, people still remember the times when they were dominated by Europe and often think in terms of the restoration or renewal of their ancient cultures. Some scholars believe that Asia's great traditions need conserving so that the world would not lose that rich heritage. But the challenge of globalization has provided a new framework for the future. In this context, we need to distinguish between the phenomenon of surface tensions and that of deep structures, with networks of economic and political relationships resting on top of structures of history and culture.

This is related to the debate about old and new globalization that has been brought forward by the work of Immanuel Wallerstein and Andre Gunder Frank and those who argue for global history.[1] The old focuses on borderless ages when humans roamed the earth or traded and conquered across vast distances. The new, however, draws its inspiration from post-modern, post-nation-state ideas of borderless communications that emphasize the tensions that affect all efforts to develop global outlooks. These are anxiety-causing tensions that threaten peace, but they are largely on the surface. In comparison, the relationships in the old globalization were dominated by civilizational differences where confrontations were often accompanied by considerable mutual respect.

Asia and Europe in globalization reminds us of shared experiences, but it also brings out such a distinction more sharply. A tentative globalization had begun at the latest during the 16th century

---

[1] Wallerstein, Immanuel, *The Modern World-system*. 3 volumes. New York: Academic Press, 1974–1989; Andre Gunder Frank, *ReOrient: Global Economy in the Asian Age*, Berkeley: University of California Press, 1998; Wang Gungwu, "Migration and Its Enemies", in *Conceptualizing Global History*, edited by Bruce Mazlish and Ralph Buultjens, Boulder, CO.: Westview Press, 1993, pp. 131–51. Wang Gungwu (ed.) *Global History and Migrations*, Boulder, CO.: Westview Press, 1997.

when the Portuguese arrived in Japan followed by the Spanish settlement in the Philippines. Two names used by them that have survived are Formosa and the Philippines, and they are symbolic of
that Iberian circling of the globe that reached two areas that did
not have historic polities in place. This was a beginning that involved
peripheral peoples from the Atlantic coasts of Western Europe and
the edge of East and Southeast Asia. Other Europeans then followed
the Iberians into the heart of Asia. These Europeans built their own
trading structures on top of the structured networks that they found
in Asia, and they organized new power relationships in their own
way to suit their own interests. In this way, economic, cultural and
normative factors were integrated in new networks of local and alien
rulers and their respective merchant partners.

During the first 300 years till the end of the 18th century, this
global outreach stretched to the ends of the earth, further than ever
in human history. All dimensions in the new relationships were deepened at the same time, with the growth of mutual respect for one
another's traditions. For example, Jesuit records on China show how
there had been a meeting of minds, and various philosophers in
Europe, notably the Physiocrats, proposed their own reading of what
their global counterparts in Asia had to offer. Their equivalents
around Asia were impressed by European weaponry, but were more
dismissive of their trading products and commercial ideas. This was
their loss and they had to pay heavily for that later on.

The truly new factor in that early globalization was the way the
missionary zeal of the Europeans deepened the cultural and normative dimensions of their contacts. It was no accident that their
adventurous reaching out was further emboldened by the post-
Reformation imagining of a personal God concerned for their wealth
and well-being on earth. This message was eventually diluted if not
superseded by secular values of nation-state structures, on the one
hand, and scientific technology on the other. But the spirit underlying their missions remained within the deep structure of a globalizing process that was evolving through the centuries. It did not
challenge the matching deep structures that were still being vigor-
ously upheld among the various Asian elites.

In short, the globalization of deep structures came in stages. These
were, firstly, a trade globalization, with the European scarch for
Christians giving way to the greed for gold, spurred by viable local
commercial structures. This was led mainly by the Portuguese, Spanish,

Dutch and English merchant companies interacting with Asian traders. Then an imperial globalization followed, mainly inspired by the British, with the greed for gold being partly replaced by a new objective of political domination. Finally, there came the global anti-imperialist reaction that replaced empires with nation-states. This was encouraged by the United States and the Soviet Union during the years of the Cold War. The two contending superpowers offered their relatively shallow global outlooks that were distinguished by ideology and different types of industrialization. These global surface tensions lasted for only about four decades. With the failure of the Soviet Union, the struggle left the world with the American set of surface tensions, and these are now expressed through the rapid delivery of economic pressure and financial services around the globe. Of particular interest here is the knowledge economy that this has spawned and its impact on the globalization of a particular kind of social science.

For example, when social science emerged in Western Europe during the 18th century, it was inspired by natural science on the one hand, and philosophy and history on the other. There was organic change as the new methodologies found their feet in economics, then sociology, and then politics, ethnology and psychology. All kept their links with philosophy and history. This spread of the scientific method, notably in geology and biological sciences, helped to push social science to try to become more like natural science. This modern secular knowledge challenged the wisdom of the East rooted in ancient scriptures and classical texts. The impact was powerful, especially through the wonders of natural science. Doubts still remain about social science, but the practical institutions in government, business and the economy, supported and explained by social science, eventually impressed even the traditionalists.

For East and Southeast Asia, the age of social science arrived in the 20th century at a time when Asia-Europe still had an asymmetrical power relationship. With decolonization, a fresh start might have driven the two regions towards equality and mutual respect. This was not to be. European self-destructiveness in a 30-year period had given all initiatives to the United States and the Soviet Union. The old Europe lost credibility and the two new powers had no deep structures to share with Asia. In this way, a great divide pushed an earlier social science apart. One part sought to be science, while the other knew that society is human and culture-bound.

That this intellectual division occurred at about the same time that decolonization was taking place around the world gave globalization a built-in bias towards the processes that had no deep structures. Instead, it persuaded smaller countries to count on the use of fast-moving science to calculate the world's will and destiny. For example, before the 1950s, key social scientists, especially economists and political thinkers, were found in Europe, and Asian elites learnt the languages necessary to learn new theories and methods. Afterwards, the dominance of English and the power shift to the United States were only feebly challenged by the compulsory study of Russian in captive states.

Forty years later, young East and Southeast Asian social scientists followed the engineers and business school graduates in the United States to accept the supremacy of their particular skills. The trend is obvious in the institutions of higher learning, although the long-term impact of the shift is still unclear. What is clear is that Asia and Europe, estranged partly by Europe's own agonies and partly by Asia's painful experiences of decolonization, are more distant now than they had been. This apartness deprives both sides of the will to return to the deep structures that had once aroused mutual respect. Furthermore, they are now both drawn to the business and technological power of the new centre in the United States, especially because it would seem that the globalization of surface tensions is less demanding and this is what really matters.

This volume of essays provides fresh perspectives on the subject that would help to question some of the easy speculations about the effects of globalization. I congratulate the authors and, in particular, the editors for drawing together these alternative visions of the past and the present. The essays here illuminate many of the complex interactions that have allowed both Asia and Europe to grow and change over the past millennium.

INTRODUCTION

ASIA AND EUROPE IN THE CONTEMPORARY WORLD

The almost everyday use of the word "globalization" has nearly robbed itself of any great theoretical import or empirical value. American sociologist Ritzer's (2004) employment of the phrase "globalization of nothingness" portends the potential emptiness of the concept of globalization. In order to save globalization from hollowing out, becoming all "sound and fury" signifying little or nothing, the multi-dimensional processes of globalization should be situated in concrete historical and spatial locations. It is putatively argued that globalization is simultaneously economic, technological, political, and cultural processes of interconnectivity that tends to "de-territorialize" rendering space somewhat insignificant. Compression of the world notwithstanding, history is shaped, nations, cultures and individuals are made in time and space. These complex processes occur, work themselves out, and mutate at the level of continents, in regions, and nations. Space is not withering; its meaning is changing both as a concept as well as in substance. Space is reinvented as regions re-configure themselves in the intensified flow of world-encompassing relationships that some people call globalization. This books attempts to capture some aspects of this dynamic.

The book may be read in the context of a recent reconnection of Asia and Europe, which has included the governmental Asia Europe Meetings since the mid-1990s, the EU-ASEAN summit in Bangkok, as well as mutual studies of each other, and the various networking initiatives of the Singapore-based Asia-Europe Foundation. Intercontinental exchange and comparisons are developing. Over the post-World War II decades, as the euphoria of political liberation subsided and gave way to a new chapter in history of post-colonial economic transformation, where some of the erstwhile peripheral regions broke into the arena of rapid economic growth, Asia has managed to secure global attention on the world stage. Over the past four decades, though the center of gravity has shifted around, Asia has remained the main site of rapid economic growth and a model for solving problems of underdevelopment. In the 1970s and

1980s, Japan was "the number one", the leading light, followed by East and Southeast Asian "tiger" economies in the 1980s and early 1990s which became models of economic development. China was then already taking off at high speed. However, with the slump and the subsequent "Asian economic crisis" of the late 1990s, the centre of economic growth clearly shifted from Southeast Asia to the giant economies of Asia, China and India. Both these populous countries accounting for about 40 per cent of the world population began to hog headlines on news of sustained high economic growth rate.

China's economy has been growing at a rate of 8 per cent to 10 per cent since capitalist economic reforms were introduced in post-Mao China in 1978. India launched important reforms since 1991 and in the past decade, was growing at a rate of 6 per cent to 7 per cent. The economic ties between these two giants have also grown significantly. Trade between China and India stood at US$13.6 billion in 2004, a marked improvement from US$3 billion in 2000 and it is likely to reach US$20 billion in 2008. During a visit to India by the Chinese Prime Minister Wen Jiaboa in April 2005, the idea of a synergy between Indian software technology and China's hardware manufacturing technology was mooted. That visit marked an important step towards what they termed "strategic partnership for peace and prosperity". These developments are likely to have long-term consequences in the geopolitics of the region and may ultimately shift the balance of the global system. However, it would be more appropriate to use the word "re-emergence" rather than "rise" since in 1820, China and India accounted for 32.4 per cent and 16 per cent of the global economy respectively. The United States' share at that time was a meagre 2 per cent, which changed dramatically by the middle of the 20th century when the US economy dominated the world, and China and India between them accounted for a paltry 9 per cent of world economic activity (Maddison, 1998:40 Table 2.2a). In the middle of the first decade of the 21st century, the two Asian giants' share is about 20 per cent between them, and is likely to grow. The Asian re-emergence has also been spectacular in terms of combating hunger and poverty. By 2005, China has become a donor rather than a recipient of food aid. Sure, inequality has grown as an inevitable companion of high growth, yet 250 million to 400 million people have been lifted out of poverty in China in recent years.

The reawakening of Asia portends not just a saga of economic growth but also a massive social transformation portending a renewal of global connections between Asia and the rest of the world especially Europe and North America. The case of Europe is interesting because here it means a renewal and re-evaluation of historical linkages.

As Asia grows, we see new sets of relationships forging among the major actors. The logic of economic relationships is sometimes overridden by political animus. Some old foes become "strategic partners", as the developments in the relationship between China and India exemplify, while other relationships flag. As we made our entry into the new century, China replaced the United States as Japan's main trading partner. On the other hand, despite the close economic ties between China and Japan—two historical rivals—political tension shows no sign of easing. Japan's position on Taiwan remains murky and the animosities over both Japan's candidacy for permanent membership in the UN Security Council and her history textbooks that tend to gloss over Japanese atrocities in China during World War II created a serious diplomatic row between these two Asian giants in April 2005. China's sharp reactions were viewed as a reflection of her new assertiveness pumped up by a robust economy. History continues to cast a large shadow on Asia's modernity and its future. The present book takes a historical view of things as the contributors wrestle with historical materials to make sense of contemporary realities.

The post-colonial reconnection is part of a broader process of global extension-cum-regionalization, which characterizes the current period, although commentators and social scientists have not kept pace with it. Economically this process takes the form of transnational flows of trade and capital showing increasingly marked regional patterns in Europe, North America, and East Asia particularly, and also in South America and Southern Africa.

Political economics is raising the regional profiles of both Asia and Europe. Dynamic Asia is no longer mainly one country, Japan, but the whole of East Asia, and the South and the North. ASEAN is playing a nodal part in the regionalization of Asia, through its own enlargement to ten countries, through its northern interface in the ASEAN + 3 grouping, with China, Japan, and South Korea, and through several other regional initiatives. India is increasingly "looking east", with an active interest in regional Asian cooperation, underlined at the ASEAN-India summit in November 2002, and in the

Sino-Indian rapprochement. The outward-oriented take-off of the Indian economy, and similar developments in Bangladesh and Pakistan, raise concrete prospects of closer links between the two huge regions of East and South Asia.

The regional profile of Europe has become much more pronounced in recent years. With the end of the Cold War, Europe is coming out of the shadow of "the West", helped by the strident militarism and Christian fundamentalism of current US policy. The "West" was originally a European cultural demarcation against Asia, well expressed by Kipling for instance, but after 1945 it became a synonym for the US and its allies. Through its integration in the European Union, "Europe" is becoming a continental organization and institution— economically successful, politically ambitious, even if servility to the US is still present in many European politicians. In 2004, it went beyond Western Europe to include the east-central part of the region. Like ASEAN, the EU is a very attractive, much solicited club and partner, eagerly courted by Turkey, for example, which at least in terms of physical geography is overwhelmingly a West Asian country.

The mounting intellectual interest in civilizations and in cultures of globalization is also likely to bring the regionality of globalization into focus. Civilizations usually, if not always, have a large territorial base, more extensive than that of a nation-state, although here again Europe may be drowned in a "Western civilization", a notion particularly peculiar to American scholars. Although cultures are being globalized, in production as well as in consumption, they also operate through important regional (and sub-regional) codes, as any MTV manager could tell you. The post-modernist critique of modernist universalism, as well as the anti-colonialist critique of "modernization", is also having their impact on the social sciences, in the form of an increasing sensitivity to "Eurocentrism", "West-centrism", and other provincial biases, a sensitivity and self-reflexivity which should facilitate both an awareness of and an interest in cultural variation. True, post-modernism has so far mainly promoted "local knowledge", but in critical social science we perceive a new interest, more reflexive than before, in the importance of regional social experiences, be they Asian, European, African, or Latin American.

A common Asian-European look at the world will bring out the enduring importance of nations and nation-states in the contemporary world. Northeast and Southeast Asia provide the most eminent and successful examples in modern history of National Development

States. As such they had to be original, creative, and stepping outside of conventional modes of thought and practices. They have done so in ways varying from being innovative through novel combinations of state initiatives and private enterprise, of outward orientations and maintenance of national autonomy and integrity. In South and West Asia the contemporary state has been much less successful, but it remains the central social institution nevertheless.

The welfare state is the distinctive European contribution to world political economy, also an institution inconceivable, or at least hardly viable, in conventional traditions of thought, whether in liberal economics or in Marxist politics. The institution combines generous social security and high taxation—between a third and a half of GDP—with high employment and highly competitive private enterprise. Actually, the most generous welfare states are in small countries most dependent on trade in the world market, such as Scandinavia, Belgium, and the Netherlands. In spite of repeated cries of crisis, and in spite of repeated neoliberal attacks, the European welfare states are still intact. The Asian National Development States survived despite the blows they received in the financial crisis of 1997–1998.

From their varying perspectives, Asian and European experiences of globalization demonstrate the enduring importance of nation-states. The most successful East Asian and Western European experiences underline the compatibility, indeed the mutual support of an open competitive economy and a strong state. However, strength and success in today's world are not permanent features. Both the Asian and the European types of recently successful nation-states are now facing new challenges, of new parameters of competition, of ageing demography, and of integrating renewed tendencies of social polarization.

This book comes out of a conference on "Asia, Europe, and Global Processes: Economic, Cultural, and Normative Dimensions" in Singapore in March 2001, but it does not purport to report that conference, and the papers have been written for this volume. The conference was the launching pad for this book. It was organized by the Committee on Global Processes of the Swedish Board for Planning and Coordination of Research (one of the Swedish public research councils, FRN) and by the Departments of Geography and Sociology at the National University of Singapore. The conference was part of a series of regional ones initiated by the inter-university and inter-disciplinary Swedish Committee, outside Europe held in

Istanbul, Beijing, Buenos Aires, and Cape Town. A South Asian conference was planned, but could not be realized because of a reorganization of the whole system of research councils in Sweden.

In organizing the conference in Singapore we had the enthusiastic and efficient collaboration of Kris Olds (now at Madison) and Henry Wai-Chung Yeung of the Geography Department of NUS. We, the current editors, keep their cooperation in grateful memory. The conference comprised a wider set of topics than the book, but many of the contributions could not, for various reasons, be incorporated into this work. However, all of us who participated in the conference learnt a lot from, and remember the most stimulating and informative contributions made by Zainah Anwar from Sisters-in-Islam (of Malaysia), Cynthia Bautista of the University of the Philippines, Daniel Bell of the City University of Hong Kong, Suvajee Chanthanon-Good of Mahidol University (Thailand), Allen Chun of the Academia Sinica (Taiwan), Kenichi Kawasaki of Komazawa University (Japan), James Mittelman of the American University, V.V. Bhanoji Rao (then at National University of Singapore), Kerstin Sahlin-Andersson of Uppsala University (Sweden), Mohd Hazim Shah of the University of Malaya, and Wilfrido V. Villacorta of the University of Philippines. Thank you all.

This book, like the other publications of the Global Processes Committee, starts from two basic assumptions. First, the buzzword "globalization" had to be deconstructed into a set of different, multidimensional processes, requiring multi- and inter-disciplinary research. Given the overwhelming economic emphasis of the globalization literature, we have found it fruitful to put a particular emphasis on cultural and institutional processes of various kinds.

Second, a proper understanding of global processes requires regional, national, and local knowledge. This was the rationale of the above-mentioned conferences, which is the rationale of the weightage given in this volume to comparing national orientations and experiences of globalization. The contributors have come together on the basis of related research perspectives and expertise, but not as a work team with a division of labour. Each contributor has chosen his/her topic and approach to it.

The contents may be grouped under four sub-themes, all dealing with different aspects of Asian and European orientations to practices and experiences of global processes.

Empires and their Legacy

Empire-building is an old global process, striving at conquering and ruling the whole known world. It is also an ambition on the part of certain nations in our own time. The Mongol empire of the 13th century was the largest continuous empire in world history, encompassing most of the Eurasian continent from Korea to Hungary. It was the most important political bridge between Asia and Europe. Ronald Findlay and Mats Lundahl, two historically interested economists (American and Swedish, respectively), present an economic theory of the rise of this Mongol empire, as well as a historical narrative. One of the enduring legacies of empires and of colonial rule has been a complex legal structure in the ex-colonies, with imported statutory law, domestic religious law, and local "customary" law. The Swedish legal historian Kjell-Åke Modéer highlights the importance of coloniality for a proper understanding of comparative law. "Coloniality" is an enduring effect of colonial domination, and as a key concept for grasping modern world history, has been developed by the Peruvian scholar Aníbal Quijano, and presented at the above-mentioned Buenos Aires conference.

Asian Nations and Globalization

Global processes are not flying over nations and nation-states. The former run through the latter, and what is moulding or affecting what, the former or the latter, cannot be determined *a priori*. It has to be studied empirically. Nations and national identities do not only look different, they are also formed in different ways. Nations and nation-states relate differently to, and have very different experiences of global processes. They form crucial vantage-points from which to look at world processes. National identities in modern transnational history, national conceptions of, and national strategies towards the world and to globalization should not be put on the shelf with "nationalism" or "national policies". They are central to an understanding of global processes.

Bangladeshi-Singaporean sociologist Habibul Haque Khondker analyses the changing roles over time of the national (Bengali), the religious (Muslim), and the global in the construction and reconstruction of national identity in Bangladesh. The Korean sociologists,

Kim Kyong-Dong and Lee On-Jook, present a comparative study of how North and South Korea have dealt differently with modernization and globalization in a dialectical interplay of international acculturation and adaptive change of indigenization. Because so little is known about it, they pay particular attention to North Korea and the interaction between external influence and the Korean culture in the shaping of that peculiar regime. The second Korean paper, by Chang Kyung-Sup, also a sociologist, looks more closely at the mutations of South Korean socio-economic policies under the trajectory of globalization.

Our two Chinese papers deal with different Chinese perspectives on the relations between Chinese national development and globalization. Yu Keping, of the China Center for Comparative Politics and Economics, treats the main variants of interpretations and conclusions in the lively 1990s debate. The Turkish-American sinologist, Arif Dirlik, who as Yu Keping points out, played a significant part in that debate, contrasts the Maoist and the post-Maoist views on Chinese national development in the world.

One important transnational flow, in current Europe as well as in Asia, is the traffic in women. Le Thi Quy from the Vietnamese Research Center for Gender and Development, adds the important dimension of sexual domination and exploitation to national and global relations.

Religions and Other World Values

The transethnic, transpolity diffusion of religions, the establishment of what is now called "the world religions", was arguably the first wave of globalization, an "axial age" (Karl Jaspers) of human civilization. In terms of diffusion, its heyday were the 4th to 8th centuries Christian era, beginning with the Christianization of the Roman Empire, and ending with the Muslim conquest of West Asia and North Africa, which was interrupted by Indian Buddhism reaching China and Japan during that period. In the new, increasingly hot war, between Islamic fundamentalism worldwide, Jewish fundamentalism in Israel/Palestine, and Christian fundamentalism in the US, religion has re-emerged as an essentialist, totalitarian, and irreconcilably conflictual phenomenon.

While religious fundamentalism is a formidable reality, it is only part of it, and studies of religion had better stay clear of unchanging essentialism and determinism. The Swedish Islamologist and polyhistorian Jan Hjärpe is arguing for a cool anthropology of religions, free of theological heat, and illustrates his argument with recent theses of anthropological Islamology.

Human rights have become a central part of global discourse in the last two decades, although the latter goes back at least to the 1948 UN Declaration of Human Rights, which managed to get through both the gathering clouds of the Cold War and the gun smoke of the first Palestinian war. Virtually universal violations apart, human rights have become principally controversial with some "Asian values" talk in Singapore and Malaysia in particular, and with invocations of Islam and of Shari´a law in Muslim nations. Elisabeth Gerle is an ordained Lutheran clergywoman (in Sweden), but also an active scholar of human rights. She presents a set of experiences from Asian-European discussions of human rights.

Continents and Regions

To what extent are "Asia" and "Europe" comparable entities in any socially meaningful sense? What is their respective location in the world? Swedish sociologist Göran Therborn answers these questions. First, by arguing that while there might be one Europe, there are at least three, for some purposes at least four, Asias. Second, he distinguishes locations in two different world systems, in the well-known system of political economy, and in the so far little conceptualized and little empirically systematized world cultural system. Therborn sets out the "cornerstones" of the latter, and indicates the position of Europe and the Asias in the world cultural system as well as in the global political economy.

The relationship between Europe and Asia has, so to speak, come full circle starting with a long and contentious colonial struggle, which gave way to political nationalism that overlapped with another European (and what was believed for a while, a universal) ideology, namely socialism. Then came in its heels, a phase of the Cold War, where the superpowers of the post-World War II scrambled for domination with profound implications for the life and death, economic prosperity and social stability of teeming millions in Asia. As the Cold War lost its meaning with the collapse of Eastern

European communism, new modes of economic transactions and politico-diplomatic relationships replaced the old alignments.

It is in this context that we need to rethink and renew our understanding of this complex web of relationships with simultaneous regional and global significance. This is the task this book sets itself. The "Asian drama", that so impressed another Swedish scholar of great insightfulness, Gunnar Myrdal nearly four decades ago, is still on. In some sense, under a new script of globalization, the drama is about to gather a new momentum.

Singapore and Uppsala in April 2005
The Editors

References

Maddison, Angus (1998) *Chinese Economic Performance in the Long Run*. Paris: OECD.
Ritzer, George (2004) *The Globalization of Nothing*. Thousand Oaks, California: Pine Forge.

EMPIRES

THE FIRST GLOBALIZATION EPISODE: THE CREATION OF THE MONGOL EMPIRE, OR THE ECONOMICS OF CHINGGIS KHAN*

Ronald Findlay
Columbia University

Mats Lundahl
Stockholm School of Economics

> *Ja, nu skall vi ut och härja,*
> *supa och slåss och svärja,*
> *bränna röda stugor,*
> *slå små barn*
> *och säga fula ord*

(Lundaspexet Djingis Khan, 1954)

When communism fell in the Soviet Union in 1989, the Mongolian economy and society in general received a tremendous shock. All of a sudden Soviet foreign aid disappeared completely and foreign trade virtually collapsed. GDP fell by more than 20 per cent in a mere four years, and in spite of a gradual improvement thereafter, the 1989 level has so far not been reached anew. Mongolia was thrown abruptly into a rapidly globalizing world without being prepared for it. The fall of communism, a system that had been in place for approximately 65 years, forced globalization on Mongolia in a dramatic way, with little to cushion its immediate impact. The country became, as it were, a "victim" of globalization.

The fact that Mongolia was victimized by globalization stands out as a bitter irony of history once we begin to extend the perspective

* Draft versions of the essay were presented at the conference "Asia, Europe, and Global Processes: Economic, Cultural, and Normative Dimensions," at the National University of Singapore, 14–16 March 2001, in two seminars at the National University of Mongolia, Ulaanbaatar, at the Faculty of Social Sciences and the School of Economic Studies, 14 March 2002, and at the First SSAPS Asia-Pacific Annual Conference in Gothenburg, 26–28 September 2002. We are grateful for the constructive comments received on all four occasions, and to Stanley Engerman, for the same reason. The research has been funded by a Sarec grant, which is gratefully acknowledged.

backwards in time. In the present age of information technology, increased international trade and factor mobility, it is easily forgotten that globalization is not a latter-day phenomenon (Findlay and Lundahl, 2000). On the contrary, such a view implicitly views globalization not as a process but as a *state*: an impossible perspective, given the label. The only sensible way of approaching globalization is by taking the term literally, as the story of how the world became global, and then the roots have to be sought considerably further back in time. We will not attempt to provide a clear-cut answer to the question of when and how globalization "began". That would be both out of place and futile. Even the most cursory inspection of the rapidly accumulating literature on this subject indicates that there appears to be about as many answers to the question as there are authors who have posed it.

A definite answer is hardly needed for our present purposes. It is more than sufficient to note that if we go back eight centuries, what was up to that point the strongest wave of or effort at globalization hitherto in history emanated from the Mongols. They were the main agents of the process, i.e. they "pushed" globalization, as it were. Needless to say, from the Mongol point of view, the early globalization episode has virtually nothing in common with the present one. On the contrary, the contrast between the two could not be more evident. They should be viewed as opposite endpoints on a scale. At one extreme we find the Mongols in the 13th century, as the active agents of the process, in virtually complete control of it, and with more or less total power to decide the distribution of the benefits and costs that arose in the course of the episode. At the other end of the scale, in the current situation, we find them as passive recipients, or even victims, as suggested above, with no power whatsoever to influence the course of events and their effects.

The present essay deals exclusively with the first of these globalization episodes. The Mongol conquests are remarkable in at least two ways. The first is of course the sheer size of the undertaking:

> The Mongolian explosion was the first real global event. It deeply affected China, Persia, Russia and eastern Europe. Indirectly, and at one remove, it affected India and Southeast Asia. Negatively, it affected Japan, Egypt and Western Europe, by not conquering them, and giving them their chance, so to speak, in their respective cultural areas. More remotely, it entered the causal network which led to Christian expansion in America, Moslem expansion in Africa and Southeast Asia. (Adshead, 1993:5)

The Mongol empire is the largest continuous empire that the world has ever seen up to the present day. At the time of its peak, after Khubilai Khan's final conquest of southern China, in 1279, it extended from the coasts of southern Siberia, Manchuria, Korea and China down to Amman in the east all the way into Hungary, Poland and Belarus in the west, and from the northern borders of Indochina, Burma and India, the shores of the Persian Gulf, the southern border of Iraq across Syria and the southern coast of Turkey in the south up to a latitude of approximately 60° N in Russia and Siberia (Bat-Ochir Bold, 2001:xi).

The second remarkable quality of the Mongol conquests is their unlikelihood. In the 12th century the Mongols "were not a linguistic or an ethnological group but simply the dominant tribe of one of the tribal confederations that inhabited the Mongolian steppes" (Fletcher, 1986:13). The Mongols gave their name to the Mongol confederation as well, but neither the tribe nor the confederation is likely to have consisted simply of ethnic or linguistic Mongols. The same applied to the Tatars, the Naimans and the Kereits, the three other main confederations in Mongolia. All of them contained ethnic or linguistic Turks as well. Altogether, the population of the Mongolian steppes is likely to have numbered no more than around a million people or so in the 12th century (Fletcher, 1986:22), and perhaps only half that number (de Hartog, 1989:53), an incredibly small number for a people who just after the turn of the century would embark on a territorial expansion that would not end until the largest continuous empire that the world has yet seen had been created.

In the following we will present a model which combines the main features of the approaches set forth in Findlay and Wilson (1987), McGuire and Olson (1996), Olson (1965) and Findlay (1996) in order to explain why the Mongols could be unified in spite of a tremendous free rider problem, how the unification took place and why they were able to create their continuous empire.

The Unification of the Mongols: The Installation of a "Stationary Bandit"

Before the epic conquest could be launched the Mongols had to be united. This in itself stood out as an almost impossible task. The logical point of departure for an analysis of the unification of the Mongols is the observation by Joseph Fletcher (1986) that their steppe habitat determined not only their mode of production but also the form of their society (cf. also Lattimore, 1951:53–83). The ecology of the Central Asian steppe would in general not sustain sedentary activities, in particular not much agriculture:

> The aridity of the Inner Asian steppe, from which no rivers flow out to the sea, has made extensive agriculture impossible. Lacking adequate water resources, the high uplands of Tibet and the grasslands of Mongolia have had a very sparse population. The 'barbarians' lived in areas roughly twice the size of China, but had perhaps no more than one-fortieth of the population. (Fairbank and Reischauer, 1979:154)

As Owen Lattimore (1951:63) has observed, when Chinese agriculture moved from the Yellow River bend towards the steppe it encountered diminishing returns. Hunting and herding became the two main productive pursuits. Both required a nomadic lifestyle. The harsh climatic conditions of the steppe forced not only the herders but the entire population to migrate periodically in search of grass and water. Migration was imperative for the "livestock of a camping group, most of the animal wealth of a tribe, even most of the herds of an entire confederation, could be lost virtually overnight to disease or starvation" (Fletcher, 1986:13). The survival algorithm (Lipton, 1968) of the Central Asian steppe—the strategy that minimized the risk of ending up below the subsistence level was periodic mobility, usually, but not always, along fixed and proven routes. "The nomad's migration was not an aimless wandering but occurred on a seasonal basis, usually to move his flocks and herds from summer pasture on the open plain to winter pasture in some more sheltered area such as a mountain valley, and back again" (Fairbank and Reischauer, 1979: 155). The hunting pattern, in turn, was determined entirely by the movements of the game animals. All that the hunters could do was to follow them.

The ecology of the Central Asian steppe thus gave rise to a highly mobile population. This population was also dispersed since the meagre vegetation could not sustain large concentrations of people (Lattimore, 1951:54, Fletcher, 1986:13–14). A nomadic population poses worse problems of large-scale organization than a sedentary one. We may think of the starting point as resembling the Hobbesian state of nature (Hobbes, 1985:Ch. 13), where no laws exist. There are no accepted rules safeguarding human lives and no property rights. The individuals can prey on each other without fear of any other retaliation than what may be occasionally forthcoming from the disorganized prey. "In such a society, life was simple, selfish and precarious" (Chambers, 1999:5), and presumably also, "nasty, brutish, and short" (Hobbes, 1985:186).

It is then quite obvious that there were gains to be made by entering into some kind of binding contract which regulated life on the steppe. Before the rise of Chinggis Khan, the Mongol people "longed for unity and for a state of order in which human life and property would be secure", claims Paul Ratchnevsky (1991:14). The various tribes were either at war or in some "state of suspended enmity" with each other (Ratchnevsky, 1991:12). Law and order is a collective benefit for all the parties concerned. Without a strong supra-tribal ruler the road lies open to casual plunder, i.e. the various tribes and tribal groups must count on being raided periodically, by marauders who will presumably take as much as they possibly can, since they cannot be sure of when the next suitable occasion for plunder will present itself.

Should these marauding raids turn out to be a recurrent phenomenon, those raided will eventually find that they have an incentive to install a "stationary bandit" instead (Findlay and Wilson, 1987; McGuire and Olson, 1996; Olson 2000:6–12). This bandit can be invited to "tax" the group regularly, a solution that is likely to be cheaper in the long run than unorganized raids. To see how this works, let us introduce our model.

Let us assume that the maximum production of a nomadic tribe amounts to Y, and that actual production is I. The maximum output is a function of the inputs of labour (L), land (T) and law and order: a public good created by a bureaucracy (G). The maximum production function is taken to be linearly homogeneous, with diminishing returns to all three factors and positive cross derivatives. The bureaucracy has no other use than as an input in private production. It has to be paid for out of tax money. Hence, there is always a risk that incentives will be distorted by taxation so that actual production (I) will fall short of Y. I will hence depend negatively on the proportional tax rate t:

(1) $I \equiv r(t)Y(L, T, G), \qquad r' < 0, r(0) = 1$

The labour force (N), which for the time being is assumed to be given, is divided between labour in production and the bureaucracy:

(2) $L + G = N$

The stationary bandit maximizes his net tax revenue:

(3) $R = tr(t)Y(L, T, G) - (1 - t)wG$

where

(4) $w = r(t)Y^L$

i.e. he obtains all the tax revenue that is left once he has paid his bureaucracy. The gross wage obtained by the bureaucrats is equal to the marginal product of labour used directly in production. Since taxation is strictly proportional, the bureaucrats pay the same share t of their income as everybody else, i.e. the net wage paid by the ruler amounts to $(1 - t)w$.

In order to maximize his net tax revenue, the stationary bandit has to find the optimal tax rate and the optimal size of the bureaucracy, i.e. he has to maximize (3) subject to the labour restriction (2). In the case of tax revenue, the restriction does not bind so taking the derivative of the net revenue with respect to the tax rate gives the first-order condition:

(5) $rY + rY^LG - (1 - t^*)r'Y^LG = -t^*r'Y$

The marginal gain of gross tax revenue from a higher tax rate plus the marginal saving on the wage bill when the net wage falls as the tax rate increases must be equal to the marginal loss of gross tax revenue as the amount of distortion increases when the tax rate increases. Thus, the stationary bandit has an incentive to stop taxation when the increase in tax revenue resulting from a higher tax rate equals the loss resulting from falling production. Since taxation is distorting the share $1- r(t)$ of the maximum production Y is lost (an efficiency or "deadweight" loss) and a share equal to t* of this loss accrues to the bandit himself. Thus, when at the margin the bandit's share of the deadweight loss due to distorting taxation exactly offsets what he gets by increasing the tax rate he will not increase the rate of taxation further. Maximizing his net tax revenue the bandit gets the share t* of the total output value.

We also need the optimal amount of the public good, which may be calculated by taking the derivatives of the net tax revenue with respect to G and L, respectively. This yields:

(6) $t^*rY^L - (1 - t^*)rY^{LL}G = t^*rY^G - (1 - t^*)r(Y^{LG}G + Y^L)$

The bandit should increase the creation of peaceful and orderly conditions until the net marginal contribution of the use of labour directly for production to his tax revenue (including the marginal gain on his wage bill as diminishing returns to direct labour drive down the gross wage rate) equals the marginal contribution by the bureaucracy (net of the marginal cost of increasing the number of bureaucrats due to the higher marginal product of direct labour, and hence higher gross wage rate, as more bureaucrats are added, as well as directly to their higher number). With shorter notation:

(7) NMRPL = NMRPG

where NMRPL denotes the net marginal tax revenue product of labour in direct production and NMRPG the net marginal tax revenue product of the bureaucracy (law and order).

To conclude, so far, the stationary bandit has an incentive to stop taxation before the 100 per cent rate is reached and, in addition, an incentive to provide public goods to the community since both measures increase his tax revenue. This Leviathan is both productive and predatory.

Law and Order in the Steppe

The problem, however, is whether any binding contracts that will lead to the installation of a stationary bandit will ever see the light of day. Law and order is a public good, i.e. all citizens in the community benefit from it and nobody can be excluded. By the same token, however, it may be difficult to find someone who is willing to organize the community and make certain that the necessary contracts are concluded. The installation of the stationary bandit is fraught with the free rider problem. This point becomes easier to appreciate if we apply Mancur Olson's (1962, 1982) logic of collective action to the problem of state foundation. If we continue to represent the degree of law and order in the steppe with G, the number of bureaucrats, the cost in terms of time, effort, money, and so forth that is required to create the bureaucracy may be assumed to be an increasing function of its size:

(8) $C = C(G)$, $C' > 0$, $C'' > 0$

Without effort, there is no order. Turning to the benefit side, the benefit for the group or community as a whole can be thought of as a function of the degree of law and order as well:

(9) $B_c = L_cG$

where lower-case c indicates community and L_c is an indicator of the "size" of the community, e.g. in terms of the total herd of grazing animals it disposes of, animals which are completely crucial for survival in a harsh environment. The bureaucracy G is a collective benefit, i.e. its utility to one individual is not diminished by the fact that it extends to other individuals as well, and no member of the community can be excluded from it. Thus, not the entire benefit accruing to the community accrues to the individual. The value of his share F_i must obviously be lower than the total value to the group:

(10) $B_i = F_iL_cG$

where $F_i < 1$ is assumed to be constant.

Will activities creating law and order be organized at all, and if they are, to what extent? To find the optimum value of G for the group we maximize the difference between community benefits and costs:

(11) $L_c + G(dL_c/dG) = dC/dG$

The marginal benefits in terms of law and order and herd size must balance the marginal cost of the effort. Likewise, for the individual, we find that

(12) $F_i[L_c + G(dL_c/dG)] = dC/dG$

These findings may be put into the simple diagram in *Figure 1*. The community benefit curve B_c rises, but we should not expect it to rise indefinitely. Efforts to install order should be subject to diminishing returns. The cost curve C, on the other hand rises monotonically, since the marginal cost should be increasing. The optimal level of G for the community is G_c^*, where the marginal benefit equals the marginal cost for the group (where the slopes of the two curves coincide, points a and b). The individual benefit curve, in turn, lies below the community curve, since $F_i < 1$. As shown in the diagram, this means that the optimal level of G is smaller for the individual than for the community. The slope of the individual benefit curve equals that of the cost curve at a lower level of G (points d and c).

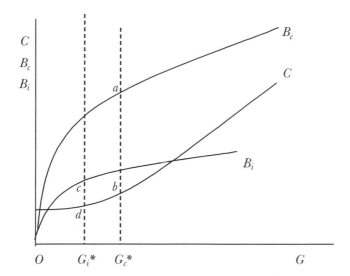

Figure 1: The Problem of Collective Organization

This is Olson's famous finding that a suboptimal quantity of the collective goods will be produced. In a group where individuals differ widely with respect to the intensity of their interest in creating the collective benefit, and all individuals by definition are less interested than the community as a whole in the benefit in question, it will be very difficult to ensure that somebody undertakes the organizing activities. Furthermore (assuming L_c to remain constant), the larger the number of individuals in the community the more severe will the suboptimization be, for this will lower the average F_i, i.e. it will rotate the individual benefit curve downwards and hence lower the optimal G level for the individual.

The problem does not end here, however. We must also ask ourselves whether any efforts whatsoever will be made to secure peaceful conditions on the steppe. This is far from certain. The pastoral economy characteristic of the Central Asian steppes if anything worked in the opposite direction: clan warfare and recurrent disputes over grazing lands and animals (Jackson and Morgan, 1990:8). If the cost curve lies completely above the benefit curve it will never be worthwhile to attempt pacification. This could be the case if the number of individuals in the community is high, so that the individual benefits are low, but the level of costs also plays an important role here. The cost curve in Figure 1 is also drawn on the assumption of a fixed number of individuals. Should this number increase, however, the vertical intercept of the cost curve will shift upwards, and with that the entire curve.

Let us assume that the community contains n individuals who must be made to agree on efforts to create law and order. All these individuals in principle have to agree with n − 1 other individuals not to bother them, i.e. the number of bilateral treaties that must be concluded amounts to

$$(13) \quad K = \sum_{m = 1}^{n - 1} (n - m)$$

and if n increases to n + 1, the number of treaties will increase with n. The intercept of the cost curve shifts upwards. (Possibly the curve at the same time rotates, also upwards, i.e. the marginal cost of increasing the probability of law and order (C) increases and enhances the suboptimization problem even further.) Thus, unless special incentives for organization can be created, what is in everybody's interest may never happen.

Thus, to conclude, if no coordination mechanisms are available, a large community size will militate against the implementation of peaceful conditions both on the benefit and the cost side. It is difficult to think of a better illustration of the free rider problem in economics than the literally free Mongolian mounted archers and herders roaming across the Central Asian steppe—difficult to reach in a vast geographical area with a dispersed population. The Mongols had no administrative system or any formal devices for organizing services before Chinggis Khan (Ratchnevsky, 1991:44). The best prediction then would be that only relatively small organized and coherent communities would be organized.

The Designation of Chiefs

This prediction receives further support once we look into the Mongol institutions for designing tribal chiefs, i.e. for concluding the treaties. Borrowing a Celtic term, Joseph Fletcher (1979–80:239; 1986:17) has called the governing principle "tanistry": the tribe should be led by the best qualified member of the chiefly house. Two mutually contradictory principles, however, existed: patrilineal succession from father to son on the one hand, and lateral succession from older to younger brother until the current generation had been exhausted and the eldest chief's sons would carry on. In this situation, succession would become subject to bargaining and active choice by the leading members of the tribe and any choice that the leading members of the tribe would make could be justified. In the tribal context the leaders usually managed to settle matters without creating too much resentment, but once the issue was the formation of a larger group faction frequently stood against faction:

> ... in a large tribe, rival candidates for the chieftaincy, each closely backed by his own retinue of personal supporters ... [nököd], might occasionally split the tribe, either temporarily or permanently. In a succession struggle, the rival candidates and their ... [nököd] competed for the support of the tribe's leading men and formed factions that could either compromise or fight. Nor were the rivals limited to the backing of members of their own tribe. If a tribe were part of a confederation, a given candidate might win the backing of the confederate ruler or other powerful elements within the confederation. Tribes or leading tribal families also commonly had special relationships with tribal (or even non-tribal) elements outside the confederation and sometimes even beyond the edges of the steppe. These too could be called upon for support or for asylum in the event that a given candidate met defeat. (Fletcher, 1986:17–18)

There was nothing in the ecological situation of the Mongols that required organization on a level above that of the tribe. "Any would-be supratribal ruler had to bring to heel a highly mobile population, who could simply decamp and ignore his claims to authority" (Fletcher, 1986:14). The situation very much resembled the one in what Samuel Huntington (1968:194) has called praetorian societies, where "no corps of professional political leaders are recognized or accepted as the legitimate intermediaries to moderate group conflict" (Huntington, 1968:196). In these societies, all social forces are politicized: armies, clergies, universities, bureaucracies, labour unions, corporations, and so forth. Political life lacks autonomy. Mongol society is a case in point. Before Chinggis Khan came to power, Mongol society was characterized by conflict and lack of unity (Ratchnevsky, 1991:12), and in principle:

> ... nomadic succession struggles tended to involve everybody. There were no "non-political" governmental functionaries to hold the realm together while military or other specialized elites determined the succession. Everybody was a warrior. Everybody was involved. Tribal chiefs had to decide which candidate to support, but everybody stood

to win by his tribe's making the right choice or to lose by its making the wrong one. Most important was predicting the outcome of the succession struggle and attaching one's tribe to the winning candidate. A tribal chief who backed a losing candidate could forfeit his position or his life, but his whole tribe would suffer, so a chief could not fail to be influenced by his tribesmen's opinions. [. . .]

Because the khan might fall sick and die or be killed at any time, the political status quo, being suspended from his person, was inherently ready to collapse. So the nomads had always to be sniffing the political breezes and to be ready to choose, form coalitions, and, at every level of society, to act. [. . .] Nomadic society was therefore more politicized at a deeper social level than the societies of the great agrarian empires northwest and south of the Eurasian steppe. (Fletcher, 1979–80:240–41)

In praetorian societies, power is fragmented, easily gained and easily lost and allegiances are easily transferred from one group to another. The Central Asian steppe was no exception:

Everything was mobile, and as a result families could move not only from region to region as climate and season required, but also from camp to camp, as the fortunes of a clan would wax and wane. A charismatic or fortunate leader would attract a large camp in a short period of time. Conversely, when a leader died or times got bad due to disease, bad weather, or war, a camp could easily break up. (Kahn, 1984:xx)

The traditional way of solving this problem among the steppe nomads was via the institution of subordinate tribes, i.e. tribes collectively under the protection of a stronger tribe, but simultaneously exploited by it (Lattimore, 1963a:59). Not all of these were conquered. Some submitted voluntarily for the sake of obtaining protection by stronger units:

Maintenance of the integrity of the subordinate tribe helped to block defection. Its members collectively and its headman individually could be made responsible for mutual loyalty. The conditions of life, however, sometimes made this safeguard ineffective. In fluid, rapidly moving nomadic warfare there were times when the subordinates could tip the scale by abandoning a detested lord and going over to an admired new leader. (Lattimore, 1963a:59)

The story of the early life of Temüjin (Chinggis Khan) bears ample testimony of the problems of organization. At the time of his birth (possibly in 1162 or 1167) (Grousset, 1966:36; Ratchnevsky, 1991:18–19) no central power existed in Mongolia. Temüjin's father, Yesugei had:

... gathered a following of his own, a heterogeneous collection of riders ... [that] were all of one stock, that of the Borjigin clan. He was
one leader in a world from which unity had flown, in which enemies
outnumbered friends and in which strength alone could hope to find
alliance. The weak fell away, their men left them, their followers found
other leaders, the tents in their camps grew fewer, the grazing for their
beasts sparser. In the end such groupings were absorbed in the train
of another chief, or disappeared under a sudden flight of arrows, to
the swift throbbing of hoofbeats and screams of anguish that fell abruptly
into silence. (Brent, 1976:12)

Yesugei, however, was not important enough politically to earn the
title of khan. His position was that of a minor chieftain (Morgan,
1986:57). Thus, young Temüjin at a very early age got drawn into
the rivalry between the Mongols and the other confederations in
Mongolia. As a member of one of the most notable Mongol families, his whole life from about the age of ten to his election as khan
some time in the 1190s is a chronicle of head-on confrontation with
the enemy, desperate struggle for survival, forging and breaking of
alliances, attacks and pursuits, flights and retirements (Prawdin,
1940:Ch. 2–3; Saunders, 1971:47–49; Brent, 1976:Ch. 1; Ratchnevsky,
1991:19–41). Organization could not be achieved without considerable bloodshed.

Peace and self-defence did not provide incentives that were strong
enough to overcome the organization problem in a durable fashion.
Temporary alliances were sufficient for that. The creation of wealth
was different. The nomad:

> ... remained precariously dependent upon nature, for a severe winter
> could destroy his flocks. The seminomads, who lived on the fringes of
> sedentary agricultural societies, shared this constant economic insta-
> bility. Their lack of accumulated resources gave both types of nomads
> a periodic incentive not only for increased trade but for military expan-
> sion. The nomads were the have-nots of antiquity, always poor in com-
> parison with peoples in more thickly populated farming regions. (Fairbank
> and Reischauer, 1979:155)

The productive base of the steppe was too meagre to allow substantial fortunes to be amassed, and preying on other nomads would
yield precisely the same type of goods as those produced by the
Mongols themselves. It was mainly when the number of animals
dropped below the minimum required for survival that plundering
other nomads was attempted. The risk of reprisals was always there
and the spoils could not be stored, but the animals had to be put

to pasturing, which of course put additional demands on the tribe's manpower.

This did not mean that wealth was not sought. On the contrary, there were strong incentives to do so. William Baumol (1990) has made a distinction between productive, unproductive and destructive entrepreneurship. Entrepreneurs are motivated by profit opportunities, but it is not at all necessary that their efforts will be concentrated on productive activities. What they will do depends on the incentives they are facing. When signals indicate that rent seeking and lobbying are more rewarding than productive efforts, entrepreneurship turns unproductive. It concentrates on the redistribution of a given cake. Should it, furthermore, be the case that war or piracy yields the highest returns, activities will turn increasingly destructive.

The first alternative for the herding nomad of course was trade. "His pastoral economy had little need of agriculture so long as it could maintain a minimal trade with settled areas in order to secure grain and also textiles, tea and other "luxuries," and "metals to make weapons" (Fairbank and Reischauer, 1979:154). Conversely, no artisan activities could be developed on a large scale in nomadic society, since that would have required a sedentary life-style (Lattimore, 1951:70). The nomads needed trade, but with that exception, for the creation of non-nomadic wealth the Mongols had no alternatives to preying on sedentary agriculturalists, and trade could never yield such huge benefits as plunder. This, however, was not something that isolated bands or tribes could carry out on their own. It required organization on a larger scale. At the same time, it provided an incentive for such organization because it boosted the benefits to the community. Organization offered not only internal peace but also an opportunity of enrichment at the expense of outside groups.

The main target was China:

> It was in the case of China, where the steppe-sown dichotomy was sharper than anywhere else in the Eurasian steppe, and where the agrarian government usually monopolized or greatly restricted external trade, that the tribes' desire to extort was strongest.
>
> Three alternative policies were available to the steppe nomads for the continuing acquisition of China's agrarian wealth: invasion, threat of invasion, and outright dependence. A fourth policy, commonly practiced by the desert nomads of Central Asia and the Middle East, namely conquest and dominion, was impractical for the nomads of the steppe because of the geographical separation of the steppe from the world of the sown. (Fletcher, 1986:15–16)

According to Fletcher (1986:16) the main purpose of the supratribal polity was precisely that of extorting wealth from agrarian societies, a very plausible conclusion in the light of the present approach. Given the formidable free-rider problem of the steppe it was only to be expected that it would take extraordinary benefits to overcome it:

> Pasture scheduling could be managed at the tribal level, and raiding could also be carried out under the leadership of the tribal chiefs without help from a supra-tribal ruler. Being nomadic, and consequently mobile, individual tribal groups could move away on their own. The grand khan could not subject his tribes to discipline without offering them a benefit great enough to win their voluntary compliance. Essentially his benefit boiled down to booty, the spoils of war – war which the tribes could not wage on a worthwhile scale without a supra-tribal leader. Social organization above the tribal level therefore came to be predicated on warfare. (Fletcher, 1979–80:237)

Not even the prospects of profitable plunder always provide enough incentive for large-scale organization, however. The basic communities remained small and their degree of cohesion was low:

> Given the mobility of nomadic life, the inessential character of supra-tribal social organization, and the fissiparousness of steppe politics, supratribal polities—being based on segmentary opposition—were unstable and frequently dissolved altogether. So there could be long periods when the largest effective unit was the tribe. [. . .] Supratribal society slipped back and forth between a supratribal anarchy (a "nation" of purely imaginary existence) and supratribal polity, which in turn fluctuated between loose confederacy and more rarely) tight autocracy.
>
> Steppe empires came into existence only through the efforts of individual aspirants for the office of supratribal ruler, who, so to speak, conquered the tribes of the supratribal society and then, to keep them united, had no choice but to keep them busy with lucrative wars. (Fletcher, 1986:20, 21)

Given the contradictory principles that governed the choice of chiefs among the Mongols it was never self-evident who the supratribal ruler would be. Coalitions were formed and backers were sought in a process with an uncertain outcome—a process that was furthermore completely centered on the person seeking office. The Mongols were ruled by:

> . . . the grand khan—the supra-tribal nomad emperor whose authority entailed kingship over a multi-tribal nomadic people, combined with a highly personal command over that people's collective military forces. Under the grand khan's rule, all authority was concentrated in him—

not in his office or in any government of officials who acted in his name, but in his person. When he died, the bonds of authority were dissolved, and his realm fell apart. (Fletcher, 1979–80:236)

All allegiances were thus strictly personal. As Fletcher (1986:22) has pointed out, in the Mongol case downplaying the historical role of individuals would be to commit a serious mistake. The system furthered the individual and it was the individual who had to forge his platform and, if he succeeded, made all the decisions:

> The grand khan . . . was not just the occupant of an ongoing institution like the thrones of the agrarian empires. He could not delegate his military function to officers of an army separable from society at large. The ruler's physical being provided the monarchy with its very existence. An active, personal, military leader was essential to the cohesion of his people. His person—indeed his personality—was the linchpin of society. (Fletcher, 1979–80:241)

Political structures were volatile and fragile and often collapsed completely. The steppe empire was the creation of its emperor, not the other way around, and when he died, his successor would have to create his own structures and allegiances—again on a completely personal basis.

One of Those Singular Figures of History

The unification of the Mongols was undertaken by Temüjin (later Chinggis Khan). This was no peaceful affair but was bound to involve civil warfare. Temüjin understood that the road to power went precisely through unification of the steppe nomads. Only after having accomplished this would it be possible to conquer the settled civilizations. Simultaneously, however, he had to hold out the prospects of plunder to achieve the unification. The two could not be separated. Mongol society was a herder and hunter society, but it was also a predatory society. Fletcher (1986:15) argues that it was impossible to forge any durable alliances without allowing plunder. From the point of view of those who entered the alliance this was easy to understand. To be ruled by a stationary bandit was better than being subjected to periodic one-shot smash-and-grab raids. As we have demonstrated in the foregoing, a stationary bandit has an incentive to limit the extent of taxation, not killing the goose that lays the golden eggs. Even better, however, is when the tax is paid by someone else, i.e. if the stationary bandit can use his community to raid others. Disregarding possible deaths during the raids this alternative is Pareto sanctioned from the point of view of the community and its ruler.

Chinggis Khan "must have been a leader of extraordinary talent, capable of iron discipline and the ability to inspire loyalty, and superior in these respects to other steppe leaders of his time" (Fletcher, 1986:34). However, his organization of the Mongol nation also rested on a number of principles. "It was by maneuvering in and out between the conventions and oppositions of the tribal system that Temüjin was able to make himself the supreme chief, strong enough to destroy the tribal system and create something new" (Lattimore, 1963a:62). This may not have been as difficult as one may think, because, as David Morgan (1986:37) has pointed out, in a sense the "tribe" was a relatively open institution where membership was determined as much by political interests as by blood relations. Thus, there was an established precedent to fall back upon for Temüjin, when he started to manipulate the structure. What is undeniable, however, is that the scale of manipulations by far outdistanced any of the attempts by his predecessors.

To obtain religious sanction Temüjin pointed to his divine mission, having been sent by the Mongol god Tenggeri. During the *khuriltai* (assembly) that elected him supreme khan of the Mongols in 1206, he had the shaman Teb-Tenggeri proclaim that the Eternal Heaven had appointed him (Grouzet, 1970:217). Yet, when the shaman became a threat to his power, Temüjin had him killed (Ratchnevsky, 1991:96–101). The Mongols in general assumed a very practical attitude towards religion, and Chinggis Khan used it to realize his own aims. He allowed complete freedom of worship, "a religious tolerance that makes the Christian Europe of his day seem barbarous by comparison" (Brent, 1976:43). This practice was not dictated simply by conviction but it could also be used to manipulate rivalries between Muslims, Buddhists and Christians in the conquered territories (Onon, 1993:xiii) and extract from each creed what served the interests of the khan best (Foltz, 1999:Ch. 6).

Chinggis Khan, however, also worked by breaking down a number of traditional power structures that militated against large-scale organization, substituting new ones that facilitated the creation of a feudal society for them. When he began his rise to power, nomad society in Mongolia was organized in a patrilineal kinship system of blood relations, supported by marriages and oaths. This system, however, suffered from the inherent weakness that it "also supplied the occasions for blood feuds that sharpened the mettle of the nomad warriors" (Lattimore, 1963a:57). This weakness was manipulated by the stationary Chinese who—like the Romans—used barbarians to control other barbarians, employing steppe tribes to defend them against other steppe tribes, dividing, and thus conquering, the nomads.

Thus, Temüjin was forced to destroy and replace a number of tribal institutions (Lattimore, 1963a:58). Instead of forging alliances through the *anda*, whereby two warriors swore alliance to one another, "as if they were descended from a common ancestor", but which by its very egalitarian nature presented problems when it came to determining leadership and pecking order, he chose to rely on another—more feudal—institution, the *nökör*, which at the time "meant a warrior who freely declared himself "the man" of a chosen leader, even to the repudiation of his own tribe or origin". The *nököd* that Temüjin had assembled when he had become Chinggis Khan became his generals and governors, and his trust in them was almost without limits (Lattimore, 1963a:59).

In the process of uniting the Mongols under his own undisputed command, Temüjin had had to destroy the traditional "double tribe": the Borjigid line, to which he himself belonged, and the rival Taijut line that had attempted to monopolize power when Temüjin's father had died (Lattimore, 1963a:60, 62; de Hartog, 1989:5). He did so by defeating the Taijut completely.

Temüjin pursued his own version of the divide and conquer method. The purpose always was to create loyalties to himself personally, loyalties that were independent of traditional tribal structures:

> At first he was dealing with men whose outlook was completely tribal. To induce them to transfer to him personally their hereditary tribal loyalties, he took care always to be able to justify each move "morally," by the standards of the very system he was going to destroy and supplant.
> He would not turn against a former ally, therefore, just because the opportunity looked good. He would first let the situation develop, and if possible help it to develop, in such a way that the other man could be accused of disloyalty in act or intent, and if there remained any shadow on his own loyalty, he would make out a case that what he did was "for the common good". The politically valuable victories were those that enabled him to divide defeated enemies by winning some of them over to his own side. (Lattimore, 1963a:62–64)

Chinggis Khan was completely loyal to those who served him, his friendship was absolute, but so was his vengeance on those whom he felt broke their obligations to him. Significantly, not a single one of his generals ever betrayed him. To ensure that those conquered did not defect or attempt any uprisings, Chinggis Khan resorted to the time-honoured system of treating them as subordinate tribes (Lattimore, 1963a:59–60). This institution had a given place in the feudal hierarchy that he built.

To reduce even further the risk that the conquered tribes would turn against him he also broke them up, distributing heir members as vassals to his trusted subordinates. Conversely, the latter received "appanages":

> These were regions, plainly in the feudal mold, in which the descendants of the first appanage-holder were to be hereditary rulers, bound to furnish military contingents to the successors of Chingis Khan. The new standard of discipline required a man to be obedient to the local ruler, who was usually not of his own tribal blood and pay his tribute within a geographically defined region from which he was not allowed to move. (Lattimore, 1963a:64)

Law and order was strictly upheld under Chinggis Khan. The extent of crimes diminished, and so did the rivalry between different groups in Mongol society. Raids upon neighbours became a thing of the past and banditry was wiped out. Grazing land was allocated once and for all among the different tribes. This removed one of the main sources of disputes. A police force saw to it that highways were made safe and returned stolen animals to their rightful owners, sanctioning theft of beasts with capital punishment (Brent, 1976:45–46).

The basic organizational rules were explicitly codified in the Great Yasa (Vernadsky, 1938; Ratchnevsky, 1991:187–96), the imperial code, supposedly promulgated in 1206[1] and further developed all the way until his death in 1227, which helped to overcome the centrifugal forces inherent in nomadic society and provided a permanent basis for his rule. The code bound not only the people but also the ruler. Functions and duties were regulated. Religious freedom was explicitly spelt out.

---

[1] This has been questioned by David Morgan, who argues that it may never have existed, but that what is usually referred to as the *Yasa* may have been nothing but "an evolving body of custom, beginning long before . . .[Chinggis'] time and being added to long after" (Morgan, 1986:99).

Chinggis Khan was also careful to learn and borrow from other people that he came across whatever he thought could be applied to his own political construction and frequently took foreigners as advisers and administrators:

> He needed and employed a few Chinese, but he kept a careful balance. An adviser who had great influence on him was Yeh-lü Ch'u-ts'ai, a Khitan who knew the Chinese culture thoroughly but who, as a Khitan, was felt to be a tribal kinsman.... [Chinggis] Khan also employed many Uighur Turks from the oases of Sinkiang and Öng-güd Turks from the fringe of Inner Mongolia. (Lattimore, 1963a:64)

Information was gathered on a regular basis from travelers and prisoners-of-war, and a spy network provided information from foreign countries (Brent, 1976:46). In the information network, Muslims (Turks, Iranians, Arabs) played a special role. Most of them were merchants who carried their merchandise across a relatively large territory, from the Near East to China. Those people accordingly saw and learned a lot during the course of their travels and Chinggis Khan understood how to make use of their knowledge:

> It was through them that... [Chinggis] Khan learned about the power of the Turkish nomads far to the west of Mongolia. This intelligence probably was influential in shaping his conviction that he must establish complete domination over all the nomad peoples, Turks as well as Mongols, before getting involved too deeply in invasion of the great agricultural and urban civilizations. He used these merchants first as intelligence agents, then as go-betweens and finally as more formal ambassadors. As his power increased he appointed some of them governors and administrators [...] In the Moslem world at this time wealthy merchants were more often well-traveled, well-educated men of the world than they were in China, where the merchants were despised by the landowners. Certainly the use of these men as administrators helped the Mongols to win over many of the Upper class in western Central Asia and northern Iran. (Lattimore, 1963a:66)

Temüjin was elected *khan* some time in the 1190s, after having forged a number of political alliances during the course of the previous fights and skirmishes. The fact that he had been elected *khan* did not mean, however, that he ruled all of Mongolia. This was not the case even during the first years after the turn of the century (Ratchnevsky, 1991:82). For that more was required. Above all the new ruler must demonstrate his military prowess, i.e. his ability to defeat his rivals in battle and secure booty for his followers. To this end Temüjin reorganized the Mongol army. After his defeat of the ruler of the Kereit confederation in 1203, his men were divided according to a metric or decimal system:[2]

> He divided his men into . . . units of a thousand [*mingghan*]. These were then metrically subdivided into ten companies [*jaghun*], each of ten platoons [*arban*]. Later, when his army grew, he would form ten . . . [*mingghans*] into that division of ten thousand men called a . . . [*tümen*]. These became the basic groupings that, in various combinations, made up his armies. He divided his horsemen into heavy and light cavalry, the former relying largely on their lances, the latter, who were perhaps twice as numerous, on their mobility and their skill with the bow. (Brent, 1976:31)

The use of the decimal system was current among the steppe nomads (Morgan, 1986:49). Different clans were mixed, however, as another way of neutralizing the traditional power structures. Ninety-five elite commanders—*orloks*—were appointed to lead the thousands—always on the basis of merit only—a creation that resembled a modern general staff (Onon, 1993:xiv). Two of Chinggis Khan's greatest generals, Jebe and Subedei, had risen to their high position before reaching the age of 25, and were given command over far senior officers (Liddell Hart, 1967:8). Chinggis Khan also required that commanders and subordinates serve each other with absolute loyalty and obedience. The transfer from one unit of the army to another was prohibited on penalty of death (de Hartog, 1989:42).

By the time that Chinggis Khan became the ruler of all Mongols, in 1206, his army probably numbered 105,000 soldiers, and at the year of his death, the size had increased to 129,000 (Morgan, 1986:87), not an exceedingly large figure in, for example, Chinese eyes, but one considerably larger than anything the Mongols had been able to muster hitherto under a unified chain of command (Fairbank and Reischauer, 1979:163), and definitely very large in comparison with the European armies of the day (Morgan, 1986:88).

Temüjin had also created his own imperial guard, originally 80 night guards and 70 day guards (*Secret History*, 1982:119), a military elite whose privates ranked above regular army officers. This guard

---

[2] Brent calls the thousand-man unit *guran*. We have, however, inserted the commonly used names within brackets.

built on a "double" principle: on the one hand, it professed professional, personal allegiance to Temüjin instead of traditional tribal
patterns, and on the other hand, it used a hostage system, with the
sons of army generals serving in the guard (Lattimore, 1963a:64).
The imperial guard would in the end, after the *khuriltai* of 1206,
number 10,000 (Fairbanks and Reischauer, 1979:163).

The new organization of the army was not simply a novel way
of increasing discipline or a tactical military device. It also helped
the new ruler to increase his political power. Although it did not
replace the tribes, it made it possible for the khan to bypass the
tribal system in military matters, i.e. it gave him direct and complete control over the machinery of violence. It also made it easier
for him to incorporate outside forces (Fletcher, 1986:30). The new
instrument was put to work, defeating the rival tribes and groupings
that still stood between the khan and absolute supremacy over
Mongolia. This took less than three years. His authority was confirmed
in the year of the tiger, 1206, in a *khuriltai* at the source of the river
Onon, one of the three largest rivers flowing through Mongolia.
Then he received the name by which he would henceforth be known:
Chinggis Khan (Ratchnevsky, 1991:89–96)—believed to mean either
the "hard" or "fierce" khan or the "oceanic" (presumably meaning
"universal") khan (Ratchnevsky, 1991:89–90, Jackson, 2000:195).[3]

Based on the organization of the military, his tactical moves among
the tribes and his successful military engagements, Chinggis Khan
had advanced to the point where he was the autocrat ruler of the
Mongols, but only for the time being. For power to endure more
was required. ". . . [I]f the tribes were to remain under the discipline of a steppe autocrat, he must raid and invade. The price of
autocracy was that the autocrat could not stop. He must continue
to enrich and engage his subject by continuing war" (Fletcher,
1986:32). Before setting out on his expedition against the Tatars in
1202, Chinggis Khan abolished the age-old custom that allowed plunder whenever the opportunity presented itself. "From now on all
plunder belonged to . . . [Temüjin]. He would be responsible for distributing it, and no man was to pause for plunder until the order

---

[3] Morgan (1986:60) has argued that the naming took place earlier (cf. *Secret History*, 1982:54–55).

had been given" (Chambers, 1999:39). The great conquests were about to begin.

To what extent Chinggis Khan was driven by material factors is difficult to know. A passage originally due to the Persian historian Rashid al-Din, who had entered Mongol service towards the end of the 13th century, quotes him as saying that the supreme joy was "to cut my enemies to pieces, drive them before me, seize their possessions, witness the tears of those dear to them, and embrace their wives and daughters" (quoted by Grousset, 1970:249). However, as Lattimore (1963a:62) remarks, this "is the conventional 'ideology', to use a modern word, of the barbarian warrior." Instead, he argues, all "his moves were politically calculated, and the calculation, from early in his career, was directed toward the building of a structure of power that would be capable of extension in both time and space." He did not display any "greed for booty or lust for women" in the process.

One possible interpretation of Lattimore's argumentation is that Chinggis Khan may have been seeking power for its own sake, but this is far from certain. A modern Mongol scholar, Bira Shagdar, ventures the hypothesis that Chinggis Khan never intended to build a world empire, only to ensure his supremacy over the steppe nomad peoples of Central Asia:[4]

> It is unlikely that . . . [Chinggis] Khan had devised a clearly formu-
> lated war strategy, it is more probable that he just preferred to carry
> out his intentions immediately. If his wide-ranging conquests are judged
> by their real outcome, it becomes clear that he did not really intend
> to build a world empire in the true sense of the word. His main aim
> was to subdue all his rivals so that all the nomadic peoples existing
> throughout Central Asia became his subjects. The most suitable pas-
> ture lands which were occupied by the nomadic peoples were in the
> east-west directions from Mongolia, but not from north to south.
> (Shagdar, 2000:129)

The Mongol Conquests

Leaving the motivation problem aside, the process of conquest itself must now be analysed in order to shed some light on the question

---

[4] Cf. also Ratchnevsky (1991:169–70).

why the Mongol empire reached the size that it did. This can be done by incorporating the central features of a model by Findlay (1996) into the framework developed above. Findlay (1996:42) conceives of the total population "as concentrated at a single point on a 'featureless plain'" (a good approximation to some of the Mongolian landscape): its "home base". In the Mongol economy, we may now conceive of two types of activities. In addition to the production of animal goods with the aid of direct labour and the bureaucracy that provides law and order, the labour force can be used for warfare. Thus the total labour force N now must be divided among three instead of between two pursuits:

(14) $L + G + A = N$

where L workers are busy directly producing, G work in the bureaucracy and A are extending the frontiers of the Mongol empire. Both the bureaucrats and the army have to be paid by state tax money.

The amount of land available is a function of the size of the army and the military technology (m) (including strategic and tactical skills):

(15) $T = T(A, m)$

Conquest, however, implies not only that the physical territory is enlarged. In addition, the population that can be used for production and warfare increases, i.e.

(16) $N = N[T(A, m)]$

Given the military technology, we can now derive the optimal size of the Mongol empire from the point of view of the ruler simply by maximizing his net tax revenue:

(17) $R = t^*r(t)Y(L, T, G) - (1 - t^*)r(t)Y^L(G + A)$

with respect to L, G and A, subject to the labour restriction

(18) $L + G + A = N[T(A)]$

This yields the first-order condition

(19) $NMRPL = NMRPG = NMRPA$

where

(20) $NMRPL = t^*rY^L - (1 - t^*)rY^{LL}(G + A)$
(21) $NMRPG = t^*rY^G - (1 - t^*)r[Y^{LG}(G + A) + Y^L]$

in direct analogy with (6) and (7) above, and

(22) $NMRPA = [t^*rY^T + NMRPL\,(dN/dT)](dT/dA) - (1 - t^*)r[Y^{LA}(G + A) + Y^L]$

The net marginal tax revenue product of labour must be equal in productive pursuits, in the creation of law and order and in the army. The latter marginal product consists of three components. Conquests extend the area that can be used for production, and the addition is valued at a (shadow) price equal to the net marginal tax revenue product of land. They also increase the population along with the territory, and the addition to the labour force is valued at a (shadow) price equal to the net marginal tax revenue product of labour in direct production. Finally we have the wage bill increase due to an increased army size.

Given the harsh conditions prevailing on the steppe, the marginal productivity of labour in production should not have been very high, even when supported by a bureaucracy creating law and order, i.e. employing manpower in the army may well have been a superior strategy, since this would increase the supply of both land and manpower, and with that the base for wealth expropriation:

> The winters were hard, the cold shrivelling all life and comfort; only the Antarctic is colder than north-eastern Siberia, the plains and uplands of which lie to the north of the Mongol territories. Long seasons of snow and darkness stretched down from these near-polar fastnesses— and they were getting longer and harder. This was the thirteenth century, when the globe's ice-caps reached towards the temperate zones and once-fertile fields disappeared under glaciers or hardened into permafrost. [. . .]
> In summer, however, the vast Eurasian landmass heats swiftly, now and then, and, where there are no rivers the soil dries and crumbles, all vegetation wilts. This was no land for agriculturalists to develop their skills. To the north, where rivers hiss through the valleys and ravines, forests of larch, birch, fir and aspen welcome the hunter, not the farmer. Between forest and desert lies the grass-ocean of the steppe, gleaming under snow in winter, flickering into a brightness of flowers in the spring, then slowly burning into the dun, khaki, yellow and pale-brown shades of the late summer. Across the plains and woodlands, through the whiplash winds of the deserts, the travelling peoples of these lands made their constant way . . . (Brent, 1976:27)

In this setting the nomads were entirely at the mercy of nature. A severe winter could easily destroy the herds upon which they were dependent:

> All through Central Asia winter pasture has always been the determin-
> ing factor for the size of the herds. Travelers and officials—the old Chinese
> and Manchu officials and the old Tsarist Russian officials—usually
> traveled through the pastures in summer, and they often wondered
> why the flocks and herds were not even larger. The reason was that
> there were not nearly enough good winter pastures. (Lattimore, 1962:32)

The inland climate of Mongolia is one of extremes since there is no
moderating sea that serves to cushion the swings. Between October
and April the regular temperature is below zero degrees centigrade
in present-day Ulaanbaatar, dropping frequently to minus 30 in
January and February. In the Gobi Desert, the temperature easily
rises to 40 degrees in the summer, to plummet to minus 30 degrees
or more during the winter. The steppe has an average temperature
of no more than 10 degrees in July, and in the winter minimum
values of minus 50 are not infrequent. The spring, in May and June,
is windy, with frequent dust storms. The short rainy season extends
from mid-July to September (Greenway *et al.*, 1997:21).

The model assumes that the contribution of the army to the territorial extension of the empire is a concave function of army size,
i.e. the marginal productivity of the army should decline with army
size. This is the conventional assumption of neoclassical economics,
and it makes marginal additions of territory possible. There is, however, also the possibility that the function is first convex and only
later turns concave. This situation is depicted in Figure 2.

The smooth curve indicates that the marginal cost of increasing
the size of the army (in terms of output forgone) is increasing. The
S-shaped curve, in turn, shows the marginal benefit in terms of
increased production through the addition of land and labour. This
curve first rises and falls only after point G has been reached. The
two curves intersect three times. To the left of point E it pays to
increase army size, since the benefits of this exceed the costs. To
the right of this point it does not, since here the cost curve lies above
the benefit curve—*unless* the addition to the army is non-marginal
so that point F can be reached. Point E is therefore a stable equilibrium point. Point F is not, however, since moving further to the
right entails an excess of benefits over costs at the margin, all the
way until a new stable equilibrium is reached in point H.

What this means is that the size of the territory may be kept down
by a failure to organize a large enough army. E is not a global maximum point, but it is not possible to move beyond it unless special
circumstances are at hand. This seems to have been the situation in

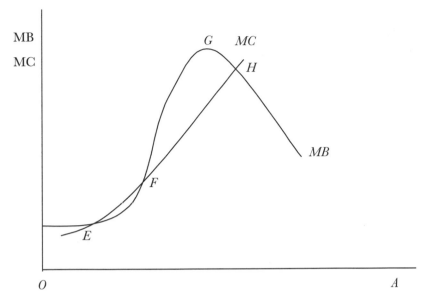

Figure 2: The Mongol Explosion

the Mongolian case, as we have already indicated in our discussion of the problem of organization. We also know that in the Mongol case the "special circumstances" translate into a single man: Chinggis Khan. Before the advent of Chinggis Khan, the Mongols had no clear sense of their identity as a people. Chinggis Khan became the "great organizer and unifier of the Mongols" (Fairbank and Reischauer, 1979:163). By organizing the tribes on a scale that was large enough he was able to trigger a cumulative process that did not end until his successors had created the largest continuous empire in the world, possibly even stopping short of point H, the point which gives the maximum return of benefits over costs. We will return to this possibility below.

The War Machine

So far we have said nothing about military technology or tactics, represented in our model by m in (15). It is, however, obvious that Chinggis Khan was an innovator in this area as well.

> With regard to the organization of their army, from the time of Adam down to the present day, when the greater part of the climes are at the disposition and command of the seed of... [Chinggis] Khan, it

can be read in no history and is recorded in no book that any of the kings that were lords of the nations ever attained an army like the army of the Tartars [. . .] What army in the whole world can equal the Mongol army? (Juvaini, 1997:29–30)

wrote Ata-Malik Juvaini, a Persian physician in the service of the Mongols, in 1260. Juvaini may be suspected of less than impartial judgment, but evidently he is not too far from the truth. Owen Lattimore (1963:66) maintains that as "a military genius, able to take over new techniques and improve on them, Chinggis stands above Alexander the Great, Hannibal, Caesar, Attila and Napoleon." It is evident that he was a great strategist who avoided many of the "classical" mistakes of earlier steppe warriors, notably that of exposing his back and his core territory to competitors while away on campaigns (Lattimore, 1963b). In his book *The Devil's Horsemen*, James Chambers (1979) offers a description of Mongol battle tactics as it had evolved by the time the Mongols were getting ready to embark on the invasion of Europe some time in the 1230s. His conclusions are extremely clear:

> In the thirteenth century, the Mongol army was the best army in the world. Its organization and training, its tactical principles and its structure of command would not have been unfamiliar to a soldier of the twentieth century. By contrast, the feudal armies of Russia and Europe were raised and run on the same lines as they had been for several hundred years and their tactics would have seemed unimaginative to the soldiers of the Roman Empire. (Chambers, 1979:51)

Mongol tactical principles were completely modern. The secret of their success in battle was the combination of fire power, mobility and endurance. Although their armies did contain artillery (light and heavy catapults and *ballistae* capable of launching heavy arrows), the most lethal weapon of the Mongols was the bow, small enough to be used from the saddle, easily the best construction in the world at the time:

> The medieval English longbow had a pull of seventy-five pounds and a range of up to two hundred and fifty yards, but the smaller reflex composite bows used by the Mongols had a pull of between a hundred and a hundred and sixty pounds and a range of over three hundred and fifty yards.[5] (Chambers, 1979:56–57)

---

[5] Saunders (1971:64) gives a range of between 200 and 300 yards. Lattimore

The Mongol bow, made from layers of sinew and horn on a wooden frame, would be superior also to the handgun for a long time to come (Morgan, 1986:91). The Mongol archer carried a wide array of arrows, for all kinds of situations: short and long range, armour-piercing, whistling for signaling and targeting, incendiary, and even arrows tipped with little grenades. His skills with the bow were hard to beat:

> He could bend and string his bow in the saddle by placing one end between his foot and the stirrup and he could shoot in any direction at full gallop, carefully timing his release to come between the paces of his horse, so that his aim would not be deflected as the hooves pounded the ground. (Chambers, 1979:57)

Each man carried two bows, one for the long and one for the short range, and at least two quivers with a minimum of 60 arrows, plus, in the case of the light cavalry, a small sword and two or three javelins. The bowstring was pulled by using a stone ring on the thumb, which allowed a faster and more powerful release than using the fingers and the stirrup provided a firm base for the firing. The heavy cavalry relied on a twelve-foot lance with a hook below the blade, and a scimitar, a battle-axe or a mace.

The entire army (with the exception of the siege artillery) consisted of cavalry, which gave it a tremendous advantage in terms of mobility:

> The prime feature of the Mongol army was ... its simplicity, due to the use of a single arm, in contrast to the inevitably complex organization of a combination of several arms which has always characterised European armies. In this way the Mongols solve the ever-difficult problem of co-operation between arms which have radically different qualities and limitations. (Liddell Hart, 1967:32)

Endurance was ensured by the system of remounts:

> The small Mongolian horse, grazing entirely on the open range with no bans and no supplementary grain feed, is amazingly tough. It can carry a man more than a hundred miles in a day – but not the next day; it must have a few days to graze and rest.... [Chinggis] Khan handled this problem by gearing his army to the average horse. His

---

(1962a:22) reports that "an inscription on a stone, a little older than the *Secret History* [*of the Mongols*] and also of the 13th century, records an arrow shot of 335 'spans', which has been estimated as about 500 meters."

cavalry were accompanied by herds of remounts, which were treated like the standardized, interchangeable parts of a machine. There was no great difference between today's horse and tomorrow's horse: both were called on only for average performance. (Lattimore, 1962:41)

Chinggis Khan never resorted to bigger horses that required hay, grain and shelter in the winter because this would have slowed him down and limited the mobility of his army. "He drew the essence of his power from archers riding tough little range-bred horses, with plenty of remounts" (Lattimore, 1963a:68), frequently as many as five (Morgan, 1986:86).

The drill was meticulous in the Mongol army. Training lasted several months and skills were thereafter kept up by continual practice. Campaigns were carefully planned:

> Before undertaking a campaign . . . [Chinggis] Khan tried to gather as much information as possible about the political and military situation of the enemy country, chiefly by means of spies. We must assume that observation and sense of direction were unusually highly developed in the Mongols, otherwise it is not possible to account for their movements over enormous distances without maps. Special officers had the task of leading the movements of the army and of fixing the position of camps. Cavalry forces of the size used by the Mongols could not be moved at short notice. It seems certain that careful planning preceded each of the major military campaigns. (de Hartog, 1989:49–50)

The Mongol officers constituted a permanent, professional corps, which it had not been before Chinggis Khan (Lamb, 1928:80). The Mongol armies also possessed a well-developed signaling system, using black-and-white flags, and communication behind the lines relied on a system, called *Yam*, of staging posts, inherited from the Khitan, but extended across the entire empire by the Mongols, connecting with a system of riders resembling the American Pony Express— only that it was faster. Urgent messages could be sent at a speed of over 200 miles per day (Morgan, 1986:103–7).

We mentioned above that the size of the Mongol army was comparatively large for its day. However, as Basil Liddell Hart (1967:7) has stressed, it was *quality*, not quantity that made it irresistible: "Alone of all the armies of their time had they grasped the essentials of strategy, while their tactical *mechanism* was so perfect that the higher conceptions of tactics were unnecessary." Friar Giovanni di Plano Carpini (1996:91) remarks that "indeed the Tartars [Mongols] fight more by trickery than by strength." Mongol battle tactics centred around the use of the light cavalry, which was used for engaging the enemy forces and showering them with arrows before the heavy cavalry moved in to strike the decisive blow:

> ... whenever possible the favourite tactic[6] was to use the *mangudai*. This was a light cavalry corps of "suicide troops",[7] but their name was more of an honourable tribute to their courage than an exact description of their duty. Ahead of the army the *mangudai* would charge the enemy alone, break ranks and then flee in the hope that the enemy would give chase. The larger the *mangudai*, the more convincing the flight and sometimes, when good open ground afforded an opportunity to regroup, it was made up of half the army. If the enemy did give chase, his ranks would already be spread out by the time they reached the waiting archers and when the quivers were empty and the heavy cavalry made their charge ... the result was devastating. The charge of the heavy cavalry was always the end of a Mongol battle plan. They advanced at the trot and in silence. Only at the last possible moment was the order to gallop sounded on the great *naccara*, a huge kettle drum carried by a camel, and by the time they had let out one hideous scream their lances were among the enemy. (Chambers, 1979:63)

The Mongol armies regularly could move 700 kilometres in two weeks, if necessary cover 300 kilometres in three days (de Hartog, 1989:49), and they moved at least twice as fast in battle as their enemies, a feature whose significance would not be fully appreciated until several centuries later:

> ... it was not until after the advent of mechanized war that the real Mongol genius came to be appreciated and the tactical principles of the Mongol army, based on the combination of fire power and mobility, were seen to be as basic and as constant as the principles of geometry. It was in the armies of ... [Chinggis] Khan that "fire and movement" first effectively became "fire in movement". In 1927 Basil Liddell Hart (1967:33) wrote that the tank and the aeroplane were the natural heirs and successors to the Mongol horsemen. At the same time surveys of the Mongol organization and tactics were being published in Germany, and British tank officers were recommended to study the Mongol campaigns. In the world war that would follow, two of the leading exponents of mechanized combat, Rommel and Patton, were both students and admirers of Subedei.

---

[6] See Liddell Hart (1967:9–10, 28, 31–32) for a more detailed discussion of Mongol tactics.
[7] The 'God-belonging' squadron (Lamb, 1928:131).

> Against the Mongols the European soldiers of the thirteenth cen-
> tury were as courageously helpless as the Polish lancers were against
> the German *panzers*. The Mongol army was a "modern" army and the
> differences between it and the armies in the twentieth century can all
> be accounted for by progress in science and in technology, but not in
> the art of war. (Chambers, 1979:66–67)

The Mongols also picked up military technology from the Chinese
(Hucker, 1975:280), notably siege warfare, an art that they had not
needed to get acquainted with before the invasions of China:

> . . . when . . . [Chinggis] Khan set out to campaign in . . . [Turkestan]
> and [Khwarazm] . . . he was able to co-ordinate the use of his cav-
> alry with elaborate siege weapons—powerful catapults, battering-rams
> and sappers who tunneled under walls and blew them up with gun-
> powder—against strongly fortified cities.
>
> He certainly recruited his first engineers in northern and perhaps
> north-western China, where the originally "barbarian" military power
> of the Jurchid, or Chin, state and the . . . [Tangut], or Hsia, state had
> acquired Chinese techniques. When he took these men westward with
> him, he brought about a cross-stimulation of Chinese and Iranian engi-
> neering and technology. This in turn almost certainly had something
> to do with the development of the cannon from the use of gunpow-
> der in sapping operations. Unfortunately we do not know the step-by-
> step details. At any rate the use of cannon both as siege weapons and
> as field weapons followed very quickly the Mongol conquest. (Lattimore,
> 1963a:66–67)

The Mongols were "modern" warriors in yet another sense. War
was total. On the one hand, this entailed the organization of all of
society along military lines:

> The nomadic social cycle began and ended with tribes in disunity,
> diffusing their military energies in internecine skirmishes. But once inte-
> grated into the grand khan's regime, the tribesmen became cogs in a
> military machine, soldiers in an all-pervasive army—an army of every-
> body, for there were no civilians. Tribal autonomy withered, and soci-
> ety itself became an army, a unitary host that directed its military
> energies outward to the defeat and despoliation of external victims.
> (Fletcher, 1979–80:237–38)

All male Mongols below the age of 60 were eligible for military service. "There was no such thing as a civilian [. . .] The Mongol rulers
therefore had available to them a cavalry force which could be speed-
ily mobilized, was highly trained, and consisted in theory—and even
to some extent in practice—of the entire adult male population"
(Morgan, 1986:85).

But war also involved the adversary, and here as well, it was total. Battle tactics was supplemented by terror measures directed against the civilian populations. "[Chinggis'] principle seems to have been much the same as President Truman's over Hiroshima and Nagasaki", remarks David Morgan (1986:93). During his Chinese campaigns he began to gather innocent civilians who were forced to march ahead of the troops when these were advancing on fortified cities. On such occasions only the inhabitants of cities that surrendered immediately were spared—and far from always. Those that resisted were ruthlessly killed. This was the case, for example, during the campaigns 1220–1222 against Jalal ad-Din, the son of the ruler of the Khwrazmian empire, that extended from the Tigris to the Syr-Darya. The army that Jalal ad-Din was leading to a large part consisted of urban Persian civilians. In this campaign Chinggis Khan set out to exterminate the enemy population:

> It was prosecuted now by calculated horror, an attempt to blot out urban life, extermination rather than simple depopulation. This was the treatment meted out to Balkh, Bamiyan, Herat, Merv and Nishapur. [. . .] If not immediately massacred, as at Merv and Nishapur, the civilian population of one city was driven on to become a human battering ram against the next. [. . .] it was warfare of unprecedented ferocity for the middle ages. (Adshead, 1993:58)

At Merv, "the jewel of the sands, the pleasure city of the Shahs" (Lamb, 1928:163), the city of the *Thousand and One Nights* (de Hartog, 1989:111), the entire population—men, women and children—was put to death. It was distributed among the soldiers who each had to execute three or four hundred people (Adshead, 1993:61). Fletcher has argued that the cruelty demonstrated by the Mongols during their military campaigns was due to their attitudes against sedentary populations:

> Their havoc proceeded logically from the legacy of the steppe wisdom about how nomads could best obtain what they wanted from the agrarian world. [. . .] . . . when the steppe pastoralist did invade the settled world, he looted and destroyed as much as his heart desired so as to remind the agrarians of the wisdom of rendering peacefully the wealth that he wanted. [. . .] With the steppe extortion pattern in mind, the Mongols did violence with a will and used terror . . . to induce their victims to surrender peaceably. (Fletcher, 1986:43, 42)

This, from the military point of view, lowered the cost of conquest, but there may have been a second reason too behind the massacres:

the numerical inferiority of the Mongols. They constantly had to fear an attack from the rear:

> Before . . . [Chinggis] Khan attacked the Kereit, he destroyed the Taijut and the Tartars, so that they could not stab him in the back. Later in China and in the Khwarazm sultanate, being so far from his own base, he could not risk the survival of forces among the defeated peoples sufficient to rise against him. (de Hartog, 1989:49)

Thus, the atrocities regularly committed by the Mongols were not the result of any "inherent" cruelty. They were calculated and what cruelty there was, was purely instrumental.

Summing up, several factors coincided in shaping the giant Mongol empire. Production conditions on the steppe made the accumulation of substantial wealth impossible, while deployment of military force displayed a high marginal productivity in terms of both land and people. Conquest became the preferred strategy. Before the rise of Chinggis Khan, organizational problems had precluded the Mongols from putting together an army that was large enough to allow for an extension of Mongol territory. It was only his political and military skills that made it possible to overcome the free-rider problem of the steppe. Finally, the Mongols were innovators in the field of warfare. The army consisted almost exclusively of cavalry which combined fire power and mobility in a way that was completely superior to anything that could be mustered by their adversaries. The Mongol conception of warfare was eminently "modern", also in the sense that it was "total", i.e. it did not spare the civilian population. On the contrary, the Mongols made a point of instilling as much terror as possible into the civilians, as a deliberate part of their warfare. The lesson was clear. "What . . . [Chinggis] Khan wanted to teach his enemies was that resistance was hopeless, that the attempt to mount it would be punished with the utmost cruelty. Only swift and willing surrender would elicit magnanimity—survival hung on instant submission" (Brent, 1976:63).

Before leaving the military theme, let us, however, sound a note of caution. As Ratchnevsky (1991:170–74) has reminded us, the solution of "the problem of how it was possible for a small, poor, backward nation of hunters and animal-breeders to conquer the most powerful and civilized states of Asia, states which disposed of inexhaustible reserves of people" (Ratchnevsky, 1991:170) should not be sought exclusively in the military context, but two other factors intervened as well. The first was the organization of the army, which ensured its elite character, already dealt with above. The second factor was Chinggis Khan's diplomatic and political skill (Ratchnevsky, 1991:172): ". . . his exposure and subsequent exploitation of the internal weaknesses of the enemy determined in advance the outcome of the wars. Genghis showed great skill in exploiting to his advantage the national, social and religious rifts in the enemy camps." Thus, it was a unique combination of military, organizational, diplomatic and political skill, united in the person of Chinggis Khan that ensured the Mongol conquests.

Once subjugation had been obtained, the time had come to deliver. Chinggis Khan was a man who kept his promises of booty and wealth for his people. For the conquered, it meant paying taxes (Morgan, 1986:100–3; Schurmann, 1956; Smith, 1970; Ratchnevsky, 1991:175–86). The stationary bandit preyed on the defeated, exactly as we would expect him to do:

> The purpose of the taxes imposed on the conquered populations was quite simply the maximum conceivable degree of exploitation. There was little pretence that in Mongol eyes their subjects had a justification for heir existence except as producers of revenue. As a rule exploitation was limited only by the consideration that it was sensible to leave the peasants sufficient to permit their survival till the next year, so that a further year's taxes could be levied. In the early days of excessive zeal the Mongols did in fact not stop even at that point. Mongol taxation was more a pragmatic series of exactions as seemed appropriate and profitable than any kind of fixed system. To judge from the experience of the Islamic lands that fell under Mongol rule, the burden of taxation was probably appreciably higher than it had been even under such unenlightened rulers as the . . . [Khwarazm shahs]. (Morgan, 1986:102, cf. Kwanten, 1979:209)

Apogee and Fall of the Mongol Empire

When the time came for the Mongols to turn eastwards, China was no longer united under a single emperor. At the beginning of the 10th century, Khitan nomads had invaded and conquered the north, including the city of Zhongdu. They were, in turn, ousted by Jurchen horsemen from Manchuria early in the 11th century who established the Ching empire with Zhongdu as their capital. Somewhat earlier, at the end of the 10th century, Tanguts had invaded northwestern China and founded the Hsi Hsia kingdom. This left only China south of the Wei and Huai rivers for the Sung. (The dynasty was known as the Southern Sung from 1127) (Fairbank and Reischauer, 1979:157–60).

Between 1205 and 1209, Chinggis Khan conquered the Hsi Hsia kingdom. Thereafter he turned against the Chin empire further east (1211–1215), sacking and burning Beijing and leaving more than ninety towns "in rubble" (Hucker, 1975:283). For this it was not enough with just Mongol forces, so whenever possible Chinese troops that chose to defect were welcomed into the ranks of the khan's armies (Morgan, 1986:66–67). Between 1219 and 1225, he conducted a campaign in the west, against the Khwarazm empire, located in present-day Turkestan, which was subjugated, gaining control in the process over such cities as Samarkand and Bokhara. By the time of his death, the area under Mongol control extended from the Caspian Sea across Central Asia and northern China to the Yellow Sea and the Sea of Japan, and from the forests of Siberia to the Hindu Kush (Brent, 1976:Ch.3). Demetrius Boulger provides the following summary judgment:

> Even the Chinese said that he led his armies like a god. The manner in which he moved large bodies of men over vast distances without an apparent effort, the judgment he showed in the conduct of several wars in countries far apart from each other, his strategy in unknown regions, always on the alert yet never allowing hesitation or overcaution to interfere with his enterprises, the sieges he brought to a successful termination, his brilliant victories, a succession of "suns of Austerlitz," all combined, make up the picture of a career to which Europe can offer nothing that will surpass, if indeed she has anything to bear comparison with it . . . (Boulger, 1900:55)

At Chinggis Khan's death his empire was divided among the four sons of his first and principal wife (or their descendants). Eventually this division was to crystallize into (1) the Khanate of the Great Khan, mainly China, ruled by Ögödei, Chinggis' third son, 1229–1241, Möngke, grandson, 1251–1259, and Khubilai, also grandson, 1260–1294, (2) the Khanate of Chaghatai, Chinggis' second son, 1227–1242, in Turkestan, the western part of which would be incorporated in the empire of Timur Lenk (Tamerlane) after 1370, (3) The Ilkhanate of Persia, built up by Chinggis' grandson Hülegü, and dissolved after 1335, and, finally, (4) the Kipchak Khanate (the Golden Horde), built up by Chinggis' grandson Batu, 1227–1255?, which dominated Russia and was taken over by Timur Lenk, and was finally broken up in the 15th century (Fairbank and Reischauer, 1979:165).

The conquest of the Chin empire of northern China was completed in 1241, by Ögödei, who had a capital built at Kharakhorum, and Korea came under Mongol rule in 1258. Ögödei also turned against the Sung empire of southern China, the conquest of which would, however, not be finished until Khubilai had become khan. When Möngke died in 1259, Khubilai had to interrupt his campaign against the Southern Sung and for four years deal with his brother Arigh Böke who had challenged him for the position as khan. In 1264 Khubilai moved the capital from Kharakhorum to Beijing and in 1271 he adopted the dynastic name of Yüan, although it would be a further eight years before full control was achieved over southern China. Mongol control over China was to last until 1368.

Before that, however, the Mongols had once more turned westwards. Already during the Khwarazmian wars, in 1221, an army under Subedei had taken the route south of the Caspian Sea through Georgia and annihilated a Russian army on the Kalka river, north of the Sea of Azov, in 1223. Less than 15 years later, the Mongols returned to the west. Moscow was burned, Kiev was taken, and in 1241 Poland, Bohemia, Hungary and the Danube valley were invaded (Chambers, 1979). The Mongols finally penetrated as far as the Adriatic Sea. The European adventure came to an abrupt end, however, since in March 1242, Batu received the notice that Ögödei had died in December, and had to return back home to elect a new khan. As it seems, the Mongol invasion of Europe thus stopped short of what was possible to achieve: short of point H in Figure 2. The superior Mongol war machine had not given the Europeans much of a chance, and the likelihood that a further westward penetration could have been successfully resisted by stationary armies unaccustomed to the mobile warfare of the Mongols is not very high (Morgan, 1986:1; Jackson, 1999:706). In this sense, the Mongol empire was too small. It did not reach its optimum extension. Europe was saved by the bell, as it were, a bell that tolled for the supreme Mongol leader, and subsequent plans of reassuming the conquests in the west were effectively checked on the one hand by the death of Möngke in 1259 and the civil wars that followed (Jackson, 1978; Morgan, 1986:156–57). An ecological factor also intervened, however. In May 1260, Hülegü withdrew most of his forces from Syria, for lack of grazing facilities, and the smaller contingent left behind suffered a defeat at the hands of the Mamluks at Ayn Jalut, in Galilee, on 3 September 1260. The Mamluks had a thorough understanding of Mongol warfare and cleverly used their weaknesses to their own advantage. Subsequent efforts in Syria foundered on the same problem: pastoral limitations and inadequate water supply in Syria (Smith, 1984).

In the south and the east, climatic and geographical factors were responsible for putting a "natural" end to the extension of the empire. India proved too hot for conquest. It escaped with occasional raids of plunder (Saunders, 1971:61, 248, note). The Mongols attempted to invade Japan on two occasions, in 1274 and in 1281 (Rossabi, 1988:99–103, 207–12). On the first occasion, they were forced to withdraw by a violent storm, and on the second occasion a typhoon, interpreted by the Japanese as a *kamikaze* (heavenly wind), wiped out the invasion forces. The Mongols were also checked in Vietnam. The efforts made by Khubilai Khan to conquer Annam in the north and Champa in the south between 1281 and 1287 forced the Mongol troops into a guerilla war in hot and disease-infested forests and mountains: the kind of warfare for which they were least suited (Rossabi, 1988:215–18).

In another sense, the empire was far too large. Yelui Ch'u ts'ai, Chinggis Khan's trusted adviser is reputed to have said: "The Mongol Empire has been won from the saddle—it cannot be ruled from the saddle" (Brent 1976:60). He was right, and as it seems, the Mongol rulers understood it (Shagdar, 2000:129). Chinggis Khan did not make any effort to occupy the land he had conquered on any permanent basis. For that, his forces were insufficient. But permanent occupation was hardly necessary as long as a sufficient part of the output value produced could be skimmed off by means of taxation. To this end he left behind a number of military governors who could simultaneously act as tax collectors and representatives of the Khan's power, providing a credible threat to those who refused to comply. Failure in thus respect would lead to sporadic punitive raids. In this he may simply, as Bira Shagdar (2000:129) suggests, have been following "the traditional form of submission typical of all steppe empires". According to this tradition:

> ... it was more important to master the peoples as appanage (*ulus*) rather than to govern the territories of the conquered countries. With regard to sedentary societies, ... [Chinggis] preferred to ensure the

economic exploitation of those countries by establishing a system of tax collection and of receiving tributes. Keeping this in mind, he distributed the conquered peoples among his four sons. The empire of . . . [Chinggis] Khan was more a nomadic confederation than a world empire which ruled, in the real sense, the countries of sedentary civilizations. (Shagdar, 2000:129)

Chinggis Khan did not divide his troops between garrisons in the conquered territories across his wide empire. Instead he stationed smaller contingents, known as *tamma*, on the borderlands between the steppe and the settled populations (Morgan, 1986:93–94). He preferred to keep his main forces as a mobile reserve in the steppes of Mongolia. Southern Russia and Turkestan. From there they could easily be deployed wherever the political and military circumstances called for it. But of course, in the end, a more settled governance and life style was inevitable (Lattimore, 1963a:68). In the end the *tamma* became the nuclei of the permanent military forces in the subsidiary khanates (Morgan, 1986:95). The very size of the empire required a large-scale sedentary administration—but this also sealed its fate. Significantly, the part of the empire that lasted longest—until 1502—was the Golden Horde:

> The Golden Horde settled in the nomadic zone and incorporated the nomadic population into its state structure; and from the nomadic zone it controlled the conquered sedentary areas, primarily Russia. The Horde preferred to follow the steppe tradition of acting as distant overlords rather than directly. It contented itself with collecting taxes and tribute, which was gathered for it by the subjected population, appointing princes, and acting as arbiters in disputes. This policy meant that the Horde rarely became embroiled in local politics and it never identified its interests with those of its Russian subjects. (Kwanten, 1979:252, cf. Morgan, 1986:174)

The other parts of the empire that Chinggis Khan built had already fallen when the end came to the Golden Horde. The Chaghatai Khanate was a loosely structured coalition between a handful of peoples. It had no formal capital and it was located in nomadic territory. However, it failed to control the nomadic population and was subject to constant intervention by the other three parts of the Mongol empire. As a consequence, the Chagatai Khanate never stabilized. It had no less than 19 rulers between 1227, the year of its creation, and 1338, when it was split into two parts. The Mongols ended up being absorbed by the Turks (Kwanten, 1979:250–52). In the Ilkhanate,

the Mongols converted to Islam and began to intermarry with the
Persians and, even more, with the Turkish speakers. In fact, they
were never driven out but had simply been absorbed by the time
of the death of the last Ilkhan in 1335 (Morgan, 1986:170). China,
in turn, had an almost proverbial ability to absorb foreign elements
into its own immense population, and the descendants of Chinggis
Khan constituted no exception in this respect:

> It was when his successors—notably . . . [Khubilai] Khan in China—
> turned their backs on the steppe and began to concern themselves
> with civilization that the old nemesis of civilization began to erode the
> empire of the great barbarian genius, as it had the empires of man
> similar but lesser barbarian conquerors. (Lattimore, 1963a:68)

The logic of collective action defeated the Mongols. Keeping the
largest continuous empire the world has ever seen together called
for extraordinary administrative measures, and a large mobile administration is a contradiction in terms (Dardess, 1972–73; Morgan,
1982). As Lattimore (1962b:257), has observed, "it is the poor nomad
who is the pure nomad." The mobile nomads reached their maximum control over wealth when they conquered China, but by the
same token, their mobility was undermined. They became dependent on "the swarming bureaucracy needed to collect revenue and
to allot patronage" (Lattimore, 1951:77). Once the Mongols had
reached the point where their enormous conquests had made their
rulers and nobles dependent on trade and taxation of agriculturalists and urban dwellers, i.e. on "non-nomad sources of privileged
income", the capacity of their leaders for initiating for collective
action vanished. Their lust for further conquests was dulled. Once
they started to settle, the conquerors were conquered by the conquered and the impossible empire crumbled.

References

Adshead, S.A.M. (1993). *Central Asia in World History*. New York: St Martin's Press.
Baumol, William J. (1990) "Entrepreneurship: Productive, Unproductive, and Destruc-
    tive", *Journal of Political Economy*, Vol. 98.
Bold, Bat-Ochir (2001) *Mongolian Nomadic Society: A Reconstruction of the "Medieval"
    History of Mongolia*. Richmond, Surrey: Curzon Press.
Boulger, Demetrius Charles (1900) *A Short History of China: An Account for the General
    Reader of an Ancient Empire and People*. New edition. London: Gibbings & Co.
Brent, Peter (1976) *The Mongol Empire: Genghis Khan: His Triumph and His Legacy*.
    London: Weidenfeld and Nicolson.

Chambers, James (1979) *The Devil's Horsemen: The Mongol Invasion of Europe*. London: Weidenfeld and Nicolson.
—— (1999) *Genghis Khan*. Phoenix Mill, Stroud, Gloucestershire: Sutton Publishing.
Dardess, John W. (1972–73) "From Mongol Empire to Yüan Dynasty: Changing Forms of Imperial Rule in Mongolia and Central Asia", *Monumenta Serica*, Vol. 30.
de Hartog, Leo (1989), *Genghis Khan: Conqueror of the World*. London and New York: I.B. Tauris.
Fairbank, John K. and Reischauer, Edwin O. (1979) *China: Tradition and Transformation*. Sydney: Allen and Unwin.
Findlay, Ronald (1996) "Towards a Model of Territorial Expansion and the Limits of Empire". In Michelle R. Garfinkel and Stergios Skaperdas (eds.), *The Political Economy of Conflict and Cooperation*. Cambridge: Cambridge University Press.
Findlay, Ronald and Lundahl, Mats (2000) *Globalization, Economics and History*. Mimeo. Stockholm School of Economics.
Findlay, Ronald and Wilson, John D. (1987) "The Political Economy of Leviathan". In Assaf Razin and Efraim Sadka (eds.), *Economic Policy in Theory and Practice*. London: Macmillan.
Fletcher, Joseph (1979–80) "Turco-Mongolian Monarchic Tradition in the Ottoman Empire". In Ilhor Ševčenko and Frank E. Sysyn (eds.), *Eucharisterion: Essays Presented to Omeljan Pritsak. Harvard Ukrainian Studies*, Vols. 3–4.
—— (1986) "The Mongols: Ecological and Social Perspectives", *Harvard Journal of Asiatic Studies*, Vol. 46.
Foltz, Richard C. (1999) *Religions of the Silk Road: Overland Trade and Cultural Exchange from Antiquity to the Fifteenth Century*. Houndmills, Basingstoke, and London: Macmillan.
Greenway, Paul; Storey, Robert and Lafitte, Gabriel (1997) *Mongolia*. (2nd ed.). London: Lonely Planet Publications.
Grousset, René (1966) *Conqueror of the World: The Life of Chingis-Khan*. New York: Viking Press.
—— (1970) *The Empire of the Steppes: A History of Central Asia*. New Brunswick, NJ: Rutgers University Press.
Hobbes, Thomas (1985) *Leviathan*. Macpherson, C.B. (ed). London: Penguin Books.
Hucker, Charles O. (1975) *China's Imperial Past: An Introduction to Chinese History and Culture*. Stanford: Stanford University Press.
Huntington, Samuel P. (1968) *Political Order in Changing Societies*. New Haven and London: Yale University Press.
Jackson, Peter (1978) "The Dissolution of the Mongol Empire", *Central Asiatic Journal*, Vol. 22
—— (1999) "The Mongols and Europe" In David Abulafia (ed.), *The New Cambridge Medieval History, Volume V c. 1198–c. 1300*. Cambridge: Cambridge University Press.
—— (2000) "The State of Research: The Mongol Empire, 1986–1999", *Journal of Medieval History*, Vol. 26.
Jackson, Peter and Morgan, David (1990) "Introduction" to *The Mission of Friar William of Rubruck: His Journey to the Court of the Great Khan Möngke 1253–1255*. London: The Hakluyt Society.
Juvaini, Ata-Malik (1997) *Genghis Khan: The History of the World Conqueror*. Translated and edited by J.A. Boyle. Manchester: Manchester University Press.
Kahn, Paul (1984) "Introduction". In *The Secret History of the Mongols: The Origins of Chingis Khan*. San Francisco: North Point Press.
Kwanten, Luc (1979) *Imperial Nomads: A History of Central Asia 500–1500*. Philadelphia: University of Pennsylvania Press.
Lamb, Harold (1928) *Genghis Khan: Emperor of All Men*. London: Thornton Butterworth.
Lattimore, Owen (1951) *Inner Asian Frontiers of China*. (2nd ed.) New York: American Geographical Society of New York.

—— (1962a) *Nomads and Commissars: Mongolia Revisited*. New York: Oxford University Press.

—— (1962b) *Studies in Frontier History: Collected Papers 1928–1958*. London: Oxford University Press.

—— (1963a) "Chingis Khan and the Mongol Conquests", *Scientific American*, Vol. 209, No. 2.

—— (1963b), "The Geography of Chingis Khan", *Geographical Journal*, Vol. 129.

Liddell Hart, Basil H. (1967) *Great Captains Unveiled*. New York: Books for Libraries Press.

Lipton, Michael (1968) "The Theory of the Optimising Peasant", *Journal of Development Studies*, Vol. 4.

McGuire, Martin C. and Olson, Mancur, Jr. (1996) "The Economics of Autocracy and Majority Rule: The Invisible Hand and the Use of Force", *Journal of Economic Literature*, Vol. 34.

Morgan, David O. (1982) "Who Ran the Mongol Empire?", *Journal of the Royal Asiatic Society*, Vol. 14.

Morgan, David (1986) *The Mongols*. Cambridge, MA and Oxford: Blackwell.

Olson, Mancur (1962) *The Logic of Collective Action: Public Goods and the Theory of Groups*. Cambridge, MA.: Harvard University Press.

—— (1982) *The Rise and Decline of Nations: Economic Growth, Stagflation, and Social Rigidities*. New Haven: Yale University Press.

—— (2000) *Power and Prosperity: Outgrowing Communist and Capitalist Dictatorships*. New York: Basic Books.

Onon, Urunge (1993) "Introduction" to *Chinggis Khan: The Golden History of the Mongols*. London: The Folio Society.

Plano Carpini, Giovanni di (1996) *The Story of the Mongols Whom We Call the Tartars*. Translated with an introduction by Erik Hildinger. Boston: Branden Publishing Company.

Prawdin, Michael (1940) *The Mongol Empire: Its Rise and Legacy*. London: Allen and Unwin.

Rossabi, Morris (1988) *Khubilai Khan: His Life and Times*. Berkeley: University of California Press.

Saunders, J.J. (1971) *The History of the Mongol Conquests*. New York: Barnes and Noble.

Schurmann, H.F. (1956) "Mongolian Tributary Practices of the Thirteenth Century", *Harvard Journal of Asiatic Studies*, Vol. 19.

The Secret History of the Mongols (1982) Translated and edited by Francis Woodman Cleaves. Cambridge, MA and London: Harvard University Press.

Shagdar, Bira (2000), "The Mongol Empire in the Thirteenth and Fourteenth Centuries: East-West Relations". In Vadime Eliseeff (ed.), *The Silk Roads: Highways of Culture and Commerce*. New York and Oxford: Berghahn Books.

Smith, John Masson, Jr. (1970) "Mongol and Nomadic Taxation", *Harvard Journal of Asiatic Studies*, Vol. 30.

—— (1984) 'Ayn Jālūt: Mamluk Success or Mongol Failure?" *Harvard Journal of Asiatic Studies*, Vol. 44.

Vernadsky, George (1938) "The Scope and Contents of Chingis' Khan's Yasa", *Harvard Journal of Asiatic Studies*, Vol. 3.

MIXED LEGAL SYSTEMS AND COLONIALITY: PARTS OF THE CONSTRUCT OF A GLOBAL LEGAL CULTURE[1]

Kjell-Åke Modéer
Lund University, Sweden

Legal Systems in Global Legal Cultures

Post-modern and post-colonial theories have created quite new categories in the field of comparative law. Legal research in comparative law of the 20th century was very much driven by the need for new legislation in the nation-state. Post-war comparativists (after the World War II) were eager to make the Western legal systems transparent, to harmonize and identify universalities within the Western legal systems. It was a consequent position in a cognitive structure dominated by the nation-state, the cold war, and still enduring imperial or colonial structures. Since the early 1950s the pan-European concept was in focus in Western Europe. Within legal historical research *"Rezeptionsforschung"* and identifying of "legal transplants"[2] were the research models of the day. The transparency between European legal systems was essential for the voluntary reception of legal phenomena from one legal culture into another. The diversity was to be seen in the difference between the continental-European *civil law* system and the Anglo-American *common law* system. These two systems interfered and interacted in a human and cognitive way when German Jewish jurists during the Third Reich were established as immigrants in law schools in the US. They were excluded from a civil law country and were included in the English and American legal cultures. German comparativists such as Sir Otto Kahn-Freund (London, Oxford) in England as well as Max Rheinstein (Chicago),

---

[1] Revised speeches at an international conference, "Asia–Europe and Global Processes", at the National University of Singapore, 14–16 March, 2001 and at University of Cape Town, November 2002.
[2] Alan Watson (1993), *Legal Transplants: An Approach to Comparative Law*, (2nd ed.), The University of Georgia Press/Athens and London.

Stephan Riesenfeld (UC/Berkeley) and Rudolph Schlesinger (Cornell/ Hastings) in the US demonstrated their common aim to identify *universalities* and *similarities* between the Western legal systems in their important and dominating research.

Post-war concepts in comparative law have been very loyal to the Western legal tradition.[3] The systematization into "legal families" identified to a great extent those of the West European legal cultures, the Romanist, the German, the Anglo-American, the Scandinavian and the Soviet "legal families".

Comparative law has to a great extent been a legal discipline rooted in European and North American legal science.[4] The concept of "legal families", introduced by Konrad Zweigert & Hein Kötz, included, for example, the Latin American legal cultures within the European Romanist family. The Western legal tradition dominated and was regarded as universal. The recent break-up in legal science from modernity and colonialism has resulted in a change in the evaluation of the political and legal cultures of the former empires and colonies. Post-modern, late-modern and post-colonial perspectives on comparative law, have contributed to and introduced new perspectives, in which the colonial Western "We and the Other" perspective has been succeeded by a more non-Western and global one.

Legal Mapping

The great changes of the political systems in the decolonized countries, including transition to democracy, during the last 20 years in Asia, Africa and Latin America, have initiated a need for a new post-modern legal atlas of the world's legal cultures. The need for such a map has, for example, been emphasized by Boaventura de Sousa Santos,[5] who emphasizes three cultural metaphors to explain

---

[3] René David & J.E. Brierley (1985), *Major Legal Systems of the World* (3rd ed.) London: Stevens; Konrad Zweigert & Hein Kötz (1998), *Introduction to Comparative Law*, (3rd ed.), translation T. Weir, Oxford: Clarendon Press; Cfr Harold J. Berman (2000), "The Western Legal Tradition in a Millennial Perspective: Past and Future," 60 *Louisiana Law Review*, 739ff.

[4] Vivian Grosswald Curran (1998), "Dealing in Difference: Comparative Law's Potential for Broadening Legal Perspectives," 46 *The American Journal of Comparative Law*, 657ff; Pierre Legrand (1999), "John Henry Merryman and Comparative Legal Studies: A Dialogue," 47 *American Journal of Comparative Law*, 3ff.

[5] Boaventura de Sousa Santos (1987), "A Map of Misreading: Toward a Postmodern

the break-up from the old Western paradigm: The Frontier, the Baroque and the South.

De Sousa Santos argues "that we must reinvent the future by opening up a new horizon of possibilities mapped out by new radical alternatives." In the construction of a new paradigmatic knowledge and law those three metaphors are made useful tools.[6] "To live in the frontier is to live abeyance, in an empty space, in a time between times . . . To live in the frontier is to live in the margins without living a marginal life." (De Sousa Santos, 1995) The centre is shifting; we experience no longer just the centre but also the frontier which is no longer in the margin (periphery). De Sousa Santos also uses the Baroque as a cultural metaphor. He looks upon the Baroque as an eccentric form of modernity. "Its eccentricity derives, to a large extent, from the fact that it occurred in countries and historical moments in which the centre of power was weak and tried to hide its weakness by dramatizing conformist sociability." In Latin America, the baroque has dominated the colonial territories as an important cultural pattern since the 17th century. "It is the manifestation of an extreme instance of the centre's weakness." "Because it takes shape in the furthest margins, the baroque becomes surprisingly congruent with the frontier." Just like the East, the South is a product of the empire, de Sousa Santos argues. It is expressing all forms of subordination brought about by the capitalist world system; exploitation, expropriation, suppression, silencing, unequal differentiation and so on. "The South signifies the form of human suffering caused by capitalist modernity." The paradigmatic change means that we are conscious of the existence of the South. This topoi is a part of a universal and globalized view on culture. De Sousa Santos looks upon these three metaphors as a whole. We cannot solve fundamental problems with traditionally modern solutions. When we are breaking away from one paradigm of legal culture, we have to find new parameters, located beyond traditional

---

Conception of Law", in *Journal of Law and Society*, 279ff; de Sousa Santos (1995), "Three Metaphors for a New Conception of Law: The Frontier, the Baroque and the South," 29 *Law & Society Review*, s. 569ff.

[6] Boaventura de Sousa Santos (1995), "Three Metaphors for a New Conception of Law: The Frontier, the Baroque and the South," 29 *Law & Society Review*, 569ff. Cfr Boaventura de Sousa Santos (1995), *Toward a New Common Sense: Law, Science and Politics in the Paradigmatic Transition*, New York, London: Routledge, chapter 8.

cognitive frontiers and observing not only time (the Baroque) but also space (the South).

New Concepts of Legal Culture

Legal cultures are increasingly defined as the jurists' cultures. Within the Western paradigm this has meant an emphasis on legal ideologies[7] and the cognitive structures of jurists in different countries.[8] John Bell has defined legal culture as "a specific way in which values, practices, and concepts are integrated into the operation of legal texts."[9] Mark van Hoecke and Mark Warrington, who put the individualistic and rational "Western legal culture" in relation to the non-Western, which they characterize as collective and irrational, have introduced one example of a new systematization of legal systems.[10] Ugo Mattei has presented another construct.[11] In his taxonomy (an intellectual framework of the law, a grammar of the legal discourse) and its changes in the world's legal systems because of the revision of the geo-legal map of the world, he makes a difference between three patterns of law, *the rule of professional law, the rule of political law* and *the rule of traditional law.* In this article, the examples are to be found on the line between the traditional law (including Chinese, Vietnamese and Islamic law) and political law (African and Latin American law), which is interesting.

Mattei emphasizes the Euro-American centrism and lack of cultural context within comparative law. The three main sources of social norms or social incentives which affect an individual's behaviour: politics, law and philosophical or religious tradition create for him the three patterns of law which are the cardinal points for a map of world legal systems and their deeper structures.

---

[7] Roger Cotterrell (1997), "The Concept of Legal Culture", in David Nelken (ed.), *Comparing Legal Cultures,* Aldershot: Dartmouth, 13ff.

[8] Pierre Legrand (1996), "European Legal Systems are not Converging," 45 *The International and Comparative Law Quarterly,* 52ff.

[9] John Bell (1995), "Comparative Law and Legal Theory," in W. Krawietz, N. MacCormick & G.H. von Wright (eds.), *Prescriptive Formality and Normative Rationality in Modern Legal Systems,* 19ff.

[10] Mark van Hoecke and Mark Warrington (1998), "Legal Cultures, Legal Paradigms and Legal Doctrine: Towards a New Model for Comparative Law," 47 *The International and Comparative Law Quarterly,* 498ff.

[11] Ugo Mattei, "Three Patterns of Law: Taxonomy and Change in the World's Legal Systems," 45 *The American Journal of Comparative Law* (1997), s. 5ff.

The rule of the professional law represents the Western legal tradition. This concept distinguishes between the political and the legal arena and the secularized legal process are the dominant characters of this pattern. The rule of political law is characterized as "The Law of Development and Transition". The majority of the ex-socialist legal family and the less developed countries in Africa and Latin America belong to this pattern. The third pattern, the rule of traditional law, represents the oriental view of the law. The different structural nature of law in this pattern because of philosophical (Confucian) or religious (Islamic law) dominance, gives it a special complexity. Even if formal legal institutions are to be found within these cultures "their working rule is different from what we are used to in Western societies."[12]

Mattei's concept gives an alternative to the traditional Western-orientated legal family concept, which has dominated the discourse in the post-war times. It is representative of the post-modern concept of law.

Coloniality—Enduring Colonialism

Late-modern concepts in legal science, therefore, have a conscious relation to both time and space. The break away from the modern nation-state concept with constitution and codification as the dominant legal instruments, to supra-national, multi-national and even natural law inspired legal systems are increasingly involving the nation-states in a pluralistic legal process. The study of politically geared norm systems is competing with the study of those of deep structures we find in time and space.

Historically, in the 19th century the American constitution and the French civil code became well-known examples of global legal phenomena. They were received as legal transplants as in the liberation process in Latin America. In Africa and Asia, instead of a voluntarily reception an imposition of the codification was made. This was the case of the German colonies in Africa and of the French colonies in Indochina at the end of the 19th century. In the German case, Darwinist ideology highly influenced colonial laws,

---

[12] Mattei (1997), 39.

which became models for legislation during the Third Reich.[13] But after the abolition of the Western empires and colonies we have quite a new situation. Which are the ruins of Western legal tradition in the former colonies?

Coloniality is a term used by Latin American researchers to describe the enduring rests of colonialism in the postcolonial area.[14] Such a cultural coloniality identifies the still existing parameters of (1) language, (2) Roman Catholic social ethics (canon law), (3) bureaucratic hierarchies and (4) aristocratic property of the land. English, French and Spanish remains have become a part of the cultural import in the former colonies. Left-side traffic in the former British colonies, the Catholic cathedrals in the French, Spanish and Portuguese colonies, the lack of land reforms in Latin America and Africa are examples of such coloniality. Also the legal cultures, the deep structures of the norm systems and their tradition of values in the former colonies apply to coloniality.

One part of this type of *longue durée* coloniality is the role religious systems play. Religious traditions not only play a role as universal autonomous systems, they also represent important norm systems. The Roman Catholic church, its canon law and social ethics have been important elements of the European heritage kept in the former European colonies throughout the continents.

Family law is in this respect an important part of the legal heritage, where the patriarchal family norms collide with both traditional law and modern (secularized) law. The role of family law in modern Germany and in contemporary South Africa demonstrates this dimension of legal culture.

The Modern Concept of Mixed Legal Systems

Within comparative law, the imposition of legal transplants into the colonies has been described as homogeneous or as "mixed systems".[15]

---

[13] Re: Germany and constitutional law in the German colonies (Schutzgebiete), Michael Stolleis (1992), Geschichte des öffentliches Recht, Vol. 2 (1800–1914), Beck München, 351.

[14] Anibal Quijano (1999), "Coloniality and Modernity/Rationality," in Göran Therborn (ed.), "Globalizations and Modernities—Experiences and Perspectives and Latin America," FRN-Report 99:5, Stockholm, 41ff.

[15] David & Brierley, *Major Legal Systems*, 78f.

Decolonization in Africa and Latin America has to a great extent resulted in confirmation of existing law. Law of western inspiration established by the colonial powers in Africa has been confirmed in the new independent states.[16] In Asian countries, in which the USSR influenced the political systems, as in for example Vietnam and Cambodia, the colonial influences were totally destroyed—and were succeeded by other forms of ideological imperialism.

This post-war *Zeitgeist* inspired the French comparativist René David to format the *"The Major Legal Systems of the World"* into "legal families".[17] David succeeded Max Weber in trying to formulate a model of "macro-comparison" of entire legal systems.[18] David covered the world by identifying the Romano-Germanic family, the family of the common law, family of socialist laws and of philosophical and religious systems.[19] His systematization was problematic. To some extent he found it more attractive to talk about Western law, as "the laws of some states cannot be annexed to either family, because they embody both Roman-Germanic and Common Law elements. The laws of Scotland, Israel, the Union of South Africa, the Province of Quebec and the Philippines would fall into this group."[20] In a footnote he regretted that "unfortunately, these laws have not been dealt with in this book".[21] On the other hand, he included the Romano-Germanic family in a chapter on "Extra-European Laws", including the vast territories outside Europe to which the Romano-Germanic family had been brought due to the colonization. As far as South Africa is concerned, David suggested, "the law of South Africa is 'mixed'."[22] So when David talked about mixed legal systems, he

---

[16] David & Brierley, *Major Legal Systems*, 564f.

[17] René David & John E. Brierley (1968), *Major Legal Systems in the World Today: An Introduction to the Comparative Study of Law*, London Stevens & Sons.

[18] Max Rheinstein (1979), "Legal Systems: Comparative Law and Legal Systems," in Hans G. Leser (ed.), *Max Weber, Collected Works*, vol. 1, Tübingen: J.C.B. Mohr, 245.

[19] R. David & J.E. Brierley (1968), 14ff.

[20] R. David & J.E. Brierley (1968), 17.

[21] He referred to Adde Smith (1965), "The Preservation of the Civilian Tradition in Mixed Jurisdictions," in *Yiannopoulos, Civil Law in the Modern World*, 3–26.

[22] R. David & J.E. Brierley (1968), 60: "Before their annexation by England, the countries which make the Union of South Africa belonged to the Romano-Germanic family by reason of their Dutch colonization. The Roman-Dutch law applied there was endangered by English rule. Under the latter influence, changes have been made which suggest that today the law of South Africa is 'mixed'."—The same was the case in North Africa where French and Italian laws competed with Muslim

identified systems which did not fit into his more general categories. They were miscellaneous to the legal families as such.

In observing "Reception of English Law in Quebec", David's co-author John E.C. Brierley, professor at the Faculty of Law, McGill University in Montreal (Quebec), defined the legal system of Quebec as "a mixed or bi-jural system and it thereby imprints the same general characteristic upon Canada as a whole, of which [Quebec] forms an important part." Brierley regarded the *"mixité"* of the legal system of Quebec in positive terms. In his view the implantations of elements of English law had been beneficial.[23]

When the German comparativists Konrad Zweigert & Hein Kötz in their major work *"Introduction to Comparative Law"*, first published in German around 1970 (and later translated into English), tried to review the systematization done by David in legal families and identified them by *"style"*, they found some what they call *"hybrid"* systems of law which were "not easy to put in the right family".[24] They mentioned Greece, Louisiana in the US, and the Province of Quebec in Canada, Scotland, South Africa, Israel, the Philippines, Puerto Rico, the People's Republic of China "and some others".[25] In a typical phrase they stated: "With them the question must be which family they are closest to in style. This calls for delicacy." And they stated: "In any case, as the example of 'hybrid' systems shows, any division of the legal world into families or groups is a rough and ready device." They realized that this form of "putting the confusing variety of legal systems into families or groups into some kind of loose order" could be useful for the novice, but "the experienced comparativist will have developed a 'nose' for the dis-

---

law: "their laws, which today combine ideas from both systems, must also be considered 'mixed'."

[23] John E.C. Brierley (1994), "Reception of English Law in the Canadian Province of Quebec," in Michel Doucet & Jacques Vanderlinden (eds.) *La reception des systèmes juridiques: Implantation et destin*, Bruxelles: Bruylant, 103ff. Cfr M. Tancelin (1980), "How can a Legal System be a Mixed System?" Introduction to his edition of F.P. Walton, *The Scope of Interpretation of the Civil Code of Lower Canada*, Toronto: Butterworth, 1–34.

[24] The term "Style" (Stil) was introduced by Konrad Zweigert in a *Festschrift* article in 1961.—Konrad Zweigert (1961), Zur Lehre von den Rechtskreisen, in Kurt H. Nadelmann (ed.), *Twentieth Century Comparative and Conflicts Law, Legal Essays in Honor of Hessel E. Yntema*, Leyden, 24.

[25] K. Zweigert & H. Kötz (1987), *Introduction to Comparative Law*, vol. 1 (2nd revised edition), translated by Tony Weir, Oxford: Clarendon Press, 74.

tinctive style of national legal systems and will either not use the device of legal families at all, or will use it with all the circumspection called for by any attempt to force a schematic order social phenomena as highly complex as living legal systems."[26]

When Zweigert & Kötz used *style* as a marker for their categorization, it resulted in a concept with eight legal families: Romanist, Germanic, Nordic, Common Law, Socialist, Far Eastern systems, Islamic systems and Hindu law.[27] This categorization became the dominant one in the comparative discourse for about 25 years. Max Rheinstein used the same concept when he talked about "*Rechtskreisen*" and "*Mischrechte*" in the German translation of his coursebook.[28]

The French comparativist René David is often referring to "mixed systems" when two or more legal systems interfere, but he never goes into how and in what ways they are mixed. Mixed systems, however, are most interesting for legal cultural research. Four examples of such mixed systems will be analysed in this survey.

Vietnam

Vietnam's legal history demonstrates how its legal culture has been influenced with elements from several other legal cultures. Ideologically, Chinese Confucianism and French francophone style as well as Soviet political law have characterized the legal culture of the country in a long perspective *(longue durée)*. During the time of French colonialism, the former Chinese law (The Xin Code) in the 1880s was succeeded by important parts of *code civil*.[29] But even if the French colonialists looked upon the code as a universal one, the influence was restricted to major urban areas. In Hanoi and Saigon, impressive courthouses were constructed in a French neo-classical style, but their services were only provided to "the Europeans and the relatively small group of Vietnamese who needed the services that only

---

[26] K. Zweigert & H. Kötz (1987), 74.

[27] K. Zweigert & H. Kötz (1987), 75.

[28] Max Rheinstein (1974), *Einführung in die Rechtsvergleichung*, München: Verlag C: H. Beck, München, 81. Rheinstein states that even if most of the "mixed legal systems" formerly were dominated by the common law, since the 1920s a contra force has been identified, most of them today belong to a civil law culture.

[29] Robert Lingat (1952), *Les régimes matrimoniaux du sud-est de l'Asie*. Paris: E. de Boccard, 30f.

the colonial system could provide".[30] Even if the French authorities
tried to impose French regulations, the traditional system remained.[31]
The colonial influences on the legal culture were also evident in the
creation of the French-inspired Law School in Hanoi (Faculté de
droit de l'université de Hanoi) 1917.[32] After the independence of
France in 1954 and the period of struggle for socialism in South
Vietnam, which led to a homogenous Vietnam in 1975, there was
a clear break from the colonial system, and the Marxist view on the
political and legal system became dominant. Directives and decrees
explicitly prohibited the authorities from practising traditional and
colonial law. The courts had to implement the new political order
and interpret contract law so it fitted into the planned economic targets. The colonial institutions (such as the Ministry of Justice and
the College of Law) were abolished. The Faculty of Law in Hanoi
was abolished in 1954 and in Saigon after the liberation in 1975.[33]
The political and legal elite was educated and trained in Moscow,
East Berlin and other universities in the Soviet Union. The *nomen-
clatural* system ensured Party hegemony within the judiciary and the
political administration.[34] The differences between political and legal
culture became invisible. The "socialist legality" was introduced as
a relevant system. The traditional Confucianism was transformed
into a new political pattern called political Confucianism. The
Confucian support of social relations with an emperor or king at the
top and a class of gentlemen-scholars manning a centralized bureaucracy below him was transferred into the new socialist cognitive
structure.

To which extent has globalization affected the Vietnamese legal
system and is it possible to find coloniality in contemporary Vietnam?
The Soviet system is in a state of change. The adjustment to an
open market system in the economy has resulted in a double command system, the *Doi-moi*, in which tradition and modernity are the

---

[30] Per Bergling (1999), "Legal Reform and Private Enterprise: The Vietnamese
Example," *Umeå Studies in Law* No. 1/1999, 50.
[31] D.G. Marr (1981), *Vietnamese Tradition on Trial, 1920–1945*, Berkeley and Los
Angeles: University of California Press, 338f.
[32] Per Bergling (1999), 51.
[33] Per Bergling (a.o.) (1998), "An Introduction to the Vietnamese Legal System,"
Umeå, 11.
[34] Per Bergling (1999), 52.

two main forces. Tradition in this system means the upholding of the monolithic Soviet-inspired system. Modernity means legal reforms in a more market-orientated system with the introduction of several international affiliations including ASEAN and UNDP and several reform programmes within the law, including adopting (American) commercial law and contract law.[35] Instead of the unacceptable rule *of* law, a rule *by* law has been introduced. Ugo Mattei regards Vietnam as an example of traditional law not of political law. "Legal sinology had long achieved a position of independence within the field of sovietology. Without the common denominator of the Soviet Union, the Asian republics have little or nothing in common with their European counterparts when it comes to language, culture, religion, and tradition."[36]

The retraditionalization as a global (post-modern) phenomenon can be observed also in the Asian countries, as China and Vietnam. The renaissance of emphasizing Confucianism is such an example. This concept is still relevant within several Asian legal and political systems, including the Vietnamese. The renewed, current French francophone activities in Hanoi and Ho Chi Min City are also affecting the legal culture. France is not only supporting Vietnamese jurists to go to Paris to study law, they are also sponsoring the francophone "Institut de droit francais" affiliated to the Hanoi Law School. And the Supreme Court in Hanoi, Hue and Ho Chi Minh City are still acting in the old French court buildings with the statute of "Justitia" as a Western icon in the entrance hall. As an example of contemporary *legal transplants* bar associations akin to those in the US are organized in Vietnam.

Argentina

In Latin America, Argentina can be used as an example of legal culture of "the South" in transition. Even if the liberation from the Spanish colonialism started in the 1850s, there is still a coloniality in this country. The Argentinean constitution of 1853 (with its federal system) was inspired from the Constitution of the US[37] and the

---

[35] Per Bergling (a.o.), (1998), 93ff.
[36] Mattei (1997), 32.
[37] Ricardo Zorraquín Becú (1996), *Historia del derecho Argentino*, Tomo II, Buenos Aires: Ed. Perrot, 349.

codification, had its archetype in the French *code civil*, as interpreted in the Spanish version[38] and in the Louisiana version (Louisiana Civil Code) 1825.[39] The Western legal tradition in Argentina came not only via Spain but also via United States.

The democratization of Argentina after the military regimes in the early 1980s has brought Argentinean legal culture into new influences. The legal education of today is much more inspired from the US than from Europe (Spain), and the Argentinean legal profession is to a great extent Americanized and inspired from the global market economy and multinational industry and trade. Traditionalism, however, is visible here as in many other Latin American countries. The role of the law of the indigenous people (the Indians) becomes increasingly important. The claims for ethnic (collective) human rights are an example of this Latin American concept of constitutionalism. (These claims are to be compared with those of the Chiapas in Mexico and the Indian claims in Peru and other Andine countries.)

South Africa

The South African legal culture is mixed into three general parts: (1) Dutch-Roman law of the 17th and 18th centuries, (2) English common-law and the 19th and 20th centuries, as well as (3) African native/traditional law. In the Mattei scheme, the African legal cultures rest between the political and traditional line. The legal hearing with South Africa's Truth and Reconciliation Commission (TRC) in 1997 demonstrated a new way to handle the past with respect to political and legal cultures. The new South African constitution consciously distances itself from the colonial heritage by putting the legal traditions of the tribe in the forefront. The collective human rights in conflict will be interpreted and decided by the South African Constitutional Court. In the South African context, coloniality means a conscious distance from the colonial "apartheid" system and its separation between "We and the Other." The South African legal system has been described as an extremely internal affair for the South African lawyers, "simply because [they], like their counter-

---

[38] Becú (1996), 361f.
[39] Shael Herman (1993), *The Louisiana Civil Code: A European Legacy for the United States*, New Orleans: Louisiana Bar Foundation, 32f.

parts all over the world tend to create law primarily with reference to the intellectual concerns raised in statutory documents, authoritative court decisions, and learned treaties."[40]

Estonia

Estonia is the Baltic state which has been decolonized most rapidly from the Soviet Union in the new geopolitical situation of the 1990s. Estonia had before its occupation a west-European legal system influenced by the French and German constitutions and codifications. After 1940, up to the liberation from the collapsing Soviet Union in the early 1990s, Estonia was under its political totalitarian system not only concerning its constitution and laws, but also regarding its legal education and legal professions. In the 1990s, there has been a dramatic change regarding both the constitution and the statutes. Western *Rechtsstaat*-ideology has clearly been implemented, including the separation of power principle, an autonomous judiciary and a market economy signed law of contract. Even if the normative situation has changed, the legal culture, however, has been changing more slowly. Comparing with former German Democratic Republic whose revolutionary change into the New Bundesländer in Germany in October 1990 meant a clear break from the former Marxist legal profession, the Estonian legal actors to a great extent were kept in the new system. The only way to change the legal culture was to recruit a younger generation for the top positions within the legal profession. The position of the Chief Justice of the Supreme Court was given to a 35-year-old law professor at the Tartu University Law School. This dramatic change has resulted in cultural clashes between, on one hand, an older traditional part of the judiciary with cognitive structures and ideologies kept from the old regime and, on the other hand, a younger generation with both international (Western) attitudes to the political system and with a nationalistic (historical) argumentation in trying to give national identity to the legal culture.

---

[40] Reinhard Zimmermann & Daniel Visser (1996), *Southern Cross: Civil Law and Common Law in South Africa*, Oxford, Clarendon Press, 6.

The Post-/Late-modern Concept of Mixed Legal Systems

In late modern legal doctrine, the differences between the legal systems—not the similarities—have been emphasized as a method of
comparison. With such a diversified perspective the *mixed legal systems*-
concept has been regarded as a more convenient construct. Every
legal system is a mixed one. The chthonic legal cultures are rare,[41]
if they have ever existed.[42] The history of a system of law has been
described as more or less "a history of borrowings of legal materials from other legal systems".[43]

Therefore the post-Second World War universalistic construct has
been heavily criticized in recent times. In the postcolonial discourse
it has been used as an example of the "We and the Other" syn-
drome. The critics have challenged Hein Kötz to respond. In an
article he stated that until any other categorization has proved to
be better, the legal families (*Rechtskreisen*) could be used.[44]

Consequently, within comparative law in recent times, different
alternatives to the "legal family" concept have been introduced. If
we return to Ugo Mattei and his "taxonomy of the law", we remember he is locating the legal systems in the world within a triangle
with the rule of traditional, professional and political laws as the
polarized three edges.[45] Mattei's model is first of all representative
for the private law systems. It is much more difficult to find a relevant model for public law systems. Other researchers have also been
interested in constructing new categories for legal law.[46] Also the
Turkish Örücü has elaborated on the topic "mixed and mixing systems" from the author's Turkish experience.[47]

---

[41] H. Patrick Glenn (2000), *Legal Traditions of the World: Sustainable Diversity in Law*,
Oxford University Press.
[42] Rolf Nygren (1998), "*Vad är egentligen 'riktigt svenskt' i den svenska rätten?*" 83 *Svensk
Juristtidning*, 109.
[43] Alan Watson (1974), *Legal Transplants: An Approach to Comparative Law* (1st ed.),
22.
[44] Hein Kötz (1998), "*Abschied von der Rechtskreislehre?*" In 6 *Zeitschrift für Europäisches
Privatrecht*, 493ff.
[45] Ugo Mattei (1997), "Three Patterns of Law: Taxonomy and Change in the
World's Legal Systems," 45 *The American Journal of Comparative Law*, 5ff.
[46] Mark van Hoecke & Mark Warrington (1998), "Legal Cultures, Legal Paradigms
and Legal Doctrine: Towards a New Model for Comparative Law," 47 *International
and Comparative Law Quarterly*, 497ff.
[47] Esin Örücü (1996), "Mixed and Mixing Systems: A Conceptual Search." In

Time and space are close connected in these perspectives in comparative law. The renaissance of using history and culture in late modern legal science has given comparative law new methods. With help of critical methods the modern, post-war (and anachronistic) views on legal transplants have been under attack within the legal cultural discourse.[48]

Historical Layers as Deep Structures of Legal Culture

The Finnish legal theorist, Kaarlo Tuori, has formulated a three-level theory of law, in which he identifies the "living law" as the first level which draws from the second level: the nation-bound historical legal culture. Tuori argues that there is a third bounder-less level, which he calls the *deep structures* of the law. General principles, justice, theological and religious arguments are mentioned as examples of such deep structures.[49]

By emphasizing legal history and legal culture as methodological instruments in the comparative analysis, new results have been observed. "Mixed legal systems" is therefore a term which is well suited for the current constructs. In current legal systems, the difference between civil law and common law has diminished.[50] And, as the deeper understandings of the systems include cultural explanations, a *multileveled structure* of a legal system seems to be a more adequate term to be used from a late-modern and postcolonial perspective.

E. Örücü, Eslpeth Attwooll and Sean Coyle, *Studies in Legal Systems*, The Hague-Boston: Kluwer Law International.

[48] Re: the recent discourse on *legal transplants*, Pierre Legrand, What "Legal Transplants"?; Roger Cotterrell, "Is There a Logic of Legal Transplants?" and Lawrence M. Friedman, "Some Comments on Cotterrell and Legal Transplants." In David Nelken & Johannes Feest (eds.) (2001), *Adapting Legal Cultures*, Hart Publishing Oxford, 55ff, 70ff, 93ff.

[49] Kaarlo Tuori (1997), "Towards a Multilayered View of Modern Law." In Aulis Arnio, Robert Alexy, Gunnar Bergholz (eds.), Justice, *Morality and Society: A Tribute to Aleksander Peczenik on the Occasion of his 60th Birthday 16 November 1997*, Juristförlaget i Lund, 432ff.

[50] James Gordley (1993), "Common Law and Civil Law: eine überholte Unterscheidung," 1 *Zeitschrift für Europäisches Privatrecht*, 498ff.

Legal Pluralism and Legal Culture

"Mixed legal systems" are by definition pluralistic and polycentric. Such legal systems were politically incorrect when the strong modern welfare-state argued for a homogeneous national legislation and a monolithic legal culture.[51] In the new geo-political situation in the 1990s, however, the nation-states developed a transparency over the political borders, and an increased mobility of minorities with multicultural influences in the national states created quite a new situation, which has resulted in pluralistic and transnational legal systems. The affiliation to the European Union has for the 15 member states resulted in an implementation of different supranational layers of legal sources as the European Convention for Human Rights (ECHR), EC-Law, conventions and customary law.

In many of the African postcolonial countries south of Sahara, mixed legal cultures are to be observed. In Senegal, 90 per cent of the population are regarded as Muslims and 10 per cent as Roman Catholics. The postcolonial legal system is still francophone, with a French-trained judiciary and a French codification. As member of the World Trade Organization (WTO), Senegal has also implemented a global commercial law. Traditional law in Senegal is represented mainly by Islamic law, and by informal *sharia*-courts. They are jurisdictions only for the members and their opinions are looked upon as arbitrary.

Also in Southeast Asia, the global economy and memberships in the WTO have resulted in an attack on traditional legal patterns in Asian legal cultures. I will underline a couple of legal phenomena which can be regarded as instruments for the globalization of law.

Constitutional Supremacy in the Legal Culture

The revised constitutions in the postcolonial and developing countries have been regarded as a global indicator of the 20th century. The constitutional reviews have had the American constitution as an

---

[51] Kjell Å Modéer (2001), "The Ongoing Dream: Legal and Political Culture in Postwar Sweden." In *Zweden en de europese cultuur* [Koninklijke Vlaamse Academie van Belgie voor Wettenschappen en Kunsten, Studia Europaea VIII], Bruxelles, 37ff.

archetype with the *rule of law*, the Bill of Rights and the judicial review as the three main parameters. The international climate, especially the economic life, has been important for the growth of constitutionalism in Africa.[52] In South Africa, this has also been the case. The political transition that created the final South African constitution in 1996 has been called a "local miracle".[53] Political revolution was made with the help of the law. In reconstructing the South African state legal formalism, democracy and a postcolonial rule of law have been such constitutionally based legal transplants.[54] The transition was made with the help of "the advice of a plethora of constitutional carpet-baggers—both individuals and government agencies—as well as the symbolic capital gained by 'western' law through the interaction of corporate lawyers and human rights advocates in the transnational realm".[55]

"Claims for the recognition of ethnicity posed the greatest threat to the democratic transition."[56] The new South African Mandela constitution of 1996 could not solve these problems, so even if the constitution gives all tribes in the country the same rights, the Constitutional court has to mediate and find solutions in the cases brought to the court.[57] In post-apartheid South Africa, therefore, traditional law has to be considered in quite a new way. The role of this court is to a great extent to mediate between the parties and reconcile those involved. From the parties' perspective, the constitutional court can also make an unjust decision which is not so astonishing (and can even be tolerated) in a country where the traditional tribes for centuries have regarded the unjust as the rule and not the exception.[58]

---

[52] Samuel C. Nolutshungu (1993), "Constitutionalism in Africa: Some Conclusions." In Douglas Greenberg, Stanley N. Katz, Melanie Beth Oliviero, Steven C. Wheatley (eds.), *Constitutionalism & Democracy: Transitions in the Contemporary World*, Oxford University Press/New York & London, 376f.

[53] Kader Asmal (1995), "The Making of a Constitution," *Southern African Review of Books* 11, March/April.

[54] Martin Chanock (2001), *The Making of South African Legal Culture 1902–1936: Fear, Favour and Prejudice*, Cambridge: Cambridge University Press, 511.

[55] Heinz Klug (2000), *Constituting Democracy: Law, Globalism and South Africa's Political Reconstruction*, Cambridge University Press, 7.

[56] Heinz Klug (2000), 111.

[57] Heinz Klug (2000), 160f, 167ff.

[58] Albie Sachs in a talk at UC Berkeley, Boalt Hall, November 2001.

The constitutional reform in South Africa has been an archetype for the late-modern political transition from a totalitarian/authoritarian regime into a democratic state with the help of law and judicialization. As Heinz Klug formulated it: Rule of law and Bill of Rights have been the global vehicles for a political transition, not made with the help of economic and technological factors, but legal ones.[59] Globalization and international political culture gave nutrition to the legal revolution in South Africa.

However, in the South African postcolonial situation, suppressed tribes are lobbying for their ethnic rights, hence the Constitutional Court in Johannesburg is in a unique and delicate position both to uphold democratic principles while mediating between the tribes and their legal traditions. The open form of constitution has given law and justice important political roles in creating a democracy upholding not only individual rights but also collective, ethnic rights.[60] The Constitutional Court is creating a dynamic form of constitutionalism.

The 1954 Chinese Mao Zedong constitution upheld the principles of equality, mutual benefit, mutual respect for sovereignty and territorial integrity. The communist Chinese constitution in that respect continued to uphold the concept of a closed nation. The legal culture was influenced by Soviet legal culture. The revisions of the Constitution in 1975 and 1978 emphasized that "China was prepared to combat the subversion and aggression by social imperialism". As Professor Xin Chunying noted, "Provisions as such left very little room in effect for the legal system on foreign related matters."[61] The opening-up of global economy initiatives started with the 1982 Constitution. It gave permission to joint ventures with international enterprises and to foreign investors to establish in China.[62] The "reform and opening-up" has also resulted in an ongoing discourse on Western democracy and human rights principles as rule of law and fair trial.

---

[59] Heinz Klug (2000), 58.
[60] Heinz Klug (2000), 111ff, 139ff.
[61] Xin Chunying (1999), "Chinese Legal System & Current Legal Reform," *Konrad-Adenauer-Stiftung-Schriftenreihe* 01/1999, Vol. 4, 764f.
[62] Xin Chunying (1999), 766.

Southern Cross—Reception into a Mixed Legal Culture

Even if the constitutional problems were resolved with the help of the Mandela Constitution 1996, the South African legal culture still upholds traditions and customs related to the legal history of the country. In recent literature different views are demonstrated. Some years ago, Reinhard Zimmermann and Daniel Visser published a study on South African private law from the early 1800s up to today.[63] They describe the South African legal culture as a mixed legal system. The Dutch-Roman law—with its roots in the continental European *ius commune*—is the "internal" legal system, which is attacked through reception of the English legal system.[64] The legal culture is the public one, instrumentalized by the jurists. This perspective gives an internal dimension on the legal culture. For Zimmermann & Visser, it is difficult to observe any African elements at all in the legal culture.

Martin Chanock, in his major work on South African legal culture on the other hand, emphasises the bureaucracy as an important part of the legal culture: "In any highly bureaucratic state the main generators and users of the law are the bureaucracy, and they are a major influence on the growth of a legal culture."[65] The retraditionalization of the South African legal culture after the apartheid regime has again discovered and introduced the chthomic elements, the law and legal culture of the black people. During the apartheid period it was impossible to identify this dimension of the law, due to the "internal" perspectives of the judiciary itself. The understanding of the legal culture extended "not simply to what officials may, or must, legally do, but how they do it". "There was a culture of hostility and intimidation . . . [The] face presented by authority. . . was a war against people who were unenfranchised."[66] The oppressing of the black and Indian population during the apartheid regime

---

[63] Reinhard Zimmermann & Daniel Visser (eds.) (1996), *Southern Cross: Civil Law and Common Law in South Africa*.

[64] Reinhard Zimmermann (2003), "Gemeines Recht heute: Das Kreutz des Südens." In Jörn Eckert (ed.), *Der praktische Nutzen der Rechtsgeschichte* [Hans Hattenhauer zum 8. September 2001]. C.F. Müller Verlag Heidelberg, 604f.

[65] Martin Chanock (2001), 514.

[66] David Dyzenhaus (1998), *Judging the Judges. Judging Ourselves: Truth, Reconciliation and the Apartheid Legal Order*, Oxford Hart Publishing, 61.

resulted in a very monolithic legal culture, to which only the whites had access. During the Mandela regime a new constitution was set up. In this the indigenous tribes were given a new legal position. In principle, every native tribe had its rights guaranteed in the constitution.

In Chanock's view, the rule of law has been imposed on the late modern legal culture in South Africa. "South Africa was colonised in the 1990s by a new kind of internationally sanctioned state: . . . the Constitutional State".[67] And he concludes in a general remark: "The land represents the link between the past and the future; ancestors lie buried there, children will be born there. Farming is more than just a productive activity; it is an act of culture, the centre of social existence, and the place where personal identity is forged."[68]

The Great Wall—Protecting an Insular Legal Culture

The Asian legal cultures demonstrate quite a different concept. The courts are first of all penal courts; the private conflicts are traditionally solved by mediation and reconciliation. Mediation is an important part of the Chinese legal culture, mandated by its Constitution. There are one million people's mediation committees and some six million mediators in China.[69] The peaceful organization of society in Confucian thinking lays the fundamentals for the traditional and internal Chinese legal culture.

In 19th century imperial China, after the Opium Wars of the 1840s, the possibilities for feudal China to keep "the foreign dragon" out of Chinese territory declined. China turned into a semi-feudal and semi-colonial society.[70] The insular jurisdictions offered to the foreigners became diasporas within the Chinese empire. After the Chinese defeat in the Sino-Japanese War 1894–1895, there was a critique against the traditional Chinese political and legal culture. Japan was successful because it was open to modern reforms. The "Wuxu" reforms in 1898 were the first modern legal reform inspired by the West. Foreign commerce and trade followed the legal reform.

---

[67] Martin Chanock (2001), 513.
[68] Albie Sachs (1990), *Protecting Human Rights in a New South Africa*, 115.
[69] Laurence Boulle & The Hwee Hwee (2000), *Mediation: Principles, Process, Practice*, [Singapore Edition] Butterworths Asia/Singapore, 187f.
[70] Xin Chunying (1999), 315.

The Emperor Guangxu in the Hundred Days Reform adopted 110 laws. The Empress Dowager Tz'u-₂shi, however, was against the reform and ordered that the Emperor be put in jail and arrested the six most important reformers. They were executed in jail Cai Shi Kou in Beijing on 28 September 1898. The Westernization reform ended in failure and was followed by the reactionary Boxer rebellion in 1900.[71]

The hostile reactions in 1898 and during the Boxer rebellion in 1900 indicated to Europe and Japan the difficulties of introducing modern Western reform in China. They demonstrated the attitudes to tradition and reform in late imperial China. Traditionally the "rule of men" has dominated Chinese legal culture even as an ongoing discourse on rights and human rights 1900–1949 has been documented.[72] Totalitarian China under Mao Zedong did not allow any influence from Western capitalist culture. During the last 20 years, however, the rule-of-law concept has been introduced in China, especially in current legal reforms.[73] Globalizations in law and Chinese membership of the WTO have together contributed to Western (American) legal reforms.

Since the 1980s, harmony, consensus and mediation again have been in focus in post-modern Asian legal culture. Those traditional elements in Chinese legal culture have been increasingly important in contemporary China.[74]

A renaissance of Confucian ideology is found in the reforms. However, there are also tendencies brought about by globalization within the Chinese legal culture. Since the membership of the WTO, transparency, openness and fairness have been important keywords in the transformation process. Fairness can be especially regarded as an integral principle in the revivalist movement for Confucian thinking in contemporary China. Confucian mediation has also adjusted

---

[71] Xin Chunying (1999), 316ff.; Hu Sheng (1991), *From the Opium War to the May Fourth Movement*, Vol. II, Foreign Language Press, Beijing, 138ff.

[72] Stephen C. Angle & Marina Svensson (1999), "On Rights and Human Rights: A Contested and Evolving Chinese Discourse, 1900–1949," 31 *Contemporary Chinese Thought*, Fall 1999.

[73] Xin Chunying (1999), 344ff.

[74] Shin-yi Peng, "The WTO Legalistic Approach and East Asia: From the Legal Culture Perspective." 1 *Asian-Pacific Law & Policy Journal* 13:1, http://www.hawaii.edu/aplpj.

to modern industrial China. "A Chinese individual defines his or her identity, rights, and obligations according to the perceived relationship between the parties. As such, his or her sense of procedural and distributive justice varies according to that perception. . . . As such, litigation is generally shunned by the Chinese because of the incongruence between the concept of fairness of the Chinese people and the basic principles of the modern law. It has also been noted that Chinese, even in modern industrial societies, still observe the basic tenets concerning social relations attributable to Confucianism."[75]

Mediation is not only an integral part of Chinese legal culture and in the Chinese diasporas. It is a conflict-solving model related to the globalization of legal culture.

Conclusions

The retraditionalization of the legal cultures has made them more complex than they would have been analysed with modern instruments. The role of the increasingly Evangelical culture within the contemporary South African community indicates a neo-colonial phenomenon also related to the legal culture. Today 72.6 per cent of South Africans claim to be Christians. In 1911, the figure was 46 per cent.[76] The upcoming "negritude" African culture is increasingly dichotomized reflecting the West European culture's fundamental content in terms of values and economic practices which also include the identification of legal customs related to the different South African tribes.[77] Global constitutionalism has also given legitimacy to traditional values and legal principles embodied in ethnic groups.

The general trend towards alternative dispute resolutions in contemporary Western societies have resulted in a privatization of the conflict-solving methods, where the traditional solutions have been used again, in South Africa during the reconciliation process under

---

[75] L. Boulle & T. Hwee Hwee (2000), 189.
[76] Ann Bernstein (2002), "Globalization, Culture and Development: Can South Africa be more than an offshoot of the West?" In Peter L. Berger and Samuel P. Huntington, *Many Globalizations: Cultural Diversity in the Contemporary World*, Oxford: Oxford University Press, 227.
[77] Ann Bernstein (2002), 199.

Bishop Tutu.[78] In China, Confucian thinking on "dispute resolution" in contemporary postcolonial times still dominates, and has always been looked at from the perspective that harmony should prevail between individuals. Dispute should be dissolved rather than resolved.[79]

This comparison between South Africa and its weak state[80] and China, upholding a political concept with a strong and stable state, has shown not only differences in the deep structures in their legal cultures. It has also demonstrated the influences from the contemporary political forces, e.g. globalization of Western constitutionalism within legal cultures. Still more interesting, however, are the contra-forces: the retraditionalization of legal cultures. In South Africa, this has been observed in the emphasis of the traditional ethnic-based legal systems, and in China with the renaissance of Confucian thinking. The upheaval of ethnic and collective human rights and mediation as an alternative dispute-solving methods are two examples of legal phenomena, which give new dimensions to Western legal cultures, which since the Enlightenment have emphasized individual human rights and conflict-solving with the help of public institutions.

---

[78] David Dyzenhaus (1998), *Truth, Reconciliation and the Apartheid Legal Order*, Juta & Co. Ltd., Cape Town.
[79] Shin-yi Peng (2000), 1 *ASLPJ* 13:10.
[80] The South African State has never been stable. Chanock (2001), 514.

ASIAN NATIONS AND GLOBALIZATION

THE NATIONAL, THE RELIGIOUS, AND THE GLOBAL IN THE CONSTRUCTION OF NATIONAL IDENTITY IN BANGLADESH

Habibul Haque Khondker
Zayed University, Abu Dhabi, UAE

Introduction

This chapter seeks to examine the processes through which the ideological contents of nationalism have changed in Bangladesh in the interplay with the forces of globalization. By exploring the changes in the global ideological regimes, this paper will examine how Bangladesh having originated as a secular state was transformed into a religious state when it officially declared Islam as the state religion. The secularist nationalism was replaced by an Islamic nationalism in less than a decade of the country's independence in 1971. However, with the electoral victory of secularist Awami League in 1996, a return to the secularist bases of nationalism took place, but this was quickly dismantled as soon as a coalition of Islamicist parties came to power in 2001. Such changes reflect deep ambivalence concerning national identity and the shifting basis of nationalism has profound impact on the consolidation of democracy and national development in Bangladesh. The Bangladesh case presents a fertile ground for rethinking transformation of nationalism and its engagement with globalization. This chapter uses the argument that nationalism is a product of the processes of globalization as a point of departure. The case of Bangladesh illustrates some of the theoretical underpinnings of the relationship between globalization and nationalism with a renewed emphasis on the role of religion.

Most writers of nationalism—more or less—viewed it in terms of a modernist project. Gellner (1983) was explicit about it so was Eugene Weber (1979). The rest were more implicit. This is not to suggest that there is a singular narrative of modernity or modernist project that would capture all the diverse histories of nationalism. Various taxonomies of the theories of nationalism can be found ranging from primordialists to constructionists, or ethnic vs civic, or integrative vs disruptive, or colonial vs anti-colonial, or official vs popular and so on. In all these dualities, we see an implicit position of linearity. Now, with growing skepticism of the idea of linearity and progress, one might be tempted to reject the entire history of nationalism as a "meta narrative" which might even be congruent with the seeming absurdities of our time. However, such an interpretation will empower the forces interested in reconstructing nationalism and rewriting history. We need to find a theoretical middle ground that would help us understand the shifts and swings of nationalist discourse.

Benedict Anderson (1999) points out that there are two "common kinds of misunderstanding" concerning nationalism. I would add a third.

The first is that nationalism is something very old and is inherited from "absolutely splendid ancestors." Thus it is something that arises "naturally in the blood and flesh of each of us." (Anderson, 1999) Anderson (1999) reminds us: "In fact, nationalism is something rather new, and today is little more than two centuries old." The First Declaration of Independence (of USA) proclaimed in 1776 Philadelphia said not a word about ancestors or Americans. The utter dismay—not to say incredulity—of the co-author of the "invention of tradition", Eric Hobsbawm (1993), at a book produced in Pakistan entitled *Five Thousand Years of Pakistan*, may easily be appreciated. Pakistan gained independence in 1947, while the proposal for the formation of such a state was mooted in 1940. The very name Pakistan was supposedly the brainchild of Choudhury Rahmat Ali who while at Cambridge in 1933 invented the name Pakistan for a separate north-western region of India with no mention of Bengal. Yet, Shahid Javed Burki, a Pakistani scholar with World Bank credentials, claims "Pakistan's history really begins with the arrival of Islam in India in the eighth century" (1999:2). Bangladesh has not claimed a thousand-year scale history yet and the country's constitution drafted a year after her independence in 1971 did have the word "nationalism" as one of the state principles. We will come back to that in a moment. Anderson tells us: "the mania for seeking "absolutely splendid ancestors" typically gives rise to "nonsense, and often very dangerous nonsense" (Anderson, 1999:3).

"The second misunderstanding", according to Anderson, "is that 'nation' and 'state' are, if not exactly identical, at least like a happy husband and wife in their relationship. But the historical reality is often just the opposite. . . . Nation and state 'got married' very late on, and the marriage was far from always happy. The state—in general—is much older than the nation" (Anderson, 1999:4). Here Charles Tilly's (1990) distinction between nation-state and national state is helpful. National state appeared on the scene much earlier rivaling city-states and other non-national entities.

The third misunderstanding that I would like to add concerns the much celebrated "nation as an imagined community". Here so-called "social construction" theory or phenomenological tradition in sociology seems to overstate the case to the extent that it falls in to the abyss of subjectivism or perspectivism. Nations are imagined; but they are not imaginary, they are not fabrications or constructions. In fact, Anderson rebukes Ernest Gellner for claiming that "nationalism is not the awakening of nations to self-consciousness; it invents nations where they do not exist". Anderson points out that Gellner confuses "invention" with "fabrication" and "falsity" rather than "imagining" and "creation" (McCrone, 1998).

Definitions of Nationalism

A good starting point in defining nationalism as always is Ernest Renan's speech in 1882 at the Sorbonne, a speech that, in part, reflected the French nationalistic aspirations of the late 19th century. In that famous speech Renan stated: "A nation is a soul, a spiritual principle. Two things, which in truth are but one, constitute this soul or spiritual principle. One lies in the past, one in the present. One is the possession in common of a rich legacy of memories; the other is present-day consent, the desire to live together, the will to perpetuate the value of the heritage that one has received in undivided form" (Renan quoted in Bhabha, 1990:19). Renan used the phrase "a daily plebiscite" in the definition of nation so as to stress on the dynamic aspect of the nation's existence. For him a nation is a soul, a mental principle. It is also a store of memories . . . (awareness of the past sacrifices). And there is the wish to live together . . . the desire to continue a life in common."

To quote Gellner, for example: "Nations are not inscribed into the nature of things," . . . and "Nations as a natural, God-given way of classifying men, as an inherent though long-delayed political destiny, are a myth; nationalism, which sometimes takes pre-existing cultures and turns them into nations, sometimes invents them, and often obliterates pre-existing cultures: that is a reality" (Gellner, 1983:49). "Nationality, though very important in certain circumstances, which has prevailed for the past two centuries, is not a universal characteristic of human beings" (Gellner, 1993:19). Or to quote Bhabha (1990:1), "Nations, like narratives, lose their origins in the myths of time and only fully realize their horizons in the mind's eye." The view that nation is a myth featured in the writings of Jose Carlos Mariategui, a Peruvian in the 1920s: "The nation . . . is an abstraction, an allegory, a myth that does not correspond to a reality that can be scientifically defined" (quoted in Brennan, 1990). Hans Kohn also emphasizes the point that a nation is a state of mind, a political principle which holds that the political and the national unit should be congruent. According to Peter Sahlins, national identity is a socially constructed and continuous process of defining 'friend' and 'enemy'. Nationalism does not express or reflect a natural, primordial reality. Joseph Stalin's definition is quite inclusive. "A nation is a historically constituted, stable community of people formed on the basis of a common language, territory, economic life, and psychological make-up manifested in a common culture" (Stalin, 1994:21). This is an ideal-type of nationalism. The real life nationalisms are only approximations of it.

Partha Chatterjee raises some important points about the problems of historicism. Despite the problems raised by Chatterjee, history—and certain universal categories with it—is unavoidable. I don't share the Henry Ford version that "History is bunk". A Fordist or postmodernist denial of history is bound to play in the hands of the powerful. History is one of the resistors against arbitrary power. "Nationalists make use of the past in order to subvert the present" (Kedourie, 1994:51). In some sense history makes nations and nations make history. Duara (1998), amongst others, makes this case and finds a corrosive influence of nation on history. In any case, the relationship between history and nation cannot be ignored. History unifies, history divides. For example, the demolition of Babri Mosque in India in 1992 divided the nation of India not so much between the Hindus and the Muslims but also between the secular liberals on the one hand and the religionists and conservatives on the other. History is both a matter of interpretation as well as evidence.

It is the meaning of history that has led Partha Chatterjee to contest Ben Anderson's notion of "modularity of nation". Chatterjee avers: "If nationalisms in the rest of the world have to choose their imagined community from certain 'modular' forms already made available to them by Europe and the Americas, what do they have left to imagine?" (Chatterjee, 1993:5). At the risk of oversimplification, Anderson's thesis can be presented in the following, though schematic manner. Anderson (1991) provides a historical sketch and does not worry about east/west difference. He grants print-capitalism a main role in the development of nationalism which, in concrete terms, led to an explosion in book publications and the spread of vernaculars. Print-capitalism not only gave fixity to language, it also paved the way for the rise of national consciousness. Unless we find a more plausible explanation, Anderson's schema seems to be sound.

Nation-state in particular and the state systems as such bear striking similarities around the world. John Meyer and his team have found a certain isomorphism in the pattern of state systems around the world and they have considered the academic curricula around the world. Isomorphism refers to a correspondence between two sets or similarities despite difference in origins.

The same argument for isomorphism can be made with regard to "nationalism" or for that matter various institutions of the national state such as national constitution (Markoff and Regan, 1987) or symbols such as national flags (Weitman, 1973) or any other concepts or categories we use in academic or public discourses. Chatterjee continues, "History, it would seem, has decreed that we in the post-colonial world shall only be perpetual consumers of modernity. Europe and the Americas, the only true subjects of history, have thought out on our behalf not only the script of colonial enlightenment and exploitation, but also that of our anticolonial resistance and post-colonial misery. Even our imaginations must remain forever colonized" (Chatterjee, 1993:5). A good example of colonization of imagination can be found a few pages later in criticizing certain English claims of the achievements of British rule in India when he says: "Having read our Michel Foucault, we can now recognize . . . etc." (Chatterjee, 1993:15).

Chatterjee argues that ". . . nationalist imagination in Asia and Africa are posited not on an identity but rather on a difference with the 'modular' forms of the national society propagated by the modern West" (1993:5). Chatterjee uses the term identity in the sense of similarity. Ironically, the focus on difference is an outgrowth of identity politics. Chatterjee's main point that there is a difference between inner/spiritual and outer material and so on are well rehearsed in the politics of Gandhi and Nehru and clearly stated by Tagore. This was a popular position in the nationalist ideological circles. The West is strong in the material aspects of civilization, the East is strong on the spiritual side. Therefore, the East and the West are complementary to one another. Who can disagree with platitudes? We can all live happily ever after.

Ashish Nandy is more critical of the West and presses charges of imperialism of categories: this is fine. Here he is repeating some of the criticisms earlier made by Susantha Goonatilke (1982). But let us consider the story of Keshab Sen's visit to England in 1870 drawn from Chatterjee. "He had been astonished to discover in England an institution he certainly did not expect to find in this country—I mean caste. Your rich people are really Brahmins, and your poor people are Sudras" (Chatterjee, 1993:38). Now is this an example of imperialism of categories? No. In my opinion, we need concepts and categories to communicate. Categories are always provisional—we use them in different contexts with great success. Most sociologists would jump to accept Sen's analysis—where caste would mean a rigid, ossified stratification without accusing him of reverse imperialism of categories.

Peter Alter (1989) viewed nationalism both as an ideology and a political movement. Such a combination is often manifest in the nationalist struggle in the Third World. "In the doctrine of Pakistan, Islam is transformed into a political ideology and used in order to mobilize Muslims against Hindus; more than that it cannot do, since an Islamic state on classical lines is today an impossible anachronism" (Kedourie, 1994:51). Nationalism, in sum, is not the awakening of an old, dormant force; rather a consequence of new conditions. Once the historical link between nationalism and modernization has been made; now it would be useful to show nationalism as an expression of globalization.

Nationalism in a Globalized World

Paraphrasing Marx, one can say the whole world is now being haunted by the spectre of nationalism. Nationalism is back. In the past two centuries, history has witnessed the rise and ebb of nationalisms sometimes with deadly consequences. The verdict is out: globalization viewed as global modernization is not going to erase differences and create a homogenized world. Nationalism and globalization are destined to coexist. Interestingly, some of the processes of globalization, i.e., formation of supra-national entities and the perceived threat to the local and national enhanced an awareness of self vis-à-vis "others", thus keeping the issue of national question alive.

A society, that is, a people living in a state juridically defined, bordered, and so forth, becomes an official nation only under certain favourable historical junctures. Such nations have certain definable and taken for granted characteristics. It has become a part of our everyday idiom, we know what it is—sort of. Let's say, we speak of the Swedes as a nation which seen in another light refers to the people who inhabit the state known as Sweden. Nation and state do overlap in certain instances. Are French Canadians a nation? Those who say no are thinking of the overlap between state and nation. In a referendum held in late 1995, the majority of the voters in Quebec voted against separation from Canada, therefore, French Canadians are not a nation. They are part of the Canadian nation. However, if the results of the poll had swung the other direction, they would be known as Quebecois. Those who insist that Quebecois are a nation despite the outcome of the referendum, see nation and state as different and not as overlapping categories. There are, indeed, many possibilities.

First, there are nations in the making either with long-held national aspirations, or twists and turns of history produce national sentiments and aspirations where there were none or very little. Certain markers, in part objective, in part subjective, separate one group of people from another. Group identity based on religion or language or some other criterion or criteria can give shape to a nation.

Second, there are multinational states. The former Soviet Union or the former Yugoslavia are examples of multinational states that have since dissolved into multiple states, each claiming its own historical nationhood sometimes with outside help. Does this mean multinational states are potentially unstable and it is only a matter of time before each "nation" achieves its own "state"? Here the possibilities are as immense as the problems of fairness, authenticity and justice. Let's take the example of India, a federal state with 25 odd states. Kashmir is often in the news these days but the problems of this sad but beautiful place go back to the days of the partition of the British India in 1947. Is Kashmir a nation? The flame of nationalism has been alive since 1947. But what about the Punjab?

Do the Sikhs have a rightful claim to nationhood? Militarily, they are now subdued. The high tide of nationalist fervour of the 1980s in the Punjab ebbed in the 1990s, thanks to an effective handling of the crisis by the Indian government. But is there any guarantee that the flames of nationalism will remain extinguished there permanently and that a new wave will not recur? During the 1965 war between India and Pakistan, the Sikhs were the most valiant fighters on the Indian side as were the Bengalees on the Pakistan side. Barely six years later, Bengalees fought the Pakistanis for autonomy and then, independence, and succeeded (with the help of the Indians) in attaining their own homeland. In India, barely a decade or so later, the Sikhs became vociferous in their demands for a separate homeland and failed. The Sikhs also fought valiantly in the 1971 war between India and Pakistan over Bangladesh. Many Bangladeshis who lived through that war identified Sikhs with India so much so that the Sikh separatism was rather baffling to them.

The functioning democracy and its attendant flexibility in India seems to be more successful in fusing diversity than, say, a command polity as represented in the former Soviet Union or the militaristic Pakistan regime. Here we have another point worth pondering—the relationship between nationalism and democracy. Nationalist movements often emerged hand in hand with a call for democracy, especially in the colonial situations. But then in several instances, the call for a heightened nationalism ended up mingling with the rise of fascism of various sorts. The critics of nationalism and, especially, patriotism have that fear in mind. The idea of nationalism has historical connections with romanticism. Sociologists and other sceptics question the sham of nationalism in a class-divided, individualistic society. Empirical studies of nationalism reveal that the idea of nationalism often originates with the elite or with an aspiring middle-class, the bourgeoisie; the rest of the society are conned into it. From a rational choice perspective, it is often self-seeking elites and certain groups who play the game of nationalism for their own individual or group benefits. Such a view borders on a conspiracy theory. Conspiracies are not unknown in history, but we do not belong to just a conspiratorial world. The scheming elites may have political ambition or the aspiring bourgeoisie may have economic gains in mind, but the masses of the people may have other, non-economic gains in mind. A sense of nationalism can give a group of people a sense of group-worth. Such sentiments and psychic satisfaction are important both to the rich as well as to the poor. The popularity of nationalist leaders lies not simply in the demagoguery of the leaders or its converse, the naiveté of the ordinary people, but in a coalition of interests. Objective conditions provide the realm of possibilities, the contexts that are "constructed" or "reconstructed" subjectively. Here the role of intellectual elites is crucial. It can be said that a discourse of nationalism is a precondition for and a prelude to the rise of a nationalist movement. National sentiments are not primordial, they emerge in the interplay of a variety of historical and contingent social forces most significant of which are the forces of globalization.

In the last decade of the 20th century, the rise of various ethno-nationalist movements in the wake of the collapse of the Soviet system led many to doubt the inevitability of the globalization process. If globalization is conceived of as a steamroller erasing all forms of differences leading to homogenization; only then the ethno-nationalistic, particularistic movements around the world can be seen as reversing the process. But if we view globalization as a complex, transnational, and multicultural project then it is not only congruent with but to some extent dependent on plurality and heterogeneity. As some of the globalization theorists have argued, I think quite convincingly, that the spread of nation-states around the world, the rise of a common set of diplomatic norms and conventions guiding the relationships among the nation-states, are markers of the processes of globalization (Robertson, 1992; Meyer, 1980).

Historically, certain key processes of globalization coincided with the flowering of nationalism in the last century. For example, the laying of intercontinental submarine cables, the standardization of time (internationally), and the initial thrust for international war conventions took place in the second half of the 19th century. Nationalism, first as a sentiment then as a movement, emerged as a discourse that emphasized differences. It was "we" versus "they". The intellectual discourse of nationalism of the present century was in itself an appendage to the nationalist movements. What is interesting in the recent globalization theory is that it pointed out how similar the rhetoric of differences was. Nationalism assumed a modular form. For the emergent intellectual and political elites in various parts of the world, there was a model of nationalism which they adapted to their own circumstances. They did not blindly emulate. Globalization, according to Robertson, implied unity, not integration, of the world.

Nor does it imply homogenization. Globalization as Hannerz and Appadurai argue is the celebration of hybridity, creolization and heterogeneity. The new wave of nationalism in the twilight of the second millennium was surely not a reaction, but a sub-plot in the drama of globalization.

According to Giddens, "Globalization is not a single process but a mixture of processes, which often act in contradictory ways, producing conflicts, disjunctures and new forms of stratification. Thus, for instance, the revival of local nationalisms, and an accentuating of local identities, are directly bound up with globalizing influences, to which they stand in opposition" (Giddens, 1994:5). However, to see the revival of nationalism as a redoubt, or as a resistance to the forces of globalization presents a view that is only nominally true. A careful analysis must entail an examination of the interface of the global and local in understanding issues of nationalism and national identity.

Globalization can be defined as deterritorialization and compression of the world to the extent that a singular society can hardly be studied without reference to the broad ideological and cultural currents at the global level. Deterritorialization refers to increasing irrelevance of territorial space and its corollary, the disjuncture between space and events. An example of deterritorialization would be the demonstrations against Salman Rushdie in Bangladesh where the controversial book was not even allowed in the first place. The controversies in England where the book was initially available freely kicked off a controversy that had direct repercussions in Bangladesh. As one writer has recently shown, there is a great deal of influence of radical Islamic views on Bengali youth in certain neighbourhoods in London which is caused both by a sense of alienation and generation gap but also due to the forces of ideological/religious globalization (Glynn, 2002). Compression of the world refers to the speed at which controversies, debates, and ideas can travel from one part of the world to another.

In order to explore the sources of national identity, we need to examine how much of it is generated by local culture and how much of it can be attributed to the differences in social structures, historical experiences, maintenance of memories, construction of memories and so forth. In contemporary societies media images, movies, and self-presentation of the nations are powerful means in shaping the national identity. Although constructivist position has gained a good deal of popularity, it would be erroneous to neglect certain essential attributes of social structure whether language, or political economy, ideology, religion, a shared culinary or aesthetic preference or a shared memory on which national identity or nationhood can be built. I would argue that the national identity is historically constructed both by the impersonal forces of social institutions, events and processes; the deliberate "construction" via "invention of traditions" constitute only one facet of these processes.

According to Raymond Williams, "nation" as a term is radically connected with "native". We are born into relationships which are typically settled in a place. This form of primary and "placeable" bonding is of quite fundamental human and natural importance. Yet the jump from that to anything like the modern nation-state is entirely artificial (Williams, 1983:45). In the context of Bengal, a sense of "nation", though highly ambiguous, arose by the middle of the 19th century, long before the emergence of the nation-state of Bangladesh. The embryonic notion of nation was embedded in the notion of the native. The "native" which is the basis of a nation with all its appearance as a given is also, to a large extent, a construction especially in the context of colonial legacy. Surely, in the initial stage, the natives saw themselves as passive subjects of the colonial rulers and tried to emulate their habits but with time and growing self-confidence they became more assertive and challenged their rulers. Chinua Achebe's *Things Fall Apart* (1958) depicts the construction of native— a self-reassured, coherent community losing its meaning and bearings in the face of colonial incorporation. In the context of Bengal, the process of nativization began somewhere in the first quarter of the 19th century. In the first quarter of the nineteenth century, with the British solidly entrenched, the colonialists influenced the structure of society as well as its culture. The construction of Bengali identity took place largely in the context of the British colonial rule. The acceptance of the colonial masters and their definition of the subjects as "natives" began to be accepted by the natives themselves.

Writing in 1840, Thomas Babington Macaulay waxed as eloquent about the resources of Bengal as he was derisive of the Bengalis: "Bengal was known through the East as the garden of Eden, as the rich kingdom. Its population multiplied exceedingly. Distant provinces were nourished from the overflowing of its granaries; and the noble ladies of London and Paris were clothed in the delicate produce of its looms. The race by whom this rich tract was peopled, enervated

by a soft climate and accustomed to peaceful employments, bore the
same relation to other Asiatics which the Asiatics generally bear to
the bold and energetic children of Europe. The Castilians have a
proverb, that is, in Valencia the earth is water and the men women;
and the description is at least equally applicable to the vast plain of
the Lower Ganges. Whatever the Bengalee does he does languidly.
His favourite pursuits are sedentary. He shrinks from bodily exer-
tion; and, though voluble in dispute, and singularly pertinacious in
the war of chicane, he seldom engages in personal conflict, and
scarcely ever enlists as a soldier" (Macaulay, [1840] 1907:503). In
another occasion, he wrote: "What the Italian is to the Englishman,
what the Hindoo is to the Italian, what the Bengalee is to other
Hindoos. . . . The physical organization of the Bengalee is feeble even
to effeminacy. He lives in a constant vapor bath. His pursuits are
sedentary, his limbs delicate, his movements languid. During many
ages he has been trampled upon by men of bolder and more hardy
breeds. Courage, independence, veracity, are qualities to which his
constitution and his situation are equally unfavorable. His mind bears
a singular analogy to his body. It is weak even to helplessness for
purposes of mainly resistance; but its suppleness and its tact move
the children of sterner climates to admiration not unmingled with
contempt. . . . What the horns are to the buffalo, what the paw is to
the tiger, what the sting is to the bee, what beauty, according to the
old Greek song, is to women, deceit is to the Bengalee. Large promises,
smooth excuses, elaborate tissues of circumstantial falsehood, chi-
canery, perjury, forgery, are the weapons, offensive and defensive, of
the people of the Lower Ganges" (Macaulay, [1841] 1907:562).

Whether Macaulay's views on the Bengali character were shared
by other colonial rulers cannot be ascertained but it can be assumed
that such a condescending and derogatory view shook the Bengali
elites and thus contributed to a renewed self-assessment. The introduction of modern education with the establishment of Hindu College
in 1817 and the rise of a middle class paved the way for the emergence of a new Bengali identity. Surely, the Bengali character was
essentially that of the middle-class origin. It was the character of the
Bhadrolok class and not that of the masses of peasantry. An urban-
based nationalist discourse evolved centering around the new educated Bengali elite which was a "derivative discourse" (Chatterjee,
1986) but surely, it was also a "different discourse" (Guha-Thakurta,
1992).

The nationalist movement was an unintended consequence of the modern education introduced by the British with the active support of the knowledge-loving local elite. Raychaudhuri finds it significant "that the very first generation of western-educated Bengalis felt attracted to the ideals of national liberation and post-enlightenment rationalism, which were by no means the only components of the nineteenth century European tradition. Mazzini and Garibaldi, but not Bismarck, were the admired heroes" (Raychaudhuri, 1988:4). The influence of the early Utilitarian thinkers, such as James Mill (1773–1836) who served the Company administration, and the humanist ideas of August Comte, the founder of sociology, on the Bengali intelligentsia was discernible in the mid-19th century (Dhali, 1985). The new consciousness, identity—a fusion of Western liberal ideas and a search for Indian traditions—arose among the Bengali elite shaping their character. The ferment of the intellectual activities was displayed in the formation of various associations and the publication of a whole host of journals and magazines. *The Partheonon* which appeared in 1830 "described itself as the organ of people who were 'Hindu by birth, yet European by education'" (Raychaudhuri, 1988:21). Here we clearly see the echo of Macaulay.

In so far as the Bengali-Hindu identity was concerned which was coterminous with Bengali identity, certain variation notwithstanding, the story can be told in a less cumbersome way, but when we begin to isolate the distinctiveness of the Bengali-Muslims, the issue becomes murkier. According to Anisuzzaman, one of the consequences of Muslim rule in Bengal from the 13th century was the large-scale conversion of Buddhists and low-caste Hindus to Islam. Despite the egalitarian ideal, Muslim society had also been influenced by the caste system. In Bengal, Islam appeared not in its orthodox form but in the mystic form preached by the Sufis (1993:19). The syncretic traditions left their marks on Bangladeshi national identity. Yet the role of Islam and the systematic effort to Islamicize in the last decades of the 19th and early part of the 20th century went a long way in their implications (Ahmed, 1981). The process of Islamization continues in Bangladesh even today under the auspices of Islamic movements which have always been transnational, hence, global.

Islam and Secularism in Bangladesh

The 4 April 2002 issue of the *Far Eastern Economic Review* (FEER), the Hong Kong-based weekly, in a lead article portrayed Bangladesh as a country with a religious-fundamentalist bent, even a potential breeding ground of the Al-Quaeda. The merit of the article, entitled "Bangladesh: A Cocoon of Terror" is less important to me than the sharp reactions that it evoked from the government of Bangladesh. The issue was banned and court proceedings were initiated against the magazine. The article among other things accused the government of "inaction" with regard to dealing with "creeping fundamentalism".

Why was the Bangladesh government so touchy about Islamic fundamentalism? Bangladesh relies on the US-led West for trade and aid. So it is somewhat understandable why the government was in a hurry to dispel any association with such a tag, especially after 9/11. Yet in the early 1990s during the previous rule of the Bangladesh Nationalist Party (BNP). Taslima Nasreen, a firebrand feminist writer who attacked Islam as practised in Bangladesh, was fiercely attacked by the religious right and the government exiled her. Many of the letters written by Bangladeshis in Bangladesh as well as overseas were particularly critical of the *FEER* article. Now it could be seen as an attempt to present a secular and tolerant face to the world for pragmatic reasons on the part of those letter writers who were embarrassed to be viewed as fundamentalists. When the leader of the opposition, in her various overseas speech engagements termed the present government as an associate of religious right Jaamat-i-Islami and so forth, she was widely criticized in Bangladesh for her seemingly "unpatriotic utterances". Many Bangladeshi intellectuals tried to present a more tolerant Islamic face of Bangladesh.

Why does Bangladesh present this Janus-like face? While religion, which for the majority is Islam, remains central, yet there is a tendency to present a secular face, at least, internationally. One writer of a letter to the popular English daily, *The Daily Star*, while commenting on the controversy over a recently mounted Arabic neon sign of Zia International Airport, Dhaka, pointed out—such a move was ill-thought out and inappropriate under the present circumstances. Why does not this tension between Islam and secular nationalism in Bangladesh go away? Does the tension between religion and secularism continue to reveal deep ambiguities about Bangladesh's national identity? This question deserves serious intellectual attention.

But before proceeding with this question let's ask: what is it about "national question" that makes it so durable?

The durability of nationalism as a force in history is to a large extent rooted in the notion of national identity which has gained importance both in sociological discourse as well as in public discussion. The historically rooted social and political conditions in Bangladesh have contributed to a return to the pendulum like movement in the construction and reconstruction of national identity. Today secular, tomorrow Islamic and again secular, and now Islamic Bangladeshis as a nation seem to be unable to make up its mind. The swings of national questions, the construction and reconstruction can be attributed to the interface of local traditions and the global forces.

Bangladesh has the fourth largest concentration of Muslim populations in the world, trailing Indonesia, India and Pakistan. Eighty-seven per cent of Bangladesh's 130 million people are Muslims predominantly of the sunni sect who follow the Hanafi school of Islamic traditions. Islam came to this deltaic agricultural land with the Turkic conquest of the region beginning in 1204. Religious preachers followed suit through the historical trade routes at the beginning of the 13th century. The religion became a mass religion under the official patronage of the Mughal rulers who ruled India incorporating Bengal (the precursor to Bangladesh) in 1576 until 1757.

There are at least four theories about the spread of Islam in Bangladesh. 1. The oldest theory, which Eaton (1994) calls "the Religion of the Sword thesis", is quite implausible. This theory gives the state, especially its military arm too much credit in the dissemination of Islam. The puzzle that this theory cannot explain is why Islam is more widely present in the rural hinterland far from the centres of power than in the surrounding area of State power? 2. The second theory suggests that migration of Muslims from the Islamic belt in the Middle East to Bengal was the main reason. This theory emerged initially as a response to the notion that the majority of the Muslims in Bengal were converted from low-caste Hindus. In 1872, soon after the publication of the first official census, Abu A. Ghuznavi proposed the thesis that the majority of the Muslims came from outside. Khondkar Fuzli Rubbee provided a similar argument in his book *The Origin of the Musalmans of Bengal*, published in 1895. 3. The third theory that Eaton calls "the Religion of Patronage theory" proposes that conversion to Islam was motivated by favours from the ruling class. Again the geographic distribution of the Muslims is incompatible with this thesis. 4. The "Religion of Social Liberation" (Eaton, 1994) suggests that in order to escape the repression of the caste hierarchy, many members of the lower-caste embraced Islam.

Although the conversion of the oppressed downtrodden classes from the yoke of the Brahminical domination thesis enjoys a great deal of popularity in Bangladesh, Eaton suggests that this is like reading history backwards and doubts the appeal for egalitarianism in the medieval Bengal. According to a number of writers, Sufi saints played an important role in the diffusion of Islam in the interior regions of Bengal. The influence of the Sufis can be found in the existence of the *mazars* in various interior parts of Bangladesh. The religious conversion resulted in a syncretic tradition in Bengal (Roy, 1983). It would be quite obvious to notice the differences in the practice of Islam in Bangladesh compared to say, Pakistan or Malaysia. Islam as practised in Bangladesh is marked by a heavy influence of local cultural traditions. Much of the religious debates between what Islam in Bangladesh is versus what it ought to be centres around the question of the degree of cultural amalgamation. For example, many of the secular minded Muslim women who would say their prayers regularly and fast in the month of Ramadan would also wear a spot on the forehead not so much to keep the evil away but to keep up with fashion. It is only the puritanical Muslims who would label such practices as "unIslamic". The puritanical Muslims would define Muslim practices in terms of their distance from those of the Hindus.

In order to understand the oscillation of the identity question in Bangladesh, it may be helpful to recount, albeit briefly, the history of anti-colonial struggle in the Indian subcontinent. Nationalist movement in India was an unintended consequence of British colonial rule itself. The emergence of a predominantly Hindu middle class and the attendant call for social reform and enlightenment gave rise to Indian nationalism. The uneven modernization of the Indian Muslims was responsible for the rise of a separate Muslim nationalism which justified the creation of Pakistan. Although the alleged differences between the two communities were exaggerated to strengthen the justification for Pakistan, the uneven economic development provided the infallible material context. The formation of Bengali Muslim identity, part of that process was based on a long historical legacy. The British colonial rule displaced the Muslims from the ruling/dominant class to class in ruins, economically decimated and politically humiliated, while the Muslims sought to maintain its cultural superiority and unity. The Permanent Settlement of 1793 by Lord Cornwallis created a mainly Hindu landed class. Then in 1843, the switch from Persian to English further handicapped the Muslims' chances of social mobility.

There was no equivalent figure such as Raja Ram Mohun Roy (1774–1833) to pave the way for Muslim enlightenment in the early 19th century. The Muslim reformists came to the scene half a century later and were unable to confront religious orthodoxies at the same level as did their Hindu counterparts. For Ram Mohun Roy and later Ishwar Chandra Vidyasagar, Hinduism as practised in India and the social customs and rituals were deeply problematic. They were critical of their culture. The birth of the first wave of Indian renaissance largely left the Muslims out. The Muslim reformers once they appeared were more interested in purifying Islam rather than criticizing various social ills directly attributable to the practice of the religion. Sir Sayyid Ahmad Khan (1817–1899) was an exception, yet rather than attacking the roots of problems, he called the Muslims to embrace modern English education which had revolutionary implications. His contribution to the establishment of the Aligarh Muslim University and his leadership pushed the Muslims out of their somnolent condition. Other social reformers included Nwab Abdul Latif (1828–1893), Syed Ameer Ali (1849–1928) and Delwaar Hosaen, (1840–1913) who was the first Muslim graduate who tried to play a role in the emancipation of the Muslims. The later two were from Bengal. Delwar Hosaen's writings were little known until recently. His collection of essays written in English was published in the early 1980s. Hosaen provides a fairly open-minded interpretation of Muslim backwardness for which he put the blame on the religion itself. For example, he takes up the issue of prohibiting the charging of interest which inhibited the formation of capital.

The Hindu-Muslim difference was given centrality in the political discourse in the first quarter of the 20th century. The creation of Pakistan was contingent upon the construction of a Muslim identity that emphasized their "differences" with the Hindus. As the movement for the creation of Pakistan was gathering momentum, Bengali Muslims were mobilized to play a key role. The Bengali Muslims sought emancipation both from the grip of British colonial rulers as well as their local Hindu overlords.

Alongside the reformist movement—if it can be called movement at all—there were two other movements. One was a movement for purifying Islam and the other was a resistance from below. The two important figures were Titu Mir (1782–1831) and Dudu Miyan (1819–1862). Their struggles were not grounded on religion as such; it was a clear manifestation of class struggle. There were other examples of peasant uprising against both Hindu and Muslim lords. There were little vertical connections between the Muslim-educated class and the rural masses. The only successful mobilization took place using religion. But such mobilization did not last long A Muslim sense of nationalism could not grow independently except as a mirror opposite the Hindu nationalist movement. The national identity of the majority Muslim inhabitants of Bangladesh today reveals a similar ambivalence towards Islam. They seek to incorporate the beliefs and ritual practices of Islam, yet they want to maintain a certain amount of autonomy in their cultural practices.

The turn of events in the early part of the 20th century that subsequently launched a new movement for the creation of Pakistan, a "homeland" for the Muslims of the Indian subcontinent, reconstructed the identity of the Bengali-Muslims. The new category "Bengali-Muslim" was a product of history and the changing political circumstances. No doubt the political movement for the creation of Pakistan accentuated the Islamic aspect of the Bengali at the expense of the Bengali identity which was syncretic. The inhabitants of Bengal in the past were identified as Bengalis as were Punjabis as natives of the Punjab. The hyphenated new category, Bengali-Muslim, was a response to the expressions of the new political demands made by the sections of the politicians. The religious identity which was implicit now came to the foreground. The national identity of the Bengali-Muslims was now reconstructed in opposition to the "essential" character of the Bengali-Hindus.

While Bengali-Hindus were painted as docile, despite such fiery leaders as Surja Sen (Masterda), Netaji Subhash Bose and others, and cerebral, Bengali-Muslims were imagined as pugnacious, as if this was an inheritance from the days of the holy wars in the Middle Ages. The result of such a reconstruction involved a process double essentializing. The Hindu-Bengalis as well as the Muslim-Bengalis were essentialized to a set of popular stereotypes. The national character of the inhabitants of the then East Pakistan was a deliberate construction. Here one might make a distinction between "social construction" and "political construction" where the latter refers to a systematic, deliberate manipulation. The Bengali-Muslims who lagged behind their Hindu counterparts in education, wealth and influence for historical reasons developed a double identity Bengali-Muslim. The English language Muslim weekly, *Mussalman*, which was launched by the Calcutta-based Bengali-Muslim elite to reflect the opinions of the Western-educated Muslims, declared in its first editorial: "Indian Muslims, politically and economically are Indian first, Muhammadans afterwards, and morally . . . Muhammadans first and Indians afterwards" (quoted in Sarkar, 1991:26). The Pakistan movement clearly reversed the sequence.

The Bengali nationalism was not independent in itself; it was incorporated within the penumbra of Indian nationalism. Bengali identity, thus, emerged primarily as a cultural force though contributing to the larger struggle of Indian national independence. Insofar as the pan-Indian nationalism was concerned the religious overtone of Hindu revivalism had to be concealed to appeal to the multi-religious, multi-ethnic population of India. The Indian National Congress emerged in 1885 as a secular party seeking to mobilize the Indian population. Its leadership as well as its aspirations were as much global as they were national. Yet, the Hindu undertone in the Congress could not be completely suppressed since that was the *raison d'être* against British colonialism. In order to fight foreign domination, the native lores and sentiments had to be revived and imagined. The deep ambivalence towards secularism and, alternately, religion in India and Bangladesh today remains a heritage of the past. The Bengali nationalism that began to emerge in the middle of the 19th century created ambivalence towards the colonial rulers. The Bengali *Bhadralok*—both Hindu and Muslim—sought to emulate the British virtues, as they were awed and impressed by the education and civilization of the British, yet they also wanted autonomy from colonial domination.

The construction of Muslim identity can also be seen as a devious ploy of the colonial administration. The partition of Bengal in 1905, mainly on religious grounds, was done ostensibly to advantage the economically and politically weaker, but numerically larger, Muslim community of Bengal. The partition was disputed both by the Hindus and a section of the Muslims in Bengal who saw in it a cynical plot of a "divide and rule" policy of the colonial rulers. The partition was annulled in 1911 in the face of growing resistance of the middle-class elites. During the years of the divided Bengal, the Muslim League was formed in Dhaka, the capital of East Bengal in 1906 and a provision for separate Muslim electorate was legislated in 1909. The annulment created resentment among the Muslims and helped form a constituency that was receptive to Jinnah's "two nation theory" which was the basis for the creation of Pakistan in the succeeding decades. Although the creation of Pakistan cannot be dismissed as either an accident of history or the manipulation of the self-serving Muslim elites, it provided an excellent example of a constructed nation. It showed that construction is not pure fabrication. There had to be some basis in the material and ideological circumstances historically formed that could be used by the leaders of the nationalist movements. With the help of hindsight, one could agree with Jinnah's detailed description of the differences between the Hindus and the Muslims and then one could ask "So what?" The two major religious communities lived in India for centuries with remarkable absence of conflict and animosity. Differences between the two communities remained unproblematic until the political need for differentiation arose. It was only in the fervour of nation construction that differences were problematized and politicized; minor differences were accentuated and amplified and substantive areas of cooperation forgotten. The invention of a nation relies on both remembering as well as amnesia.

Yet, soon after the creation of Pakistan, supposedly a homeland and sanctuary for the Muslims of the Indian subcontinent, Mr Jinnah, its founder downplayed the religious theme. In his speech as the first president of the Pakistan Constituent Assembly, he declared: "You are free; you are free to go to your temples, you are free to go to your mosques or to any other places of worship in this state of Pakistan. You may belong to any religion, caste or creed—that has nothing to do with the business of the state" (quoted in Ahmed, 1990:19). However, Pakistan as a nation-state because of its geographical separation had to use common religion as the basis for nationhood. The movement for autonomy in the eastern part of Pakistan led to the emergence of Bengali nationalism, which underlined language rather than religion as the basis of nationhood. The long-standing linguistic identity was an essential ingredient in, the formation of national identity in Bangladesh. The importance of language as a basis of nationality was recognized by philosophers, such as Herder, who maintained that "every language has its definite national character" (quoted in Kohn, 1951:432).

Both language and secularism became justification for a separate identity for the inhabitants of Bangladesh from her very inception. Bangladesh emerged as a nation on four cardinal principles which were enshrined in the constitution of this republic. Nationalism, secularism, democracy and socialism were the four pillars on which Bangladesh stood. However, the political turn of events that led to the tragic coup d'état in August 1975, which dislodged not only the rule of Sheikh Mujibur Rahman the founding leader of the country, but it also took the country towards a path of religious orthodoxy. Bengali nationalism based on ethnic, linguistic and cultural identity was redefined after the 1975 coup on the basis of political calculations (Murshid, 2001). Not that the new rulers were any more religious than the ones they replaced but in order to show that they were different, they began to pose themselves as the custodians of religion. Since 1975, the country has clearly drifted towards Islam. This came in good time with the global resurgence of Islam. The Islamic revivalism in Bangladesh was also supported by the funds received from the Gulf states that began to establish links with various religiously affiliated political parties in Bangladesh.

It is interesting to note that Bengali-Muslims too sought to maintain this dual-identity with all its ambiguities. The birth of Bangladesh in 1971 inherited this challenge of maintaining a distinctive Bengali-Muslim character which entailed an equidistance from both the manipulated "Pakistani" identity as well as the Bengali-Hindu identity. The Islamic revivalism, however, never assumed a strong fervour; it managed to whittle the secularist traditions which were essential parts of Bangladeshi cultural heritage. Today, for any visitor to Bangladesh, it would present itself as a highly religious country. One of the in-flight "entertainment" channels on Bangladesh Biman, the national flag carrier presents recitations from the Koran. Other channels present Western pop music, and of course romantic Bengali music. In a rather coincidental way, it reflects the pluralism of Bangladeshi culture. In the Hajj season, Biman gears itself up as if to face a national crisis when it has to ferry thousands of pilgrims from Bangladesh to Saudi Arabia. The same planes are filled with jeans-clad Bangladeshis returning home from the United States in the New-York–Dhaka flights. Islam alongside blue-jeans, and cricket is another patch in the multicoloured quilt of Bangladeshi culture.

There are a number of features that need serious consideration in explaining the growing influence of Islam in Bangladesh. The most important of these has been the growth of Islamic national education locally known as Madrasah education. In 1994, there were 5,762 Madrasahs in Bangladesh with a student population of 1.7 million. Compared to 4.8 million secondary school students the same year the figure may not be as overwhelming as it looks, still it is a number that one has to reckon with.

The Islamic party won more than 12 per cent of the votes in the election of 1991. In 1996, they won only 3 per cent of the votes. This is not an indication of their declining popularity. In the latest election of October 2001, the share of votes of the Islamic parties is hard to ascertain because as an electoral strategy they formed an alliance with the Bangladesh Nationalist Party which assured BNP a resounding electoral victory. Rather, one can see in it an acceptance of Islamic trappings in the political establishment. Clearly, a desecularization process has been taking place in Bangladesh. It has become a routine for the newly elected Prime Ministers to perform a Hajj before taking over the new government.

The process towards desecularization or for that matter secularization is not irreversible. The process is very much linked to the politics of the day. One political scientist who conducted a content analysis of the speeches of Khaleda Zia, the then (2003) Prime Minister and the leader of Bangladesh Nationalist Party, reported that she began every speech with Bismillah-Ar-Rahman-Ar-Rahim (in the name of Allah, the Beneficent and the Merciful). In most of her speeches, Khaleda Zia upheld the Islamic provisions incorporated in the constitution during the rule of Ziaur Rahman, namely by insertion of Bismillah-Ar-Rahman-Ar-Rahim; dispensing with secularism and substituting instead "absolute trust and faith in Almighty Allah"; (Maniruzzaman, 1992:209). Sheikh Hasina, the leader of Awami League, in her speeches accused both Zia and Ershad of rigging the elections and using Islam to increase their appeal to the people. Sheikh Hasina, in contrast, promised a living, secular democracy (Maniruzzaman, 1992:210). Jamaat-i-Islami promised to build an Islamic state strictly on the basis of the Quran and Sunnah. Its stance was anti-Indian and it attacked Awami League for the latter's secularism. "The secularists and the leftists were badly defeated

by parties who espoused various levels of Islamic orientation"
(Maniuruzzaman, 1992:211).

The chances of the spread of fundamentalism in Bangladesh are
very remote. The poverty and the backwardness in Bangladesh mea-
sured in conventional social indicators should not be seen as deny-
ing this country its rich cultural tradition of secularism which I think
is a product more of local traditions, a combination of religious syncretism and cultural mysticisms than an imposition from outside.
One of the errors in the perception of the Western media is to look
for a particular brand of (Western) secularism in every corner of the
world without any regard for cultural and historical diversities. If we
take the issue of specificity of Bangladeshi culture seriously, the emergence of both an Iran under Khomeini or Afghanistan under Taleban-
style Islamic revolution or a West-European secularizing trend are
both equally unlikely.

The Reconstruction of Nationalism in Bangladesh:
Reactions to Salman Rushdie and Taslima Nasreen

The ambivalence built into the Bangladeshi identity incorporating
Islam and secularism came to surface following the two controversies that set the Islamicist believers against the secularists. The first
controversy revolved around Salman Rushdie's controversial novel,
The Satanic Verses. The second controversy involved the author, Taslima
Nasreen, whose writings led to a major row in the early 1990s.
Taslima Nasreen attracted a great deal of attention in the early 1990s
because of her controversial writings. Taslima Nasreen, an anesthe-
siologist-turned poet, columnist and novelist has been both prolific
and polemical. She has been treated with disdain by some, mute
appreciation by others, and many chose to ignore her. Some of her
writings have evoked the wrath of the so-called Islamic fundamentalists in Bangladesh to the extent that a *"fatwa"* has been issued by
a relatively unknown group with a prize-money posted on her head.
The outspoken writer went into hiding for fear of her life since the
fatwa was declared. But this extreme move on the part of the fundamentalists and the issue of an official order of arrest on charges
of insulting Islam after an interview she gave to the *Statesman* of India
on 4 June 1994 was reprinted in the *Bangladesh Times*, a pro-government
daily in Dhaka few days later. In that interview, she was quoted as

saying that "the Quran should be thoroughly revised". From her hiding place, Nasreen denied saying that and claimed that the Indian reporter confused the Quran and the *Sharia* and that she had recommended that the *Sharia* be thoroughly revised. Her disclaimer did not satisfy her opponents. On 3 August 1994, she surrendered to the High Court and was granted a bail and the permission not to be present at court during the court proceedings. No restriction was imposed on her travels. A week later the controversial writer arrived in Stockholm at the invitation of the Swedish branch of the PEN. The pro-Islamic political parties in Bangladesh were furious and brought out processions accusing the government of complicity and harbouring the "apostate" writer. Now that the matter is in the hands of the due process of the law, a process that is known for its notorious sluggishness in Bangladesh, it seems the matter will be forgotten in due course. These two controversies revealed not only some of the deep-seated tensions between Islam and secularism in Bangladesh but also unwittingly, the possibility of a reasoned dialogue between alternative modes of modernities. The secularists in Bangladesh agree with Nasreen's identification of the negative functions of religion in society, a source of conflict, disharmony, bloodshed and so forth, yet they would be reluctant to express their support for her openly.

However, as the irreversible march of globalization continues, we will not only discover how similar we are but also how strong and divisive are our economic interests. The print-capitalism did create nationalism in the majority countries of the world, in the same vein the electronic media is creating opportunities for various "nations" to see how close they are to each other, paving the way for the rise of a global culture. The complexity of globalization is manifested in the overlap and contestation of cultural passions and economic interests. The feelings or sense of a transnational culture is, sometimes, an aspect of a globalism or cosmopolitanism. Tagore best expresses the cosmopolitan notion of nationalism as an outgrowth of Bengali renaissance. The poet in his own way championed the enlightenment project in Bengal and the Indian subcontinent at large. He wrote: "During the evolution of the Nation the moral culture of brotherhood was limited by geographical boundaries, because at that time those boundaries were real. Now they have become imaginary lines of tradition divested of the qualities of real obstacles." He continued, "There is only one history—the history of man. All national histories are merely chapters in the larger one (Tagore, 1976).

As the principles of secularism seem to be on retreat in India, Pakistan and Bangladesh in the opening years of the new millennium due to a whole host of local and global factors, the cosmopolitan secularists seem to be on the run. However, as a return to Islamism and anti-secularism leads to a sense of despondence, the very possibility that a reasonable, secular and tolerant political regime can emerge, given the oscillation of ideological swings, provides a basis for hope. The enlightenment project has not been put off; it is merely on hold. The very pendular nature of things gives us the possibility of a tolerant polity characterized by democracy and human rights; it also presents the threat of a turn to right, to intolerance and new orthodoxies. The swing of the pendulum is no longer dictated by the forces within the nation but beyond the national borders of Bangladesh by the happenings in the region as well as the global forces.

References

Achebe, Chinua (1958) *Things Fall Apart*. London: Heinemann.
Ahmed, Raffiuddin (1981) *The Bengal Muslim 1871–1906: A Quest for Identity*. Delhi: Oxford University Press.
—— (ed.) (1990) *Religion, Nationalism and Politics in Bangladesh* New Delhi: South Asian Publisher.
Alter, Peter (1989) *Nationalism*. London: Edward Arnold.
Anderson, Benedict (1991) *Imagined Communities*. London: Verso.
—— (1999) "Indonesian Nationalism Today and in the Future." *New Left Review*, 235. May–June.
Anisuzzaman, (1993) *Creativity, Reality and Identity*. Dhaka, ICHS.
Bhabha, Homi K. (ed.) (1990) *Nation and Narration*. London: Routledge.
—— (1992) "Postcolonial Authority and Postmodern Guilt." In Lawrence Grossberg, Cary Nelson and Paula A. Treichler (eds.), *Cultural Studies*. New York: Routledge.
Brennan, Timothy (1990) "The National Longing for Form." In Homi K. Bhabha (ed.) (1990) *Nation and Narration*. London: Routledge.
Burki, Shahid Javed (1999) *Historical Dictionary of Pakistan*. Edited by Jon Worono V. [publisher?]
Chatterjee, Partha (1986) *Nationalist Thought and the Colonial World: A Derivative Discourse*. London: Zed.
—— (1993) *The Nation and Its Fragments*. Princeton: Princeton University Press.
Dhali, A.H. (1985) "Humanist Movements in Bengal: Nineteenth and early Twentieth Century Trends." In Rafiuddin Ahmed (ed.), *Bangladesh: Society, Religion and Politics*. Chittagong: South Asia Studies Group.
Duara, Prasenjit (1998) "Why is History Antitheoretical?" *Modern China*, 24:2.
Eaton, Richard (1994) *The Rise of Islam and the Bengal Frontier*. Delhi: Oxford University Press.
Gellner, Ernest (1983) *Nations and Nationalism*. Ithaca: Cornell University Press.
—— (1993) "Nationalism and the Development of European Societies." In Jyrki Iivonen (ed.), *The Future of Nation-State in Europe*. Edward Elgar.

Giddens, Anthony (1994) *Beyond Left and Right.* Cambridge: Polity Press.

Glynn, Sarah (2002) "Bengali Muslims: The New East End Radicals?" *Ethnic and Cultural Studies,* 25:6 pp. 969–88.

Goonatilake, Susantha (1982) *Crippled Minds: An Exploration into Colonial Culture.* New Delhi: Vikas.

Guha-Tkahurta, Tapati (1992) *The Making of a New 'Indian' Art.* Cambridge: Cambridge University Press.

Hobsbawm, Eric (1993) "The New Threat to History." *New York Review of Books,* Vol. 40, No. 21.

Kedourie, Elie (1994) "Nationalism and Self-Determination." In J. Hutchinson & A.D. Smith (ed.), *Nationalism.* Oxford: Oxford University Press.

Kohn, Hans (1951) *The Idea of Nationalism.* New York: Macmillan.

Macaulay, Thomas Babington (1907) *Critical and Historical Essays.* London and Toronto: J.M. Dent and Sons.

Maniruzzaman, Talukder (1992) "The Fall of the Military Dictator: 1991 Elections and the Prospect of Civilian Rule in Bangladesh." *Pacific Affairs,* 65:2 pp. 203–24.

Markoff, John and Daniel Regan (1987) "Religion, the State and Political Legitimacy in the World's Constitutions." In Thomas Robbins and Roland Robertson (eds.), *Church-State Relations: Tensions and Transitions.* New Brunswick, NJ: Transaction Books. pp. 161–82.

McCrone, David (1998) *The Sociology of Nationalism.* London: Routledge.

Meyer, John W. (1980) "The World Polity and the Authority of the Nation-State." In A. Bergesen (ed.), *Studies of the Modern World System.* New York: Academic Press.

Murshid, Tazeen (2001) "State, Nation, Identity: The Quest for Legitimacy in Bangladesh." In Amita Shastri and A. Jeyaratnam Wilson (eds.), *The Post-Colonial States of South Asia.* London: Curzon.

Nandy, Ashis (1989) *The Intimate Enemy: Loss and Recovery of Self Under Colonialism.* Delhi: Oxford University Press.

Raychaudhuri, Tapan (1988) *Europe Reconsidered.* Delhi: Oxford University Press.

Robertson, Roland (1992) *Globalization: Social Theory and Global Culture.* London: Sage.

Roy, Asim (1983) *The Islamic Syncretic Tradition in Bengal.* New Delhi: Sterling Publisher.

Sarkar, Chandiprasad (1991) *The Bengali Muslims: A Study in their Politicization 1912–1929.* Calcutta: K.P. Bagchi & Company.

Stalin, Joseph (1994) "The Nation." In J. Hutchinson & A.D. Smith (eds.), *Nationalism.* Oxford: Oxford University Press.

Tagore, Rabindranath (1976) *Nationalism.* Madras: Macmillan.

Tilly, Charles (1990) *Coercion, Capital and European States. A.D. 990–1990.* Oxford: Basil Blackwell.

Weber Eugene (1979) *Peasants into Frenchmen.* London: Chatto & Windus.

Weitman, Sasha R. (1973) "National Flags: A Sociological Overview." *Semiotica* 8 pp. 328–67.

Williams, Raymond (1983) *The Year 2000.* New York: Pantheon.

FROM THE DISCOURSE OF "SINO-WEST" TO "GLOBALIZATION": CHINESE PERSPECTIVES ON GLOBALIZATION

Yu Keping

China Center for Comparative Politics & Economics (CCCPE)

"Globalization" has become a fashionable term which is globalized as associated with McDonald's, internet and the film *Titanic*. Whether one is in the West or the East, in developing or developed countries, and in capitalist or socialist countries as in China, people are talking about "globalization". All popular theories in Western countries, we can say, reverberates in China sooner or later, as modernization theory, postmodern theory and globalization theory. The modernization theory that prevailed in the West in the 1950s and 1960s did not become popular in China until the 1980s while the globalization theory that came into existence in the West in the early 1990s has been a hot topic in China since the mid-1990s. This fact itself is a good annotation that globalization has been an inevitable trend shaping the development process of the world and China. As an active member of the international community, China is necessarily facing the backlash from globalization through its opening and reforming policies. As a result, for Chinese politicians and scholars, it is a common topic of discussion how to respond to the challenges and opportunities arising from globalization.

Sensitive Chinese scholars responded quickly when the globalization issue was a lively debate in the West at the beginning of the 1990s. They introduced Western scholars' views on globalization one after another and advocated studies on it at the same time. Some of these scholars included Arif Dirlik of Duke University and Li Shenzhi of the Chinese Academy of Social Sciences, who was thought to be one of the earliest Chinese advocators on globalization.[1]

---

[1] In 1993, the Institute of Contemporary Marxism invited Professor Arif Dirlik of Duke University to come to Beijing for serial lectures on globalization and capitalism, which were published in the initial issue of *Strategy and Management* in 1993 as "Capitalism under Globalization." It was regarded as the first publication to

Asia was confronted with a serious financial crisis in 1997. The wave of crises originated from Thailand and Indonesia and expanded to Malaysia, Singapore, South Korea and Japan. China had not yet been impacted deeply from the Asian financial crisis, but the threat of a financial crisis resulting from economic globalization awakened the Chinese leaders and scholars. Jiang Zeming, then President and General Secretary of CPC, said on 9 March 1998, "We have to recognize and treat properly the issue of economic 'globalization.' Economic globalization is an objective trend of world economic development, from which none can escape and in which everyone has to participate. The key point is to see dialectically this trend of 'globalization,' i.e. see both its positive aspect and its negative aspect. It is particularly important for developing countries."[2] The top leader's interest in globalization gave a great impetus to scholars and analysts engaging in studies on globalization, which came to be a hot issue for intellectuals. It follows that a number of essays on globalization were published and some of the important Western works on globalization, such as *The Trap to Globalization*, were translated into Chinese. The Institute of Contemporary Marxism went further to have edited a globalization series which includes seven books: *Antinomies of Globalization, Marxism in Globalization, Socialism in Globalization, Capitalism in Globalization, Globalization and China, Globalization and the World* and *Globalization and Post-Colonial Criticism*.

However, globalization is so complicated that it brings forth a number of paradoxes, around which Chinese intellectuals have been debating. There are at least the following six paradoxes of globalization among Chinese scholars.

First, is globalization a fact or just a fiction? Some people think that globalization is a fact and an objective existence that deeply impact human development, and human beings have entered into a global age. Conversely, others insist that globalization is simply fiction fudged by Western scholars and is perhaps even a conspiracy of new Imperialism. In their view, globalization is a myth at most because human politics, economy and culture can never be globalized.

---

introduce systematically Western globalization theories and exerted a great impact on the Chinese intellectual circle. Professor Li Shenzhi, former Vice President of Chinese Academy of Social Sciences, wrote a few of papers to advocate and encourage studies on globalization in China.

[2] Jiang Zeming (1998), *People's Daily*, 9 March.

Second, is globalization capitalist or socialist and so forth? Many Chinese intellectuals believe that globalization is a necessary result of capitalist productive development and an inherent demand of capitalism. Globalization means that the capitalist mode of production has extended over the world and capitalism comes into a new stage of its development. Therefore, globalization, to be exact, is global capitalism. However, some scholars argue that globalization is neutral although it originates from capitalism. In nature, globalization is neither capitalist nor socialist. Like market economy, it can be combined with both capitalism and socialism.

Third, besides economic globalization, is there a political or cultural one? For many scholars, globalization is nothing but economic integration because it is based on integration of capital, products, market, technology, production and communication. They limit globalization strictly to the economic field and refuse to view its influence in other fields. Many other scholars, however, believe that the concept of globalization is beyond economics even though it originates from the economic process of integration. A process of political and cultural globalization, they argue, is coming to us as economic integration is going on. In their view, globalization has not only its economic implication but also a political and cultural one, and thus, globalization is an overall process of social change, including economic, political and cultural changes.

Fourth, is globalization more advantageous or more harmful for developing countries? Some intellectuals find that developed countries dominate and control the process of globalization with their economic and political power. Developed, rather than developing countries are true winners of globalization. To the contrary, others think that competition generated by globalization is not a zero-sum game and all players can be winners from it. Like developed countries, developing countries can find the situation advantageous while developed countries are likely to be at the losing end. It depends on what strategies they take. China is a good example of one who gained much from globalization.

Fifth, is globalization modernization, Westernization or Americanization? Many people believe that globalization means Westernization, above all, Americanization for China. In their eyes, standards, regimes and regulations used in the process of globalization are made by Western countries according to their own values and interests. However, many people do not think so. They think that globalization is quite different from Westernization or Americanization. Fundamentally, for them, globalization is a process of modernization in spite of the fact that this process originates from the West and the US leads it.

Let me begin with the definition of globalization. It is a premise for studying globalization to understand the meaning of globalization. Basically speaking, there are three different opinions among Chinese scholars on the definition of globalization.

The first view places globalization as a process of integration of human life, especially a global and holistic tendency beyond regions and nations. In other words, it stands for "an objective historic process and tendency of contemporary human development beyond nation's boundary, which is unfolding a global communication, net and interaction."[3] Some go further to explain that the essential meaning of globalization lies in the global consensus beyond spatial, cultural and institutional barriers, in the global interdependence among nations and regions, and in the fact that as communication develops and international connection becomes closer, there is a realization that human beings all over the world face many common problems and should seek to cooperate to resolve these problems.[4]

The second view regards globalization simply as global capitalism, a new stage and new form of capitalist development. In the viewpoint of some authors, globalization is nothing but a logical result of contemporary capitalist development, a universalization of the capitalist mode of production. It is said that "fundamentally speaking, the present economic globalization is a globalization under control of contemporary capitalism. So-called issues of globalization are essentially issues of contemporary capitalism, especially of developed capitalism." Concretely, "in perspective of the dynamic mechanism and realistic foundation, the historic necessity of globalization should be found in the capitalist mode of production."[5] According to this logic of thinking, globalization is only a temporary form and even an alternative name for capitalism. Thus, it is also called "late capitalism,

---

[3] Cai Tuo (1998), "Globalization and Contemporary International Relation", *Marxism and Reality*, No. 3.

[4] Tan Junjiou (1998), "Thinking and Arguing on Globalization," in Yu Keping (ed.), *Globalization and Antinomies*, China/Beijing?: [? Pls confirm] Central Compilation and Translation Press, p. 127.

[5] Yang Caoren and He Zhiwei, "Globalization, Institutional Opening and National Rejuvenation," ibid., p. 138.

developed capitalism, disorganized capitalism, transitional capitalism, globalized capitalism, post-Fordism and etc."[6]

Now that globalization is the latest form of capitalism and that Western developed countries, especially the United States, are natural representative of contemporary capitalism, it is plausible that globalization means Westernization. This is the third conception of globalization prevailing among very few of intellectuals in China. In view of this conception, globalization is characterized by identification and universalization of human values. Globalization is understood as Westernization simply because the values of Western developed countries, especially of the United States, represent human universal values. As one author pointed out, in Chinese context, intellectuals with an orientation towards liberalism are used to defining globalization by the terms such as "the world trend" and "universal values". Furthermore, those intellectuals simply identify globalization with Westernization or Americanization by defining Western or American political, economic and cultural values and standards as "the world trend" and "the universal values."[7]

It follows the debates that intellectuals in China as well as those abroad are divided into two opposite camps. Some of them are active advocates of globalization while others oppose it. The former considers globalization to be a blessing and is warmly welcomed while the latter takes globalization to be a disaster and they resist globalization. Some Chinese scholars say that the only way for a renaissance to occur in China is for the country to join in the process of globalization and that China's future, including democracy and economic prosperity, depends largely on its joining the globalization process. Other people, however, consider globalization to be a trap and they regard the supporters of globalization as traitors.

Globalization is based on the integration of capital, production, communication and technology and above all it belongs in the economic category. To put it in another way, as a scholar says, "the main sign of globalization is economic globalization as well as information

---

[6] Wang Fengzheng (1998), "Globalization, Cultural Identity and Nationalism," in Wang Ning (ed.), *Globalization and Post-Colonial Criticism*, China or Beijing?: Central Compilation and Translation Press, p. 91.

[7] Zhang Yiwu, "Globalization: Rethinking in View of Asian Financial Crisis," ibid., pp. 82, 86.

globalization."[8] However, there is a necessary tendency, more or less, of political and cultural homogenization over the world as global economy is getting gradually integration. Therefore, globalization has not only its economic contents, but also political and cultural ones. It is "a cultural, a political, and economic phenomenon."[9] There are not much further dissuasions in this regard for Chinese scholars who are studying globalization. Most essays about globalization refer to economic globalization and many scholars strictly limit globalization to the field of economy. Meanwhile, there are a few of people who identify globalization with economic integration. Fewer of them go far to refuse using the general conception of globalization, especially the conception of political and cultural globalization, because to claim political and cultural globalization, in their view, is to abandon Chinese fundamental political values and political system.

For the most part of Chinese authors, the meaning of economic globalization is self-evident: "elements of economic growth, especially elements of capital, technology and human labor flow to the global level under dynamics of market rule, so that national and regional economy are increasingly integrated into a global economic system. The interdependence, reciprocity and interlink of human economic development has been increased and varieties of commodities produced in different countries are shared by all people in the world."[10] Some researchers summarize the features of economic globalization as follows: 1) globalization of production, a new world-wide division of labour replacing traditional international division; 2) formation of a new international multi-trade system with a homogenization of international trade; 3) the process of financial integration among nations has greatly facilitated financial transactions; 4) a global framework of investments are in formation, whereby the activity of investments could reach almost anywhere in the world; 5) transnational or supranational cooperation has been the centre of international economic life and plays a more important role in world economy,

---

[8] Li Ling (1998), "Chinese Legal Development under the Background of Globalization," *Studies and Enquiries*, No. 1.

[9] Zhu Jinwen (1998), "Some Issues on Globalization," in Hu Yuanzhi (ed.), *Globalization and China*, China or Beijing:? [pls confirm] Central Compilation and Translation Press, p. 102.

[10] Mu Guangcong (1998), "Economic Globalization and Chinese Population," *Contemporary World and Socialism* (Quarterly), No. 3.

challenging the traditional sovereignty of the state; and 6) skilled persons with extraordinary ability are becoming internationalized and there have appeared "international persons" as senior experts at international trade and management meetings.[11]

For most Chinese scholars, economic globalization has been an inevitable fact and tendency of world economic development from which none can escape. So long as one country opens to the world economic market, it is destined to be in the process of economic globalization. China is not an exception. China should actively participate in the process of economic globalization rather than being forced into it. Some people say that China's participation in economic globalization is not only an inevitable fact but it is necessary for the country to realize its economic modernization. In their view, the most advantageous outcome of economic globalization is the optimal distribution of world resources. For no matter how one country's economy operates effectively, it is always suffers from limitation of domestic resources and market. Moreover, the optimal development of the whole world economy can only be reached under the condition of global integration of world resources and markets with minimum limitation of domestic resources and markets. Furthermore, economic globalization allows developing countries a good chance to catch up with developed countries economically.[12]

Globalization is a holistic process of historic development and economic integration requests all concerned nations to observe common game rules and institutional arrangements on the one hand, and in turn, tends to influence worldwide political and cultural values on the other hand. Some Chinese scholars have begun to consider other forms of non-economic globalization, such as political, lawful and cultural globalization.

Political globalization, for certain Chinese authors, means an identity of political values and political institutions among various nations and political systems, which above all is manifested as convergence upon democratic values based on political freedom and equality, and as universalization of democratic institutions which realize such basic

---

[11] See Xue Rongjiou (1998), "The Impact and Challenge of Economic Globalization," *World Economy*, No. 4.

[12] See Liu Lie (1997), "Economic Globalization: A Necessary Way by which Developing Countries Catch Up with Developed Countries," *International Economic Review*, No. 11–12.

political values as freedom, equality and human rights. As some political scholars define, political globalization simply stands for global democratization: "In view of political implication, globalization and democratization is a synonym. The recent wave of political globalization was starting by the fall of Berlin Wall in 1989, the end of Cold War and the disappearance of iron curtain. The visible dynamics of globalization is economic integration while the invisible one is integration of values, integration of democratic and global values."[13]

Other political scientists even specifically discuss the concrete democratic mode of the global age. As one of them argues, good governance will be the democratic mode of the global age. Good governance means political process to maximize public goods and its essential character is cooperation and synergy between government and citizen in public management. It is a new relationship between state and civil society, an optimal condition of state-society. Good governance consists of six elements: 1) legitimacy, i.e. public order and authority should be identified by citizens mostly with their interests in mind; 2) transparency, i.e. access by citizens to political information involved with their interests; 3) accountability; 4) rule of law; 5) responsiveness; and 6) effectiveness. Such an ideal political form is defined as "the political model at the global age."[14]

International practices and conventions, which all nations should observe, have obtained much more importance than before as we enter into the global age. In other words, globalization of law should be put on the agenda for lawmakers, as a few Chinese jurists advocated. "In view of law, adoption of conception of globalization raises a number of problems over which people have to think seriously, like the problem of conflict between world economy and national interests, problem of conflict between the traditional culture and modernization, the relation between globalization and sovereignty of state, problem of pluralism of law, and the status of state as a legislature and so on"[15] (Ling, 1998). In the eyes of some jurists, globalization of law is a new stage of law development. They explain globalization of law by saying that legislation arising out of global-

---

[13] Liu Junning (1998), "Globalization and Democracy," *Contemporary World and Socialism*, (Quarterly), No. 3.

[14] Yu Keping (1998), "From Good Government to Good Governance," *Way*, No. 1.

[15] Li Ling (1998), "Chinese Legal Development under the Background of Globalization," *Studies and Inquiries*, No. 1.

ization should be based upon global consensus on law, possible resolution to global problems, changing notion of traditional sovereignty of state and weakening ideology of nation.[16]

The issue of cultural globalizaiton is more debatable in China. In fact, there have been two perspectives on this issue: "Westernization View" (Xihua Lun) and "the Chinese Cultural Quintessence" (Guo Cui Lu) since modern China. However, the thought of Chinese cultural quintessence has gradually lost its defensibility as Western pop music, fashionable clothing, popular books and magazines, lifestyles and so forth has been accommodated and adapted one after another in China after the reappearance of China on the world scene following its isolation of about 50 years. Cultural globalization has been a reality in a sense that there has emerged a cultural identity or value identity beyond the native or national cultural identity. It is called "global culture" by some Chinese scholars. For the Chinese advocates of global culture, global identity or global value has its necessity and reality due to the global process of socialization. In their view, human socialization is always completed under certain cultural environment which has now extended beyond the national boundaries. A global culture and socialization have come into existence and brought up a global man who has been surrounded by global cultural information and enjoy the global material and spiritual civilization.A man who has been nurtured by global socialization above all is a global man rather than a Chinese, an American, a French or a Russian. So far each national culture actually is a fusion of some cultures in spite of the fact that each national culture remains independent from the others. It is a global culture that is a mixture or blend of national cultures. The existence of a global culture means universal values have emerged as a reality in the world, which surpass the national border, social system and political ideology.[17]

One of the problems that interests Chinese scholars greatly is what impact globalization will bring to China. Globalization impacts the international community both positively and negatively. From a positive perspective, globalization distributes resources more effectively throughout the world, leads to international cooperation that is of

---

[16] See Zhu Jinwen (1998), "Some Issues on Globalization," in Hu Yuanzhi (ed.), *Globalization and China*, China or Beijing?: Central Compilation and Translation Press, pp. 111–19.

[17] Tan Junjiou, "Thinking and Arguing on Globalization," ibid., pp. 131–32.

higher quality, encourages the sharing of globally scientific and technological information and resolving global problems like air pollution, illegal immigration and drug trafficking. From a negative perspective, it helps to strengthen the hegemony of developed countries in international economic and political life, increases the risks of international financial crisis, widens the gap between the South and the North, and helps international capital control more likely the economy of underdeveloped countries. The impact of globalization on the international community will apply in the same way to the Chinese society.

Globalization provides a lot of good opportunities for China's development. It is beneficial for China to absorb foreign capital, to learn from foreign advanced science, technology, management and institution, to export national products, and to participate in international cooperation. However, it is obviously unfavourable for China's development at the same time. This is one area which Chinese politicians and scholars have been particularly emphasizing since the East Asian financial crisis. Generally speaking, the negative function of globalization for China is focused on the following two aspects. First, there are threats to China's economic safety. Foreign control of capital and high technology in big domestic enterprises threaten to restructure the process of China's industry. The opening of the domestic financial market to the world at large and the huge number of foreign debts are vulnerable in a serious financial crisis arising from a fluctuating world economy. Second, there is a possibility of a weakening of the sovereignty of state. It is one of the primary conditions of participating in the process of globalization to observe established international practices and conventions, most of which, indeed, are made according to and reflect the standards and values of developed countries. Developing countries have no alternative but to follow these Western-valued practices and conventions which thus tend to weaken their sovereignty more or less.[18]

As many Chinese researchers have clearly seen, the Chinese government has participated actively in the process of globalization by carrying out the policies of opening the country to the world, striving to be a member of the WTO and signing the International Covenant

---

[18] See Wang Caocai (1998), "World Economic Globalization and China's Economic Safety," and Liu Jianping, "Economic Globalization and Our Strategy of Economic Safety," in *Globalization and China*, pp. 180–200.

on Civil and Political Rights. Most Chinese scholars claim to participate actively in globalization. The problem for China as a developing country is how to join in the progress of globalization rather than if China should join in the progress of globalization. As an author notes, Chinese people must "recognize fully the dual impact of globalization dominated by developed countries: chance coincides with challenge. It is a lucky chance in the sense that globalization provides for developing countries good opportunity to absorb international capital and modern technology, to increase export, to improve market economy and to join into world market. It is a good example that China carries out the policies of reform and opening and constructs socialist market economy. Meanwhile, it is a great challenge as well and a process of mental agony and pain for developing countries in the sense that the progress of globalization will undermine the foundation of sovereignty of state and that their economic independence will be suffered from hegemony of developed countries. The recent financial crisis in East Asia is a good explanation in this regard."[19] The East Asian financial crisis has exerted a great influence on Chinese intellectuals who are interested in globalization. Now they are more carefully and cautiously putting their emphasis on the moment and the way China participates in the globalization process.

In the first place, many people argue that China cannot compete with developed countries to participate in the process of globalization because China's socio-economic conditions are still behind and globalization is actually controlled by a few advanced countries. Joining the advanced countries in the process of globalization will certainly lead to a situation under which China's economy is integrated into the global market too quickly before it is able to manage the attendant consequences that come with globalization and will in turn, be manipulated by other economically advanced countries. An economist summarizes the "view of coincidence with globalization" in such a way that "China has entered into the gate of globalization and that will not enable it to improve its economy without coincidence with advanced countries in the progress of globalization." However, he feels that "this view is too simplistic and far from the Chinese situation, and therefore is one-sided and improper."

---

[19] Wang Weiping (1998), "Globalization and China's Political Reform," *Antinomies of Globalization*, pp. 50–51.

Second, some think that China should take part in the process of globalization as an alternative, instead of pursuing it without reservation. Compared to politics and culture, the priority should be given to economic globalization although politics, culture and economics hardly exist isolated from each other as is well known. In the view of certain Chinese scholars, as we have seen, globalization is often considered as economic globalization. For some of them, China can never follow Western countries even in economic integration. Instead, China should keep moderate pace as it opens to the global market. They warned that Chinese economists should not have any dream of economic globalization which hides huge risks and should realize the inequalities of existing global economic order by which Western developed countries manipulate developing countries including China. They emphasize that China must insist on an independent strategy of economic development, watching out for Western economic and political hegemony and defending our national economy and sovereignty of state.

Lastly, some intellectuals emphasize economic nationalization upon which, in their opinion, economic globalization should be based. As we have pointed out at the beginning of the Chapter, globalization is a unity of nationalization and internationalization in a certain sense. It is the case in the field of economy. On the one hand, economic globalization is breaking out of the traditional national barriers and hurrying the process of world economic integration; on the other hand, the trend in economic nationalization has become more apparent than before. For example, regional economy has been developing very rapidly in recent years; protectionism even in developed countries remains strong as before; and trade wars among nations take place now and then. In such a situation, how should China deal with the relation between economic globalization and nationalization? In other words, which should be given top priority—joining the global economy or developing a national economy? A few scholars frankly express their preference stating that national economy has priority over economic globalization. The fundamental goal of participating in global economy, for them, is to develop the national economy more quickly and to increase national economic power. The more global the world economy becomes, the more apparent the national interest is. It is their conclusion that "it is absolutely mistake to stress opening to the global market rather than protecting national economy. It is a basic principle to develop our national economy."[20]

Why are there so many contrary views about globalization? Why does globalization bring about such paradoxes? There might be a number of reasons to explain this. First of all, in my view, it is because of the inherent contradiction of globalization in its very nature. The process of globalization by nature is intensively contradictory: It has tendencies of homogenization and fragmentation; it is a unification with pluralization; it includes both centralization as well as separation; it is both an internationalization and a nationalization at the same time; it combines cosmopolitanism with nationalism.

First, globalization is a unity of universalization and particularization. On the one hand, globalization is a process of homogenization characterized by a convergence of lifestyles, modes of production and values among various nations' civilizations. For instance, the market economy is becoming a world abstract beyond its European origins; democracy and human dignity are being sought by all peoples in the world as basic human values while despotism is rapidly losing its supporters. However, on the other hand, universalization is always accompanied by particularization. Market economies in various countries are quietly different although it has been an international abstract. Furthermore, the differences among market economies in various countries are not decreasing as the market economy is expanding over the world. For example, the market economy in Germany is called a "social market economy" which is quietly different from a liberal market economy in the United States or the United Kingdom; the market economy in East Asia is different from others due to much governmental intervention. Democracy is the same case. All people over the world are longing for democracy which is likely to differ in different countries. For instance, Japan and South Korea adopt a representative democracy which is quite different from the one in the US or Britain.

Second, globalization is both integration and fragmentation. Indeed, it is an integration and homogenization in terms of the rapid growth of international organizations, such as the United Nations, World

---

[20] Gao Debu (1997), "Globalization or Nationalization?" *Chinese Cadres' Forum*, No. 5.

Bank, International Monetary Fund (IMF) and World Trade Organization (WTO) whose roles have grown increasingly important. It also means a higher degree of integration among nations, which leads to dissolving the traditional national sovereignty and barriers to a significant extent. Moreover, cosmopolitan ideas are being reflected in the sense that integration movements among nations are more lively, such as European integration, global floating of capital and global sharing of more and more common information. Nevertheless, there is a reverse tendency along with global integration that strengthens unprecedentedly the particularity, plurality, and independence of each nation and region. The movement of national independence and autonomy is a good example. It does not disappear but does develop more and more deeply as global integration goes on. More and more small minorities demand independence one after another, so did East Timor and the Albanians in Kosovo begin their independent movement. The tide of regional, local and communal autonomy is rising, not disappearing, at the same time as the process of globalization occurs. Community movements and communitarianism have been hot political issues in developed countries. A very special term "global localism" has appeared which specifically reflects contradiction due to the fact that local autonomy is developing rapidly under the condition of globalization.

Third, globalization includes both centralization and decentralization in its concept. One of the major aspects of globalization is increasing centralization of capital, information, power and wealth, especially in transnational cooperation. The merger of big companies has been the fashion since the 1990s. Mergers push centralization of power and wealth. A good example is the recent merger of Macdowell and Boeing, two biggest companies in the international aviation industry. At the same time, it is an outstanding trend as well to decentralize capital, information, power and wealth. Small capital is still very active and developing very well as if it has not suffered from the opposed centralization of capital. It seems a contradiction but a fact as well that the higher the degree of centralization of information is, the more difficult to monopolize it. The best example in this regard is the internet. So far the internet is the largest network receiving information and allowing access to information that transcends national boundaries. The internet provides information from all over the world, all fields of society and all aspects of human life so long as some form of this information has found its way into the network.

Lastly, globalization involves both internationalization and nationalization, and it combines cosmopolitanism with nationalism. As we pointed out above, globalization is breaking out of the traditional national barriers. As a result, more and more international conventions, covenants, agreements and norms are accepted and observed by nations all over the world. "Join the international" is becoming a common slogan and many international principles have authentic international coverage However, each nation never forgets its own tradition and characteristics while it accepts international conventions, agreements and principles. Each nation tries to deal with international principles in the light of its own specific national conditions as it attempts to nationalize these international principles and norms. For instance, while most countries in the world agree to accept the international covenants on protection of human rights and environment, they need to keep in mind their own national characteristics and needs before they are able to observe these international conventions.

Furthermore, the questions arising out of the paradoxes on globalization among Chinese intellectuals can be seen in the context of the Chinese history of modernization. We have been able to discern some new features and special meaning from this discussion although it began long before it ended. There are at least two attractive developments in this discourse, in our view, compared to the other discourses in modern Chinese history of thoughts: the discourse proposes going gradually beyond the dichotomies of the traditional paradigm of "Sino-West" and the ideological paradigm of "socialism vs. capitalism."

The discourse on "Sino-West" might be the longest discourse in modern China, which is specified as "Sinification" or "Westernization" to signify the Chinese opening to the world. It is a discourse around which Chinese intellectuals have been disputing from the period of the Westernization movement under the Qing Dynasty, through the Republic of China under the Kuomingdang regime, till the People's Republic of China under of the Communist Party of China (CPC). The dominant doctrine throughout the discourse is always the "Chinese body with Western function" (*zhong ti xi yong*).[21] The doctrine has the same essential meaning with its various expressions during the different

---

[21] The doctrine means that China can only introduce and use Western sciences and techniques as a tool while insisting on the Chinese political system and traditional values as a goal.

periods and different regimes. It is the essence of that doctrine that created fundamental differences between China and the Western countries so that China can only use Western sciences and techniques as tools while never learning from Western political, social, economic and cultural systems and values. But since the discussion on globalization took place in the 1990s, the situation is changing, as we have already seen. Participants in the discussion on globalization, for the most part, no longer regard it simply as Westernization in spite of the fact that almost all of them recognize the dominant role of Western developed countries in globalization. It seems to Chinese intellectuals that the subject of globalization must project equality among nations, no matter how big or small the nations are, although the manipulators of globalization in effect are the more advanced Western countries. It follows that China should participate actively and intuitively in the globalization process while it must never be Westernized. Here we have an insight into how Chinese intellectuals are dealing with the dichotomy of "Sino-West" which inevitably touches on nationalism.

The international community is divided into two blocs after the second world war: communist and capitalist countries. China since 1949 belonged to the former bloc while all Western developed countries belong to the latter. Because of this, Western countries are almost synonymous with capitalism. It is under such a particular context that the traditional discourse on "Sino-West" has turned into one of "socialism vs. capitalism," which is dealing with the matter in a more or less ideological manner. The ideological discourse on socialism or capitalism appeared repeatedly each time China was implementing its policies of opening up to the Western world. But now we are able to find in the discussion on globalization that Chinese intellectuals, for the most part, no longer like to regard globalization simply as capitalism, although they know clearly that the developed capitalistic countries control the process of globalization. They do not advocate capitalism publicly in China while they do welcome globalization in China. Thus the discourse on globalization is dissolving, in other words, the ideological dichotomy of "socialism vs. capitalism" which has dominated Chinese thought for a long time.

GLOBALIZATION AND NATIONAL DEVELOPMENT: THE PERSPECTIVE OF THE CHINESE REVOLUTION

Arif Dirlik

University of Oregon

I will take up a problem here that is elided in most discussions of globalization: the problem of national development in the strength of globalization. The juxtaposition of the terms, globalization and national development, points to a deep contradiction in contemporary thinking, or a nostalgic longing for an aspiration that may no longer be relevant, but is powerful enough still to disturb the very forces at work in relegating it to the past.

There is a suggestion in arguments for globalization that national development may be achieved through globalization, which in turn would be expected to contribute to further globalization, and so on and so forth into the future, which goes against the tendency of these same arguments to set the global against the national, as a negation of the latter. While it may not be a zero-sum relationship, the relationship between globalization and national development is nevertheless a highly disturbed one. Understood as the persistence of commitments to autonomy and sovereignty, most importantly in the realm of the economy, the national goals obstructs globalization, just as globalization erodes the national agenda, at the same time rendering irrelevant any idea of development that takes such autonomy and sovereignty as its premise. If we are to take globalization seriously, in other words, the very idea of national development becomes meaningless. On the other hand, if national development as an idea is to be taken seriously, as it was for most of the past century, then globalization appears as little more than an ideological assault on the national aspirations, to rid the present of the legacies of that past. I suggest below that we take this contradiction seriously, inquire into some of its implications, and consider resolutions that avoid entrapment between the past and the present, or an ideological erasure of the past by the present. We could instead seek out ways to direct the forces of globalization in directions that do not erase but rather presume the central importance of the local in globalization.

I am concerned here most importantly with Third World circumstances in globalization. That term itself is a reminder of the
distance between the present and the past, but it still enables a convenient way of mapping shifts in global power and inequality. The
Third World itself may not point to any entity identifiable on a geographical or cultural map, but it is arguable that only about three
to four decades ago there was a shared Third World response to
questions of national development, identifiable with some kind of
national liberation socialism.

I will sketch out below the outlines of these strategies of national
development. I will proceed from that to outline what some influential
analysts see as the defining characteristics of a mapping of the global
political economy under the regime of globalization. I draw extensively on the Chinese experience which offers a paradigmatic case
on both counts; first, as a foremost example of a revolutionary agrarian society challenging the globalizing forces of capital, and, subsequently, as a successful case, at least so far, of post-socialist development
through incorporation in global capitalism.

To conclude, I would like to suggest that the differences between
the two mappings of political economy and economic development
should be the point of departure for any consideration of a political
economy that aims to get past political slogans to address concrete
economic, social, and political problems. This requires close attention
not just to technical questions of the economy, but to questions of
class interest and power in the organization of the global economy.

National Development and Social Revolution in
Early Chinese Marxist Thought

For this section, I am using the title of the first article I published
nearly three decades ago (Dirlik, 1974). The original article expresses
cogently an ideal of national development that was expressed by
Chinese Marxists of various stripes in the 1920s. Similar ideas would
subsequently become quite prevalent in Third World ideals of development, as well as in efforts to explain Third World difficulties with
development in such alternatives to modernization discourse as
Dependency Theory and World System analysis.

Despite internal differences in their diagnoses of the problems of
national development, Chinese Marxist analyses were uniformly

inspired by V.I. Lenin's analysis of the contradictory role imperialism (understood as "the highest stage of capitalism") played in colonial and semi-colonial societies: that while imperialism was responsible
for introducing into these societies the progressive forces of capitalism,
it also created structural impediments to the realization of capitalist
development as in Europe and North America (Lenin, 1967; 1969).

There were two major aspects to these impediments. One was
economic. Development in these societies resulted not from the logic
of the national economy, responding to internal demand and needs,
but rather followed the logic of a globalizing capitalist economy, the
search of imperialist powers for markets for commodities and capital, as well as the conflict generated by the competition among them
in this search. As imperialists had little or no interest in the national
development of these societies, what development there was contributed not to national economic integration, and an economic structure that answered the various needs of the national economy,
including subsistence needs of the population, but to a bifurcated
economy, with a modern capitalist sector increasingly integrated to
a global capitalist economy, and a much larger sector that remained
mired in premodern economic practices, and was subject to the
exploitative forces of the modern sector just as the national economy
as a whole was subject to the exploitative forces of global capitalism.
Spatially speaking in the case of the Chinese economy, this meant
the lopsided development of coastal areas, and a few coastal cities
such as Shanghai, and the increasing "underdevelopment" of vast
areas of the interior, and the populations therein. Economic bifurcation,
needless to say, also undermined efforts to achieve integration at the
political level.

The other aspect was social: the creation of a new class structure.
As capitalism was introduced into China from the outside, the emergent Chinese bourgeoisie was itself a foreign product, aligned in its
interests with the outside forces that produced it, and with little commitment to the interests of the nation as a whole. True, there was
some distinction between an overtly "comprador" bourgeoisie and a
"national" bourgeoisie that strove for autonomy within the structural
context of imperialism. But even the latter were more closely integrated structurally with the forces of global capitalism than with the
national economy, and were condemned in their very activities, sort
of to speak, to contribute to the deepening of the almost inevitable
structural bifurcation of the economy. This was the major reason

that any hope for national development had to be preceded by a social revolution that would transfer power to social forces that had an investment in the creation of a national economy; represented most importantly by the working class and the peasantry. Ultimately, as we are quite aware, this meant the creation of an autonomous state that could use political means to establish boundaries around the national economy, and the basis for national economic integration; an autonomous economy that answered to internal needs, in other words.

This analysis led not merely to demands for autonomy, however, but for economic autarky, as occurred during the Cultural Revolution. In hindsight, it is clear that only through the institutionalization of state control and coercion could such autarky be achieved, which opened the way easily to the substitution of state interests in development for popular needs and aspirations. There is an additional complication, perhaps less evident in the case of a well-established society, such as China, than in many other Third World societies: the assumption that there already was in place a nation whose economic integrity had to be safeguarded, when the creation of an integrated national entity was itself one of the goals of economic development.

The Cultural Revolution was a response to concerns that were as old as the history of the Chinese revolution; not just the Communist but the nationalist revolution. The experience of agrarian revolution which in the end brought the Communist Party to power was also an important force in shaping the course of post-revolutionary development policies, which found their clearest articulation in the Great Leap Forward of the late 1950s and the Cultural Revolution of the 1960s, two events that were dynamically interlinked, and represented in their day by paradigmatic expressions of Third World encounters with development.

The Cultural Revolution dramatized within Marxism a new conception of the relationship between culture and a new mode of production, and, by extension, politics and the mode of production. Marxism presupposes some correspondence between a new mode of production and a new culture, but there is some ambiguity in the theory as to whether the new mode of production produces a new culture, or whether there is some autonomy in the realm of culture in facilitating the new mode of production. Not satisfied with the cultural consequences of the new relations of production that had been established by 1956, and bent upon deepening the revolution, radicals in the Communist Party (led by Mao Zedong) had no choice but to settle on culture as the next realm of revolutionary activity. In the process, they were to recognize to the realm of culture an unprecedented measure of autonomy (in Marxist terms), so that culture would come to bear the burden for the transition to socialism. It matters little in this context whether this autonomy recognized to culture was a product of China's historical legacy, the legacy of a guerilla revolution in which ideological struggle played a central part, or the logic of theory confronting the consequences of a socialist revolution legitimized by the same theory itself (the material transformation of social relations, in other words, failing to create a new culture automatically). The consequences are clearer: cultural transformation, rather than a function of socialist transformation, must play a key role in producing a socialist society. This autonomy of the cultural against the economic or the social, resonated with changes under way globally in the 1960s. Suffice it to say here that it also underlined the importance of the political and ideological aspects of the revolution, against mechanical transformations in the mode of production understood economistically or technologically, which pointed in new directions of action that broke with earlier assumptions of modernization in either its capitalist or socialist guises.

To view the Cultural Revolution simply in its relationship to the history of Marxist-inspired revolutions, or in terms of a struggle between the First and Second Worlds of post-World War II sociology, is insufficient, because what imbued the Cultural Revolution with its concrete historical characteristics may be the ambiguous status of Chinese society in the 20th century, even after the victory of the Communist Party: as a society that belonged in the Second World by virtue of its socialist revolutionary history, but also in the Third World by virtue of its political, economic and cultural relationships to the world of capitalism in Euro/America. It is important to recall that the Cultural Revolution coincided historically with decolonization in the Third World, and that, until the advent of the geopolitically inspired Maoist Three Worlds theory of the 1970s, the Cultural Revolution identified ideologically with the colonial world against both the Euro/American world of capitalism and Soviet-style "social imperialism. "The juxtaposition of the rural Third World against the metropolitan First and Second Worlds was important, I think, both to the new departures in Cultural Revolution socialism, and to its ideological claims on the procedures of revolution.

Especially for its anachronism with the present, Lin Biao's "Long Live the Victory of People's War" (Lin, 1972) must be viewed as one of the most important documents of the Cultural Revolution, because it crystallized both the hostilities and the aspirations against the worlds of industrial capitalism and socialism of the newly emerging nations around the globe, and resonated with the ideology of national liberation struggles, of which the Chinese had been the most successful to date. It matters little whether or not it was ideologically justifiable from a Marxist perspective on socialism or revolution, which was its presumed theoretical basis; though it is arguable that it carried to its logical conclusions a Third Worldist socialism that had appeared first in the Second Congress of the Communist International in 1920. What is relevant is that Lin applied globally a paradigm of the Chinese revolution itself, which had captured the cities from the countryside, and brought to the fore the fundamental meaning of that revolutionary experience: the primacy to any consideration of revolution of the agrarian world against industrial societies. The hostility, unfortunately, would overshadow the more meaningful message: that a resolution of global problems would require the resolution of the problems of agrarian societies, just as the resolution of economic problems in individual nations, especially Third World nations, called for the resolution of the economic problems of the majority population of peasants.

The significance of this piece for the purposes here was not that it called for war on industrialized societies, or that it stressed emphasis on agrarian societies, but that the call itself expressed the sense of empowerment in Third World societies that accompanied decolonization. This same sense of empowerment is visible in the articulation at the time of different notions of development than those that prevailed under either capitalist or Soviet-style socialist strategies of development. The Maoist paradigm of development was possibly the most powerful of the alternative notions of development which came to the fore as the new National Liberation struggles sought for ways to bolster economically their newfound political sovereignty. This paradigm proposed (a) that development policies take as their point of departure the necessity of all-round development nationally, and, (b) that this could be realized only by "delinking" from the capitalist world-system.

The first premise was enunciated clearly in Mao's classic 1956 essay, "On the Ten Great Relationships," which called for attention to contradictions created by "uneven development" nationally (Mao, 1979). The second premise was enunciated throughout the Cultural Revolution years by the stress on national self-reliance, and the avoidance of material or ideological dependence on the outside world. It followed logically from the first premise in its analytical assumption that involvement in the capitalist world system would inevitably substitute the economic demands of this world system for the needs of a national economy. It may be worth emphasizing here that these "Maoist" premises had deep roots in the Chinese Revolution, in the intense attention of Chinese Marxists in the 1920s to the implications for the national economy of involvement in a capitalist world economy. As these premises were re-enunciated in the 1960s, they exerted immense influence in thinking on Third World development, of which the work of the distinguished development economist Samir Amin may be exemplary.[1]

As important as the structural implications of this new paradigm of development were, equally important were the substantive issues it raised, with profound social implications, that resonated with contemporary concerns in both advanced capitalist or socialist and Third World societies. A slogan such as self-reliance, that was central to Maoist developmental ideology, implied not just avoidance of dependency, but also called for active participation on the part of the people in the process of development. Its social implications were profound. Against their marginalization in earlier conceptualizations of development (capitalist or Soviet-socialist), self-reliance recognized the "people" as both the motivating force and the end of development. No

---

[1] Of Amin's many works, the most thorough may be *Delinking*. Amin, of course, was not alone. The example of the Chinese Revolution and Maoist development policy also exerted influence on important thinkers such as Immanuel Wallerstein and those associated with him in promoting "world-system analysis," independent scholars like Andre Gunder Frank, as well as "dependency theorists" such as Fernando Henrique Cardoso It is also important to note that the Maoist development model in its concerns resonated with the contemporary dissatisfaction with modernization "theory," expressed mainly but not exclusively in world-system analysis and the "dependency theory" emanating from Latin America. In other words, the Maoist paradigm was part of a search globally for alternatives to the modernization theory. That some of the above-named scholars, most prominently Frank and Cardoso have turned their back on their earlier analyses is an eloquent testimonial to intellectual and political changes of the last three decades.

longer to be left in the hands of experts, development conceived along these lines brought the "people" onto the centre stage of the developmental process. In order for such a process to work, it was necessary also to place collective values over private ones, for cooperation and everyday negotiation were crucial to the achievement of social goals. Politically, the process required participation in collective decision-making on a daily basis, creating unprecedented possibilities for grassroots democratic participation in social life. The labouring population, that is to say the majority of the people, would be responsible also for managing its own productive life. At the most fundamental level, the insistence on self-reliance was premised on a recognition of the subjectivity of the people, and their ability to manage their subjectivities in accordance with social goals.

In its idealistic reading, "putting politics in command"—a condition of self-reliance—implied the priority of public over private values. The type of individual who could live up to this absolute priority of the public over the private was obviously one who had overcome internally the force of social divisions that generated individualism; be it class and gender divisions, the division of labour, hierarchies of experts and non-experts and, at a most fundamental level, the division between mental and manual labour. Creating such individuals required the appropriate social settings, but it also required individual effort at cultural self-transformation, because of the dialectic between social and cultural transformation. It required social institutions that would promote the welfare of the people, and enable their loyalty to collective institutions; but it would also require individuals who, rather than take advantage of such institutions, would devote themselves to fulfilling their promises.

I would like to stress here one aspect of the Maoist institutional vision that has received much criticism from the perspective of economic efficiency, but was nevertheless quite significant in its consequences for social and political organization. This was a conviction in the necessity of integrating agriculture and industry, so as to overcome the structural division between agriculture and industry, or rural and urban societies, that seemed to characterize modern societies. This was one of the institutional innovations of the disastrous Great Leap Forward in 1958, but like other aspects of Maoist developmental thinking, its origins lie in the history of the Chinese Revolution. While the communists had sought such integration out of necessity in revolutionary Yan'an years, when they had no choice but to produce for themselves, the idea itself was one that first appeared in Chinese radicalism in anarchist writings in the first decade of the 20th century (inspired by the writings of Peter Kropotkin). In anarchist writing, it is also important to note, the idea of integrating industry and agriculture to create self-sufficient local communities found a parallel in the creation of well-rounded individuals, who combined mental and manual labour, and thus overcame the class divisions that grew out of the division of labour. Needless to say, for anarchists, who eschewed nationalism, the primary goal was to avoid the alienation of modern industrial society in the reaffirmation of community. As it was appropriated into Maoist ideologies of development, these anarchist ideals were also linked to strategies of national autonomy and development (Dirlik, 1991; Chan and Dirlik, 1991).

Even so, however, the anarchist juxtaposition of nation and community may have something to tell us about Maoist conceptualizations of society, and the contradictions that they contained. The idea of self-reliance, of which these institutional innovations may be viewed as expressions, is a multi-layered idea. It did not aim just at national autonomy through self-reliance, but autonomy at every level of society, down to the locality (which is what is disturbing from an economistic perspective that stresses "comparative advantage"); so that local societies themselves had to seek to be self-reliant, without relying on the outside, symbolized in the Cultural Revolution years by the accomplishments of the Dazhai Brigade in Shanxi. Here, too, there is a conflict between the vision of autonomous communities and the existence of a hierarchical Party bureaucracy with the power to dispose of resources according to its own notion of political, social and national good. But the distinction is important. Self-reliance was a means not just to national economic autonomy, but also to community formation. Its utopian aspirations could attract even those who otherwise did not share in the goals of a Chinese nationalism.

There was a downside to all of these promises, especially under conditions of unequal power, which the Cultural Revolution would finally exacerbate rather than eliminate. But that is not the question I wish to pursue in this context, where I am more concerned with the appeals of these Maoist ideas globally (Dirlik, 2002b). The paradigm of development offered by Cultural Revolution Maoism seemed not only to answer the needs for simultaneous economic development and social cohesion in emergent postcolonial societies, but also the widespread alienation produced by development in economically

advanced capitalist and socialist societies. It is not surprising that the
Cultural Revolution should have spawned a new radical literature
on development that rejected economic efficiency in the name of
participatory development and democratic management (Andors,
1977; Bettelheim, 1974; Gurley, 1976; Hoffman, 1974). Neither is it
very surprising that it should have proven to be appealing even to
those who had little reason to be favourable to its revolutionary
goals, conservatives who saw in the social achievements of the Cultural
Revolution the promise of new kinds of social cohesion and commitment to social goals.

What I would like to stress here is the underlying spatial assumption of this argument, that the nation is comprised of a space, defined
by a bounded surface, with little tolerance in that space for uneven
development, for such unevenness calls into question not just economic integrity but the political existence of the nation. If the search
for autarky carried the logic of national integration to its extreme,
its very extremeness is nevertheless a reminder that the anxiety over
unevenness in the national economy was not just a characteristic of
extremist revolutionary regimes, but all political economic thinking
that took the nation as the unit of analysis. After all, Marxist revolutionary regimes did not invent so much as inherit the use of state
power to regulate economic relationships and, until the 1960s and
the 1970s, import substitution seemed to be the preferred route to
development against export-oriented development.

The difference here may be not so much a difference between
liberal nationalism and a revolutionary fundamentalism, but a difference
in power that is embedded in the very structure of the capitalist
world economy as it has taken shape over the last few centuries:
that the powerless have very few options in their struggle for national
economic and political integrity other than shutting out the world
economy and, with it, the promise of development that comes at a
very high social and political price. It may not be very surprising
that radical social scientists through the 1970s (and to the present)
have concurred that national economic development might not be
possible except through some measure of delinking from the global
capitalist economy dominated by nations of the First World. But
shutting out the world has proven to be an impossible task. This
has become particularly so as the controlling powers in the world
economy are prepared to use all coercive means at their disposal to
force open economies that sought to shut out a globalizing capitalism,

or whenever it seemed that they might be vulnerable to dependency on others—most notoriously in the case of energy dependency which continues to serve as an important factor in the First World's seemingly endless war against the Third. This has become even more evident in the post-Cold War period. With communist states becoming history, there is something seemingly puzzling about the perpetuation by the United States and Great Britain of what used to be viewed as Cold War era politics of continuous war. The puzzle, however, may be a consequence of the exceptional significance attributed to communism as a factor in this war. It may be more proper, in hindsight, to view the war against communism of the Cold War years as only one phase of a much longer history that has been shaped by efforts to remove all obstacles to a capitalism headquartered in Great Britain and the United States in their successive hegemonies. The "opening of China," first in 1842 and again in 1978, carries a symbolism that overflows the boundaries of the Cold War.

It is a symbolism that also relegates to the past the Cultural Revolution of the 1960s that for a brief moment appeared as a harbinger of the future. A genuinely critical evaluation of the Cultural Revolution, which is a rarity these days, must proceed by recognizing its historicity—a recognition both of its significance under its historical circumstances and a recognition that with the transformation of those historical circumstances, the Cultural Revolution appears as a remote historical event, that left behind little but memories of misdeeds and oppressions. It is not necessary in order to understand the Cultural Revolution critically to erase memories of what it meant to contemporaries. Such erasure in fact obviates the need for critical understanding not just of the Cultural Revolution, but of past and present ways of thinking about it. In the case of those who were victims of the Cultural Revolution, it would be asking too much to expect them to think of it critically, but surely that is only part of the reason for the contemporary urge to relegate memories into oblivion. While there was never any shortage of those who would condemn the Cultural Revolution on moral or political grounds, they have been joined over the last two decades by Chinese participants in the Cultural Revolution who were complicitous not only in its ideology but its misdeeds, foreigners who would forget their earlier admiration for the Cultural Revolution, and many others who seem to perceive in the vulgarization of its memories the means to producing best-sellers for the US market. Ideology and a consumptive voyeurism have come together in curious ways to obviate the need to speak about this event with any degree of intelligence, let alone critical intelligence.

The Two Cultural Revolutions

If the Cultural Revolution seems irrelevant today, it is because the problems it addressed are no longer significant problems. The Cultural Revolution appeared significant in its day as a breakthrough in the history of socialist revolutions, or revolutions in general, in defiance of the inevitability of "deradicalization." At a time when socialism, and the whole idea of revolutionary politics, have been relegated to the past, a breakthrough in revolutionary politics carries little meaning, let alone historical significance. Much the same could be said with regard to the Cultural Revolution as an expression of resurgent Third World politics. In the immediate circumstances of the Cultural Revolution in the 1960s, the idea of a Third World carried significant weight in global political discourse. In our day, when it is hardly possible to speak of the Third World as a coherent idea, let alone a promise, it makes little sense to speak of a revolutionary Third World alternative to accepted paradigms of development (Dirlik, 1995). Third worlders, including the Chinese in the People's Republic, are anxious to remake themselves in the image of the First World, pretending all the time that they are creating "alternative modernities" that build on ancient traditions. Where they have not made it already into the ranks of developing economies, Third World societies are in shambles, apparently in need of renewed colonial aid for their sustenance.

These changes are not changes on an ideological plane, but are products of transformations within global relations. I have suggested elsewhere that the whole history of socialism as we have known it, no less than the history of the Third World, need to be comprehended in their relationship to transformations within capitalism (Dirlik, 1994). Colonialism, and socialism as a response to it, especially in the Third World, were products of one phase within capitalism. While capitalism as a mode of production persists, contemporary capitalism is quite different in the global relations that it calls for than the capitalism that produced the Third World, or sought to contain the socialism that was its own product. This new phase in capitalism, whether it is called global capitalism, late capitalism, post-Fordism, or flexible production or accumulation, has made irrelevant earlier conceptualizations of global relations, as well as of the relations of exploitation and oppression informed by those conceptualizations. Euro-American transnational corporations may still be dominant globally, but they have been joined by others, some of them originating in the former Third World. There may still be dominant nations, but it makes less sense than before to speak of imperialism or colonialism, when the nation-state has lost much of its power to corporations that are transnational, both in personnel and culture. And, most importantly in the context of this discussion, it makes little sense to speak of national economic autonomy, when the paradigm of development based on the national market has been replaced by a paradigm of development that calls for export economies and porous national boundaries as a condition of development. The nation-state, indispensable to the economic operations of capital in an earlier stage, now finds itself under attack as an obstacle to the same operations. Capital still rules, but under a different regime, one that seeks to be inclusive rather than exclusive. States still exist, more powerfully than ever, but with more tenuous ties to the nation. The distinction between the inside and the outside, too, has become more tenuous.[2]

---

[2] I am making some broad statements, here, which are justified by my conviction that earlier ways of understanding the world need to be revised significantly to grasp contemporary changes. It is not my intention to suggest that these statements apply equally to all societies and all transnational corporations, let alone "capital in general." It is difficult to be certain at this point whether or not the globalization hype itself drew its plausibility from the Clinton years in the United States, with their economic foundation in the new internet and computer industries. The current regime of George W. Bush, with its basis in more conventional extraction and energy industries, certainly raises questions about what globality may mean. It is also quite apparent, however, that the nationalism of the current regime is class-based, as it is quite willing to impoverish the majority of American citizens, and compromise their rights, in order to sustain US hegemony in world politics. In any case, we need to formulate new concepts, I think, with which to comprehend the long-term changes at work that distinguish the postcolonial postsocialist world of the present—what is best described as the world of global modernity—from the world of socialism, anti-colonial movements and the Cultural Revolution. Further discussion of these relationships which entail considerations of empire, imperialism, colonialism and global capitalism, as well as of class and cultural relations globally, may be found in Dirlik (2002; 2003a; 2003b).

These structural transformations within capitalism would produce their own "cultural revolution." As theorists such as Fredric Jameson and David Harvey were the first to point out, the new phase in capitalism was to demand and produce its own culture, which may be encapsulated conveniently by the term "postmodernism" (Harvey, 1989; Jameson, 1994). This other cultural revolution, a cultural revolution of capitalism, coincided with the Chinese Cultural Revolution, although few were aware at the time of its eventual significance. It may be interesting to recall, in historical hindsight, that the launching of the Cultural Revolution in China, with the developmental policies it promoted, coincided almost to the year with the establishment of the export zones in Kao-hsiung in Taiwan and Masan in South Korea. It might not have occurred to radical critics of modernization and capitalism at the time that the future lay with the latter rather than the former. But that is exactly what has happened. And national autonomy in economic development has receded before the onslaught of export-oriented economies symbolized by these zones. The success of these economic zones, needless to say, would be made possible ultimately by new technologies that made possible the transnationalization of production. It was these same technologies that would make possible the new cultural revolution in capitalism, central to which is its self-representation as producer of images and information rather than of commodities (which still need to be produced, albeit in Third World locations, while the First World takes over as the "brain-centre" in the designing of the world). What the capitalist "cultural revolution" produced ideologically was culture commodified and rendered into an end in itself, infinitely malleable and marketable, rather than culture as a means to something else, such as community.

Viewed in this perspective, what is striking about the Cultural Revolution in China was that it was directed at the problems of a world that was already being replaced by another world dictated by the transformative powers of contemporary capitalism, that was far ahead of what its critics imagined whether they were located in the First, Second or the Third Worlds. The Cultural Revolution, as a product of the revolution against imperialism, or First World domination of the Third World, spoke to problems inherited from the past, when the First World of capitalism was already in the process of creating new global relations, and corresponding social and cultural relations, that made those problems irrelevant. The contradictions between modernism and antimodernism in Mao Zedong thought, at the moment of their enunciation, were already incorporated in post-modernist conceptualizations of the world which since then have proven to be of immense capacity in their ability to contain contradictions; so that business can utilize Maoist strategies in planning for the market while radicals continue to argue about appropriate responses to cliche-ridden conceptions of capitalism.

Whatever its failings as ideology and practice, the demise of Maoism as it appeared during the Cultural Revolution was a result not just of its own failings as a revolutionary ideology, but of its increasing irrelevance to an emergent world of capitalism that was radically different from the one that had produced Maoism. Cultural Revolution Maoism represented not a solution for the future, as it was taken to be at the time, but a last gasp of a past that was already irrelevant to a present that had overtaken it.

This, I think, is what we call globalization—the naturalization into inevitable historical process of conscious policies designed to overcome the obstruction presented by national boundaries to the spatial prerogatives of capital. Globalization as some kind of historical process, a contemporary version of diffusionism, is not particularly new. Much more interesting is globalization as an ideology that came to the fore in tandem with efforts to overcome contradictions generated by processes of capitalist development and resistance to it; that negates the viability not only of nations as units of analysis and development, but also of political internationalism that had characterized earlier radical analyses. Globalization discourse provides its own mapping of the process of development which, in its contrast with earlier mappings of national development, points not so much to the failure of the latter as to the contradictions they presented. The resolution of these contradictions that finds expression in the discourse of globalization, it needs to be underlined, does not represent the only resolution possible, but rather the most preferred resolution that sustains the structure of power under the capitalist world system while containing the very oppositional forces generated by the system itself.

The Network Society

In the first of an ambitious three-volume study of contemporary global transformations, *The Rise of the Network Society*, Manuel Castells has offered a most revealing analysis of the re-spatialization of the political economy of development both as concept and as practice (Castells, 1997). His theorization of the new situation of globality is important not because what he has to say is particularly unusual, but because he is able through the metaphor of the "network society" to synthesize much that has been written on the question of globalization. His work is particularly relevant to my argument here because a spatialization of the global capitalist economy around nodes in a network provides a cogent contrast to the spatialization around bounded surfaces discussed earlier. It may or may not describe accurately the processes at work in the contemporary world economy; but it has much to say about a shift in ways of thinking about the world economy that has taken place over the last two decades, and does so without an apparent ideological commitment to globalization.

One of the most impressive aspects of Castells' analysis is its ability to account for an intensified mobility of capital while retaining a strong sense of the persistence of structural relationships in power. Castell's metaphor of networks in the description of contemporary capitalism is derived from the central importance he assigns to information technologies, which then serve as the paradigm for the reconfiguration of global relations. The metaphor of "network" offers ways of envisaging the new global capitalism in both its unities and disunities, in its pervasiveness as well as in the huge gaps that are systemic products of the global economy. The metaphor of network shifts attention from surfaces to "highways" that link nodes in the global economy. A network has no boundaries of any permanence but may expand or contract at a moment's notice and shift in its internal configurations as its nodes move from one location to another. Marginality to the global economy may mean being outside of the network, as well as in the many spaces within that are in its many gaps. Marginality does not imply being untouched by the networks, as the inductive effects of network flows affect even those who are not direct participants in its many flows. Finally, the network metaphor offers new ways of accounting for power. It is possible to state that the most powerful nodes in the global economy—for example, Saskia Sassen's "global cities" (Sassen, 1991; 2002)—may be those locations where nodes of economic, political and cultural power coincide. The network militates against neat spatialities, but it also allows for their inclusion in considerations of power; while any location may be included in the network, the most powerful, and controlling, nodes are still located in the national spaces of commanding global presence.

Castells identifies North America, Europe, and East Asia as the locations of such commanding power that determine "the basic architecture" of global relations. "Within this visible architecture," however, "there are dynamic processes of competition and change that infuse a variable geometry into the global system of economic processes." As he explains it:

> What I call the newest international division of labor is constructed around four different positions in the informational/global economy: the producers of high value, based on informational labor; the producers of high volume, based on lower cost labor; the producers of raw materials, based on natural endowments; and the redundant producers, reduced to devalued labor. ... *The critical matter is that these different positions do not coincide with countries. They are organized in networks and flows, using the technological infrastructure of the informational economy.* They feature geographic concentrations in some areas of the planet, so that the global economy is not geographically undifferentiated ... Yet the newest international division of labor does not take place between countries but between economic agents placed in the four positions that I have indicated along a global structure of networks and flows. ... [A]ll countries are penetrated by the four positions. ... Even marginalized economies have a small segment of their directional functions connected to a high-value producers network. ... And certainly, the most powerful economies have marginal segments of their population[s] placed in a position of devalued labor. ... The newest international division of labor is organized on the basis of labor and technology, but is enacted and modified by governments and entrepreneurs (Castells, 1997:146–47).

What is pertinent to the discussion here is Castells' observation that while nation-states are by no means irrelevant to the functioning of the new global economy, national spaces no longer serve as meaningful economic units, criss-crossed as they are by economic activities of various sorts between nodes that are as much part of a variety of global structurations (subject to chaos though they may be) as they are of the national space in which they are located. As he is focused almost exclusively on labour and technologies, Castells has less to say about the organizational aspects of such structurations; on the alternative spatializations produced, for instance, by transnational corporations as well as a host of transnational organizations from NGOs to universities. His analysis is nevertheless at one with most other analyses of globalization that are premised on the insufficiency of the nation as a unit of analysis in the analysis of the contemporary global economy.

While to an analyst such as Castells this may present a problem
where the social, political and cultural implications of globalization
are concerned, ideologues of global capitalism perceive in it the end
of the nation-state, and a need to re-spatialize politics to conform
to the essential "borderlessness" of a globalized economy. One such
analyst is Kenichi Ohmae, who suggests that "the nation-state has
become an unnatural—even a dysfunctional—organizational unit for
thinking about economic activity" (Ohmae, 1995:16). The alternative
is to rethink of political units in terms of "region-states" that correspond to the "regional economies" that are on the emergence with
globalization (that also correspond to the more stable nodes in the
global networks). What Ohmae proposes for China, which plays a
large part in his analysis, provides a sharp contrast to the economic
thinking of Chinese Marxists that I described above:

> ... the people of Guangzhou [in Southern China] know that they can-
> not deny a significant, ongoing relationship with the rest of mainland
> China. That connection is real—and is part of their strength and
> appeal. What they cannot afford is to be victims of tight, centralized
> control. But they can productively—be—in fact, they would do well
> to be—part of a loose grouping of Chinese regional states, a kind of
> Chinese federation or common-wealth (ibid., 97).

Unfortunately, Ohmae has little to say on what the mutual responsibility would be of the "region-states" in such a federation, or what
role a central government would play in enforcing those responsibilities. We may glean what he has in mind, however, from his discussion of "the civil minimum," the provision of equal services,
including those that entail subsistence needs, to all the citizens of
the nation-state, which in his view is inconsistent with the efficient
allocation of resources. As he puts it:

> ... alignment of government power with domestic special interests and
> have-not regions makes it virtually impossible for those at the center
> to adopt responsible policies for a nation as a whole, let alone for its
> participation in the wider borderless economy. . . . No matter how
> understandable the political or even social pressures behind these align-
> ments, they make no sense economically. Investing money inefficiently
> never does. In a borderless world, where economic inter-dependence
> creates ever-higher degrees of sensitivity to other economies, it is inher-
> ently unsustainable (ibid., 57).

Ohmae does not tell the reader what a "an explicit commitment to
heightened regional autonomy within a 'commonwealth' of China"
might leave of a 'commonwealth of China' when the regional economy

acts or aspires to act "as a local outpost of the global economy" (ibid., 74, 94). The message, however, is clear. Globalization means the supremacy of the market in shaping all relations, social and political, and the nation-state in its social and political concerns is an impediment to the efficient functioning of the market. The nation-state must allow the regional autonomy that permits successful regions to participate in the global economy, unhampered by obligations to other parts or constituencies of the nation guaranteed earlier by the state. What he does not say is why the nation-state might be needed at all under the circumstances, except to guarantee the success of its global "nodes" in the global economy—and perhaps to suppress the dissent that might result from its own participation in the "bifurcation" of the economy. The state here becomes something more than a mere promoter of economic development; it appears as an enforcer of the interests of the "local outposts of the global economy" and, we might add, of those in charge of the "local outposts." This is the state of global capitalism.

It is interesting that for all their vaunted internationalism, socialist states, in their real or imagined responsibility to their popular constituencies, produced a totalistic empowerment of the nation-state. It is equally interesting that capitalism, which experienced its embryonic growth within the womb of the nation-state, would return the nation-state to an earlier alliance between capital and the state, where the state is no longer responsible to constituencies other than those who manage the global economy, rendering the nation into more or less an empty shell, or a mere geographic or cartographic expression. The contrast provides a clue to the predicament that faces us all at the present.

Public Responsibility in an Age of Globalization

At a time when the nation no longer serves as an exclusive or even a viable unit of economic activity, when the ties between the state and the nation are once again being blurred, what is in question is not merely the viability of the nation-state, yearning for which may simply be the product of nostalgia for the past, but the more substantial question of the relationship between forms of political governance and public welfare. Delinking from the world economy no longer seems to be an option, unless it is accompanied by a fervent anti-modernism, as in the case, for instance, of the recent Taliban

regime. Neither are revolutions understood totalistically, as total systemic transformations; revolutions as we have known them have been
products themselves of the project of modernity, with nation-states
as their premise. The question of governance presently has to take
as its point of departure contemporary political configurations which
are increasingly difficult to grasp in terms of these earlier paradigms
of politics (Jones, 2002).

   This question inevitably invites thinking about the relationship
between corporate activity and public welfare, as the behaviour of
corporations in a context of global economic competition has much
to do with the erosion of the power of the state to be responsive to
its constituencies at large. The transnationalization of corporate activity is not novel, but is now subject to a new political consciousness
of globality; which demands that corporate responsibility is not
restricted to constituencies in the country of affiliation, but wherever
corporate activity is conducted. Should a US-based corporation, for
example, be responsible for the welfare of populations in India where
the corporation may be active? If claims to globalization are to be
taken seriously, globalization should not mean just the globalization
of activity, but a globalization of responsibility as well. The question
is how such responsibility may be enforced, which raises further questions about the unevenness of power that is often elided in discussions on globalization. It has become painfully evident over the past
decade, following the fall of socialism, that such unevenness of power
has assumed even greater sharpness than before with the expansion
of the coercive power of the United States, to the point where globalization appears to be little more than the universalization of US
sovereignty (and suzerainty) globally.

   The problem with an analysis such as Ohmae's is its oblivious-
ness to the different consequences of marketization in different social
and political contexts; most importantly in the differences between
those societies which occupy the architectural centres of global power,
as Castells puts it, and those who are powerless or marginal. Such
unevenness, as is cogently manifested in Ohmae's analysis, applies
not just to political relations between countries, moreover, but to
social relations within countries. In comparison with inequality between
countries, in other words, are inequalities in class and gender relationships that cut across countries, and are in the process of being
globalized as well.

Equally problematic is the rather cavalier dismissal in such an analysis of the surfaces implied by "national development," which comes into sharp relief when contemporary analyses of globalization are placed against earlier ideas of national development. There is much to support such a position empirically. Back in 1987, then People's Republic of China premier Zhao Ziyang suggested (contrary to what the socialist revolution had hoped to achieve) that all of coastal China be converted into a special economic zone to encourage foreign investment. While coastal China has not become a special economic zone, it has developed rapidly over the last decade and a half, producing that economic bifurcation which earlier revolutionary nationalists had feared. Indeed, analysts such as Dean Forbes have perceived in the development of Southeast and East Asian economies of an urban corridor, increasingly remote from its hinterland (Forbes, 1999).

The problem is what meaning to assign to this restructuring of national economies into networks that cut across national boundaries. There is a difference between a city-state such as Singapore and a continental nation such as the People's Republic of China in judging the consequences of an urban corridor that unites them. The latter has to face the politically divisive consequences of a structural bifurcation in the national economy, which presents questions not only of national sovereignty but the very viability of the nation, that are not likely to go away so long as nations exist—which is also an empirical fact. The PRC government, with a century of nationalist/socialist revolution behind it, has so far refused to accept the bifurcation of the economy, and has made some effort at least to promote the development of western China; whether it will be successful in the effort remains to be seen.

The rapidly developing parts of the national economy in the "urban corridor" are not without deep problems either. There is little need here to dwell upon the ecological destructiveness of rapid growth facilitated by foreign investment, by investors who have little interest in the ecological welfare of places where they invest. Likewise, the exploitation of labour has reached levels where slave-like or even slave labour has made a comeback. A recent study by Anita Chan documents the horrendous condition of Chinese labour in the most rapidly developing areas which not only does not receive much help from the state, but suffers from the oppressive collaboration between

Chinese officials and foreign investors (Chan, 2001). The situation is obviously worse in the so-called developing economies, but similar phenomena are by no means absent from the most developed economies, such as the United States.

These problems, elided in celebrations of globalization and regional states, no doubt call for difficult policy decisions on the parts of states, transnational corporations, local businesses, as well as public interest groups of one kind or another. I would like to suggest here, however, that fundamental to any consideration of solutions is an ideological and cultural transformation of attitudes toward the notion of development. Celebrations of globalization, or a preoccupation with contemporary configurations as a given empirical fact, too often leads to a dismissal of insights to be derived from the past; especially when that past is associated with seemingly failed or discredited attempts to open up alternative paths to the future. Such dismissal may be described properly as ideological because it ignores that while past paradigms may no longer be relevant, the problems that produced them are still with us, even more critically than before, and call not for a cavalier dismissal of those paradigms, but their reexamination so as to produce out of them new paradigms appropriate to the present.

I can only conclude here with a suggestion of the considerations that are crucial to any contemporary cultural transformation, or even a cultural revolution, that should be a point of departure in confronting the seemingly intractable problems we confront. First, is the ideology of development itself, what we may call developmentalism, that has become something of a "global faith," driven not only by corporate and government greed, but also a globalized cultural desire to participate in endless cycles of consumption (Rist, 1997). Second is an attention to places, concrete locations of everyday life, which, rather than meaningless statistics of growth at the national or state level, ought to be the measure of economic health, social welfare and political democracy—a measure of the claims of states and corporations, in other words, to fulfill the promises of popular welfare off which they thrive. This also requires reconsideration of governance at all levels, beginning with places, and guaranteed public participation not only in the political process but in corporate decision making as well (Prazniak and Dirlik, 2001). Finally, as I noted above in passing, if globalization is to serve as more than an excuse for intensified and uncontrolled exploitation of labour globally, it must be accompanied by the cultivation of global responsibility on the part of global actors; that a corporation, say, should be responsible not only to its stockholders, or the nation or location from which it hails, but to every location where it conducts its activities.

This is a wish-list no doubt. There are seemingly insurmountable ideological and material obstacles to each of these propositions—especially at a time when we seem to be entering a period of endless war, unprecedented imperial arrogance on the part of the United States with its overwhelmingly dominant role in global affairs, and corporate contempt not only for human welfare but even the welfare of stockholders. But it is precisely the continuous crisis that we seem to be living in that calls forth an insistence on such a wish-list. The alternative is hopelessness and, possibly, catastrophe for all. Does the Cultural Revolution, or more precisely, the revolutionary Maoism that the Cultural Revolution drew upon, have anything to say to the present? I think so. The repudiation presently of Maoist alternatives in modernity is part of an overall repudiation of radical alternatives to capitalism. We need to remember that, while transformations in capitalism may have rendered irrelevant earlier socialist challenges to its domination, capitalism is still capitalism, and these very same transformations have produced, and are in the process of producing, problems that await urgent resolution. Some of these problems are as old as the history of capitalism, others are products of new departures in capitalist production and organization. The resolution of these problems must take the present as their point of departure, but that is not to say that the past does not have anything to offer to the present. Recalling earlier revolutionary challenges is necessary to overcoming the ideological hegemony of capital. But it is not only for ideological reasons that the past is important. The revolutionary Maoist vision of society in particular—what I described above as the substantive issues that Maoism raised with regard to local society—may be relevant in surprising ways to confronting problems of contemporary capitalism.

Recent years have witnessed a reorientation of radical activity globally from an emphasis on the nation-state to an emphasis on local movements. The disillusionment with the inability of socialist states to resolve social problems is certainly an element in this reorientation. That disillusionment itself is part, however, of a broader loss of faith in the state in capitalist as well as in formerly socialist societies. While the nation-state is by no means dead, as some would

suggest, for the last two decades states worldwide have been anxious to shed many of the responsibilities they had assumed earlier
for the welfare of their populations. This has been accompanied by
an increasingly visible alliance between states and transnational capitalism; so that once again the state appears nakedly as a promoter
of the interests of capital, sometimes against the interests of the populations whom they claim to represent. While the "privatization" of
the state has been proceeding at different rates in different places,
depending on the ability of the populations to resist it, such privatization nevertheless represents a global tendency against an earlier
conception of the nation-state as a defender of the public against
private interests. This, too, is a product of the new phase of capitalism. In this sense, the fall of socialist states—the most extreme
form of the priority of the public over the private—since the late
1980s may be viewed as part of a global process that includes the
capitalist state as well.

One by-product of this weakening of the "public state" is the
weakening of an earlier role that the state played as an intermediary between the transnational forces of capitalism and the needs of
local societies, so that local communities face more directly than
before the demands of a global economy. The increased stress on
local society in recent years, in other words, is a product not just
of loss of faith in the state, or in state-oriented solutions to social
problems, but of the very operations of transnational capital that
draw localities out of their isolation, utilize them to their own ends,
and abandon them when such localities no longer serve those ends.
The very operations of capital, it may be suggested, produce the
local as we know it presently. In response, local societies have to
fend for themselves as well as they can without reliance on the help
of the state. This need has been quite important in fostering local
movements.

I am not suggesting here that local movements can afford to be
merely local. In order to be effective, local movements have to seek
translocal alliances—not just nationally but transnationally—to counter
the global powers of capital; under the circumstances of global capitalism, the welfare of working people at any particular location, say,
in the US or China, may be much more interdependent than earlier seen. But the new situation suggests that radical defense of people's welfare has to take the local as its point of departure.

This is where, I think, memories of the Chinese Revolution in its Maoist guise may have much to offer to the present. As I noted above, the Maoist vision as articulated during the Cultural Revolution, linked the fate of the local to the national, but that vision was informed in the history of the Chinese Revolution by a prior alternative anarchist vision that disassociated the local and the national, and gave priority to the needs of local society apart from, and against, the nation-state. In its stress on "self-reliance" at the level of local society, the Maoist vision contained this idea of local autonomy. Its products are well known. Especially important has been the institutionalization of integrating agriculture and industry at the level of local society, which was to produce a unique social configuration not just in Maoist but also in post-Mao China. This has accounted in many ways for the ability of Chinese society, in contrast to other formerly socialist societies, to withstand the socially destructive forces of capitalism while opening up to the capitalist world-system. This social configuration also owes much of its success to the experience of revolutionary years which may have created conditions of corruption and the abuse of power, which seem to receive all the attention these days, but that were also to breed habits of self-reliance, collective activity, and cooperation between local political leadership and the population at large (Unger and Cui, 1994).

What is interesting is that while the current in Beijing retains its coercive powers, and is quick to claim for itself the developmental successes of Chinese society, much of this success is in fact due to the ability of the many localities in China to fend for themselves. While it would be misleading to state that the Communist regime in Beijing and the development of local society in China should be viewed in isolation from one another, an analytical distinction may nevertheless be useful that points to two conflicting paradigms of development in China. One is that to which the state is central, that guarantees to the Communist regime, and the new managerial class it cultivates, a position of power in the global economy and politics, but promises little beyond an authoritarian state capitalism. The other is one that is based in local society, that draws on an earlier revolutionary legacy of local development that gives priority to the welfare of the people over the power of the state, and points to a democratic socialism. What is radical politically about the latter alternative is also that, while it obviously does not reject the state, it calls for a reevaluation both of the territorial scope of the state (as expressed in new regionalisms) and the scope of its powers. In other words, it calls for a reconsideration of the boundaries and the responsibilities of the state against the claims of the present regime to define the nation, and claim it for its legitimacy.

Thanks to its revolutionary legacy, rather than the anti-revolutionary authoritarian propensities of the current Communist regime, in other words, Chinese society not only continues to offer a model of modernity that challenges the hegemony of capitalism, but also offers concrete resolutions of problems that are products of the reconfiguration of global relations under contemporary capitalism. The legacy of the Maoist vision may be more visible in China than elsewhere, but there are suggestions of it in other local movements around the world; not just in Third World locations (from India to Chiapas) where the language of self-reliance promotes the defense of local community against the ravages of capital, but also in First World societies, where it invokes memories of living communities against the "virtual communities" of global capitalism.

The Cultural Revolution may or may not lay claims to be the only, or even the most accurate, representation of the Maoist vision, which was itself rooted in the history of the Chinese Revolution. It dramatized for the world the power of that vision. That it will haunt the memories of many for generations to come may be sufficient to qualify it as a world-historical event. But it was not merely a ghostly event. Try as we might to exorcize its memories, it haunts us because, in its very historicity, it spoke to problems that are also part of our legacy. Like it or not, it will be with us so long as we demand solutions to those problems.

References

Amin, Samir (1990) *Delinking: Towards a Polycentric World*. Tr. from the French original by Michael Wolfers. London, NJ: ZED Books.
Andors, Stephen (1977) *China's Industrial Revolution: Politics, Planning and Management, 1949 to the Present*. New York: Pantheon Books.
Bettelheim, Charles (1974) *Cultural Revolution and Industrial Organization in China: Changes in Management and the Division of Labor*. Tr. from the French by Alfred Ehrenfeld. New York: Monthly Review Press.
Castells, Manuel (1997) *The Rise of the Network Society*. Vol. 1 of *The Information Age: Economy, Society and Culture*. Malden, MA: Blackwell.
Chan, Anita (2001) *China's Workers Under Assault: The Exploitation of Labor in a Globalizing Economy*. Armonk, NY: M.E. Sharpe.

Chan, Ming K., and Arif Dirlik (1991) *Schools Into Fields and Factories: Anarchists, the Guomindang, and the National Labor University in Shanghai, 1927–1932.* Durham, NC: Duke University Press.

Dirlik, Arif (1974) "National Development and Social Revolution in Chinese Marxist Thought," *China Quarterly*, No. 58 (April/June):286–309.

—— (1991) *Anarchism in the Chinese Revolution.* Berkeley, CA: University of California Press.

—— (1994) *After the Revolution: Waking to Global Capitalism.* Hanover, NH: University Press of New England for Wesleyan University Press.

—— (1995) "Three Worlds or One, or Many: The Reconfiguration of Global Relations Under Contemporary Capitalism." In *Nature, Society, Thought*, 7.1 (1995): 19–42.

—— (2002a) "Rethinking Colonialism: Globalization, Postcolonialism, and the Nation," *Interventions* Vol. 4(3):428–48.

—— (2002b) "The Politics of Cultural Revolution in Historical Perspective." In Dubravka Juraga and M. Keith Booker (eds.), *Rereading Global Socialist Cultures After the Cold War: The Reassessment of a Tradition.* Westport, CT: Praeger Publishers. pp. 55–89.

—— (2003a) "Empire? Some Thoughts on Colonialism, Culture and Class in the Making of Global Crisis and War in Perpetuity," *Interventions*, 5.2 (2003):207–11.

—— (2003b), "Global Modernity? Modernity in an Age of Global Capitalism," *European Journal of Social Theory*, 6.3 (August 2003):275–92.

Forbes, Dean (1999) "Globalisation, Postcolonialism and New Representations of the Pacific Asian Metropolis." In Kris Olds, Peter Dicken, Philip B. Kelly, Lily Kong and Henry Wai-cheung Yeung (eds.), *Globalisation and the Asia-Pacific: Contested Territories.* London and New York: Routledge, 1999. pp. 238–54.

Gurley, John (1976) *China's Economy and the Maoist Strategy.* New York: Monthly Review Press.

Hardt, Michael, and Antonio Negri (2000) *Empire.* Cambridge, MA. Harvard University Press.

Harvey, David (1989) *The Condition of Postmodernity: An Enquiry into the Origins of Cultural Change.* Oxford, UK: Basil Blackwell.

Hoffman, Charles (1974) *The Chinese Worker.* Albany, NY: State University of New York Press.

Jameson, Fredric (1994) *Postmodernism, Or the Cultural Logic of Late Capitalism.* Durham, NC: Duke University Press.

Jones, Gareth Stedman (2002) "All that's left is reformism," *The Guardian Unlimited*, Monday, 12 August 2002. http://www.guardian.co.uk/comment/story/ 0,3604,772994,00.html

Lenin, Vladimir I. (1967) *Lenin on the National and Colonial Question.* Peking: Foreign Languages Press.

—— (1969) *Imperialism, the Highest Stage of Capitalism.* Peking: Foreign Languages Press. (Published in 1916.)

Lin Biao (1972) "Long Live the Victory of People's War!" In K. Fan (ed.) *Mao Tse-tung and Lin Piao: Post Revolutionary Writings.* New York: Anchor Books. pp. 357–412.

Mao Zedong (1979) "On the Ten Major Relationships." In Mark Selden (ed.), *The People's Republic of China: A Documentary History of Revolutionary Change.* New York: Monthly Review Press. pp. 314–22.

Ohmae, Kenichi (1995) *The End of the Nation State: The Rise of Regional Economies: How Capital, Corporations, Consumers, and Communication Are Reshaping the Global Markets.* New York: The Free Press.

Prazniak, Roxann, and Arif Dirlik (eds.) (2001) *Places and Politics in an Age of Globalization.* Lanham, MD: Rowman and Littlefield.

Rist, Gilbert (1997) *The History of Development: from Western Origins to Global Faith.* Tr.

from the French original by Patrick Camiller. London and New York: ZED Books.

Sassen, Saskia (1991) *The Global City: New York, London, Tokyo*. Princeton, NJ: Princeton University Press.

—— (ed.) (2002) *Global Networks, Linked Cities*. New York: Routledge.

Unger, Roberto M., and Cui Zhiyuan (1994) "China in the Russian Mirror," *New Left Review*, 208 (November/December):78–87.

POLITICAL SELECTIVITY
AND CULTURAL RESPONSE IN THE PROCESS OF MODERNIZATION AND GLOBALIZATION: NORTH AND SOUTH KOREA COMPARED

Kim Kyong-Dong and Lee On-Jook
Seoul National University

Prologue

When North Korea's heretofore reclusive leader Kim Jong Il surprised the world by unexpectedly emerging out of a long period of isolation for a historic meeting with South Korea's President Kim Dae Jung in Pyongyang in June 2000, the global community immediately responded with media spotlight but with cautious expectation that the hermit state might be finally coming out of seclusion and joining the rest of the world on the path to globalization. While a great deal of diplomatic chess play has been going on among the two Koreas and four Powers surrounding the peninsula, the United States, Japan, China, and Russia, even the most keen-eyed political pundits are reluctant to make any reasonable predictions as to what North Korea's next step might be. Although the Pyongyang summit has rewarded President Kim of South Korea with a Nobel Peace Prize, it has also stirred up heated ideologically and politically charged debates in South Korea causing rather uncomfortable internal conflicts within the society.

If South Koreans are utterly baffled when it comes to discerning the true nature of North Korean society, it goes without saying that people outside Korea would have enormous difficulty in understanding what goes on in that society and how it is possible for such a society to exist. However, the major focus of analysis of North Korea by many local and international experts thus far has been the political nature of the state, with relatively less attention given to the social-cultural features of the society. One of the main reasons for this tendency lies with the sheer dearth of reliable, objective, and empirical social data on North Korea. Even the relatively limited social analyses have not been too keen about approaching the study

of North Korea from a perspective of the sociology of development
and modernization.

We intend to fill this gap by attempting to characterize the nature
of North Korean society in comparison with South Korea from the
perspective of their respective experience of modernization, by means
of a bird's-eye-view of the nature of social change in the two Korean
societies from that perspective. Because of space limitation, we shall
not repeat here the substance of our own theoretical views on modernization but only a very concise synopsis of our theoretical ideas
may be presented without detailed exposition. Earlier, Kim (1985;
1994; 1996) has proposed a new way of conceptualizing modernization mainly from the purview of later-joiner member societies in
the process. Basically, it holds the following views:

First, modernization is to be seen as an historical process of societal transformations started in the West, or more specifically in the
western part of Europe around the turn of the 16th century.

Second, it has since been spreading throughout the world causing international acculturation in the societies that have come into
contact with the process.

Third, these societies so exposed to the international acculturation
processes now have attempted to make adaptive changes by indigenizing those cultural elements introduced to their societies through
acculturation.

Fourth, political selectivity plays an important part in determining a whole range of matters concerning the change, from whether
or not a certain change is needed, desired, rejected, resisted, promoted, or discouraged, to the direction, speed, scope, and substance
of change. In this process, the interaction and the relative power of
the elite and the mass eventually determine the outcome of change.
And for a society to effectively meet this challenge, it would be more
advantageous if the society's structure is flexible enough to absorb
any turmoil caused by the struggle.

Fifth, as a society comes into contact with strange cultures by
acculturation from outside, it has to make some decision as to what to
do with them. In doing so, they must be able to assess what is good
and bad, right and wrong, correct and incorrect, how they might
approach to resolve the issue, with what kind of material-technical
means, and so on. It is their cultural resources they have to draw
upon in making their political selection. This process of cultural selectivity could be affected by the degree of cultural flexibility which is

open to foreign cultures and cultural preparedness to accept them. Cultural selectivity may also operate in the very process of indigenizing certain adopted cultural elements and the end result turns out to be a form of cultural mixture. Indigenization is inevitable.

Sixth, acculturation in a generic sense is an interactive, two-way process of cultural change caused by contact of different cultures, both supposedly being affected (Moore, 1963). Modernization as a form of historical, international, cross-cultural acculturation, however, happens to have yielded one-sided change instead of two-way cultural alterations because the flow of culture in the process of modernization has been from nation-states with greater military prowess, superior economic wealth, and technological know-how, to societies with weaker armed forces and inferior economic and technological power.

It is in this context that the receiving societies are left with little choice but to try their best to make selective response, and selectively adopt whatever is more immediately utilizable, relatively less repellent and threatening, or more readily acceptable to the existing culture, psychologically, material-technically, and institutionally. Despite the tilted impact of western cultures, however, we insist that all societies that have encountered the surge of acculturation from the West have attempted some adaptive change and indigenization of modernization. In this sense, the notion of modernization as equivalent to westernization is a misconception.

One final observation is in order. Some (Dirlik, 1999) recently have presented the view that the language of globalization in the latter half of the 20th century has replaced modernization as a paradigm of change. We prefer to view globalization as a continuation of the historical modernization process since the 1500s. Modernization is inherently an expansionary process, due to the capitalist economic system embedded in modernization as the main driving force behind this extensive diffusion. Now, even with the information and communication technologies having enabled societies to go global in almost every sense of the term, the driving force behind globalization still is the worldwide capitalist system. The central argument we are presenting is that the process of globalization in itself does not constitute any qualitative alterations in the very nature of international acculturation initiated from the West and ensuing adaptive change of indigenization in the receiving societies around the world. We also regard the discourses on "postmodern" phenomena still premature by the same token.

Modernization of the Two Koreas

The period of comparison between North and South Korean modernization covered here is confined to the post-World War II era. At the end of the war, the Korean peninsula was arbitrarily divided along the 38th parallel and occupied by the two powers, the United States in the South and the Soviet Union in the North. The divergent paths of modernization of the divided Korea was thus determined initially by the external political decision. Division has not yet ended and we have witnessed the most historically peculiar development in the northern part of this tragic nation. How are we to understand this strange phenomenon?[1]

Political Selectivity in the Two Koreas

Viewing from the perspective of our modernization theory, the most outstanding fact about the incipient modernization on the Korean peninsula is that political decisions played the foremost part in determining the fate of the divided Korea.

1. Paths of Nation-Building

Various efforts made by nationalist leaders in both parts of divided Korea to push for a united new nation notwithstanding, the process of preparation for the establishment of an independent nation-state in Korea was virtually steered by the foreign forces occupying the nation, coupled with often violent political infighting among the competing local forces. The end-product was the establishment of two separate regimes, a liberal democratic republic in the South led by Rhee Syng Man and a soviet-style socialist dictatorship in the North headed by Kim Il Sung.

As can be expected, institution building was attempted in starkly different ways. In the South, a representative democracy was formed through free universal elections and moderate land reform and privatization of the vested properties of the Japanese colonial legacy were initiated with a view to setting up a basically capitalist economy.

---

[1] For general accounts of North Korea's development, the following may be referred to: Bunge (1981); An (1983); C.I.E. Kim and B.C. Koh (eds.) (1983); Foster-Carter (1990); Halliday (1989). For South Korea, Kim (ed.) (1987); Kim (1988); Kim and Lee (2000); Macdonald (1988); and Savada and Shaw (1992) are suggested.

In the North, a populist soviet-style government was formed and immediately embarked on a series of drastic socialistic reform programmes including land redistribution, socialization of industrial plants and other properties, equalization of women's rights, worker's revolutions and the like. Up to this point, one could readily surmise that external influence was most prevalent. The foreign political institutions with their ideological inclinations were almost blindly adopted. In the North, Kim Il Sung himself came to power not by his own merit but by the choice of the Soviet authorities.

Political selectivity definitely crept into the process of actual implementation of those foreign elements. The nature of newly formed elite corps in the politico-bureaucratic sphere made the difference. In the South, the Rhee regime, emerging out of severe political struggles, initially turned to the existing bureaucratic, professional, and intellectual elite, a group that had once served the Japanese, for the urgent task of nation-building (Kim and Lee, 1983; 1987). This was done in the face of not so mild protests from the nationalist sector that had sacrificed much during the colonial days. In contrast, the Kim regime in the North manned its party and state apparatus with the old guards who fought in the guerrilla warfare against the Japanese and/or local communist independent movement leaders before liberation and their entourage, while the local soviet organizations were largely filled with populist leaders in the communities.

As the North was being occupied by the armed forces of the Soviet Union, and the proletarian revolutions were taking place, most of the non-communist, Christian or Buddhist capitalists, professionals, bureaucrats who used to work for the colonial government, intellectuals, and wealthy farmers and merchants fled to the non-communist South, seeking refuge from the revolutionary socialist reforms and political purges of the new soviet regime. This naturally left North Korean society with only a handful of trained bureaucrats and professionals with communist inclinations because a large majority of those with training and experience suited for nation-building had vacated the North.

2. The War and Its Aftermath

In the summer of 1950, the Korean War broke out when the North Korean People's Army invaded the South with massive support from the Soviet Union and the People's Republic of China. This is to be seen as a political act on the part of the North Korean regime to re-unite the nation by means of a war, as a programme to sovietize the entire peninsula. This being the dawn of the Cold War era, the so-called free nations under the banner of the United Nations swiftly responded to bring the war to a truce in 1953. Therefore, this whole incident is to be viewed clearly as a series of political actions taken by the regimes of the days, both local and international.

The decade of the 1950s after the war was a period of struggle for the Korean people in both the North and the South to survive and recover from the devastating effects of the war, materially and spiritually. The economy had to rely heavily on economic aid from either the United States or the Soviet Union and China. The economic performance during this period, however, diverged due mainly to the different systems they adopted. South Korea was much slower in recovery because it had to follow the steps of economic rehabilitation dependent upon aid, followed by import substitute industries in the light consumer sectors, before any active development programmes were to be formulated and implemented. In the North, on the other hand, a vigorous economic recovery was pursued, with some remarkable success. Since it was a socialist economy, planning was inherent in the system, and mobilization was much easier under a populist dictatorship accompanied by strong ideological indoctrination.

Initially, North Korea was almost completely dependent upon the Soviet Union, politically, economically, and even culturally. It was a very loyal satellite state, worshiping Stalin as its hero. And the Soviet Union gave strong support to Kim in his engagement with the South in the Korean War. The support from the Soviet Union during the war, however, was restricted to the provision of advisory units, weaponry, and air power support, while China sent troops in huge numbers to fight along side the North Korean army in the days when the North was pushed almost to the border of China. Since then, China became a "blood ally" of the North. And then, Kim also adopted from China's Mao Zedong's programme called the Great Leap Forward and embarked on his own version of Thousand Mile Steed programme. Economic assistance from China also increased.

Towards the latter part of the 1950s, however, North Korea had to face an intricate diplomatic problem. As the Soviet Union began to pursue détente with the West in the aftermath of the death of Stalin, which caused an ideological squabble with Mao who accused the Soviets of being ideological compromisers, North Korea was forced to distance itself from both Communist states. Under such circumstances, North Korea began to proclaim what is known as the *Juche* ideology or the pronouncement of self-reliance.

3. The Era of Divergent Economic Development

North Korea's economic development was most prominent during the latter part of the 1950s. By implementing the Three-Year Economic Development Plan (1954–1956) in the post-war recovery period and the ensuing Five-Year Plan (1957–1961, actually completed in 1960), the economy grew rapidly. It is not possible to show exact figures due to the dearth of accurate statistics available for North Korea, but the rates of growth in national income in this period are estimated to be around 30 per cent (1954–1956) and 21 per cent (1957–1960), which were known to be beyond the planned goals of 20 per cent and 17 per cent, respectively. Beginning with the First Seven-Year Plan (1961–1967, later extended to 1970), however, growth started to slacken, the actual rate falling down to 7.5 per cent, way below the planned goal of 15.2 per cent (Lee, 1988). Then the economy began to slow down throughout the 1970s and 1980s, finally reaching an impossible point in the 1990s, as is widely known.

The growth in the recovery period after the war and in the rest of the 1950s was simple extensive growth made possible by utilizing idle industrial resources and mobilizing the huge unemployed labour force, pursuing industrialization concentrating on heavy industries according to the Stalinist planned economic policy. Resources were mobilized through domestic savings, consumption and labour force controlled by the state, and capital made available through aid from the Soviet Union and Eastern Europe.

The slowdown since the 1960s was due to the failure of the North Korean regime to overcome major obstacles and to make necessary adjustments to the changing internal and external environments. The main obstacles were shortage of arable land (North Korea is a very mountainous country) and labour force, and stagnation in the energy, transportation, and mining sectors. In addition, aid from the Soviet and the Eastern bloc rapidly decreased, depressing the chief sources of cheap capital and technology, while military expenditure began to increase drastically. This was mainly due to the North's changing relationship with the Soviet Union and China, on the one hand, and the consolidation of power of Kim Il Sung by proclaiming the self-reliance Juche ideology, both of which contributed to the self-sufficient autarky.

The failure of the North Korean economy to sustain growth in the ensuing decades of the 1970s through the 1990s is history. Basically, it was mainly due to the fundamental pitfalls of the social-ist command economy, coupled with the crucial constraints of autarky which almost completely closed the outside world. Throughout this period, North Korea further consolidated the personality cult of Kim Il Sung, systematized the Juche ideology, stepping up its application to autonomous self-sufficient economic performance, and methodi-cally preparing the succession programme for his son, Kim Jong Il. All this has resulted in the tragic national bankruptcy as witnessed by the entire world. At times, some dependency theorists would praise North Korea as one of the most autonomous non-dependent states, free from the perils of dependency that was claimed to have been preventing less developed countries in the Third World from any development. Some later have had to retract their earlier position after actually visiting and observing the pathetic conditions of North Korea (Foster-Carter, 1977; 1987). The 1960s in South Korea was a tumultuous time. In April of 1960, a student upheaval toppled the Rhee Syng Man regime which was characterized by authoritarian rule and rampant corruption. This was followed by about one year of instability under a fragile democratic regime, but such a condition did not sustain too long for it ended with a military coup by May 1961. The military junta immediately embarked on a series of five-year economic development plans beginning in 1962. The basic ori-entation of this new regime was expressed in the slogan "Guided Capitalism," which upholds the pursuit of a market economy with strong intervention from the state.

We need not go into the details of the so-called success and fail-ure story of South Korean economic development. Throughout these processes, it would suffice to simply stress the centrality of political decisions in the pursuit of economic modernization both in North and South Korea. At this point, it is more useful to look into the cultural aspect of their respective modernization. This is especially interesting after the financial crisis in Asia in the last few years of the 1990s, for it is since then that the issue of Asian values and related cultural specifics of East and Southeast Asia have drawn much attention.

Modernization in the Two Koreas as Cultural Mixture

Culturally speaking, a comparison of the two Koreas is particularly useful because they started their post-WWII modernization with essentially identical cultural legacies but treaded dramatically divergent roads of international acculturation and indigenous adaptation. The most outstanding common elements are Confucian heritage and Japanese colonial experience, whereas the distinctly different influence from outside stems from their respective exposure to Soviet and Chinese communism and socialist economic system in the North and US liberal democracy and capitalist economy in the South. Our job here is to shed some light on the relative and interactive influence of these cultural elements in the dynamic process of modernization in the two parts of Korea.

1. Confucian Heritage

Despite the relatively rich discussion in the past decade or so on the role of Confucian tradition in the economic development of East Asia, we do not find substantial agreement on the exact nature and substance of such influence.[2]

Thus far, no one has yet clearly identified the most salient elements of Confucian tradition that have affected the modernization process. Moreover, there still is a lack of an embracing theoretical scheme whereby one could pinpoint the dynamics of Confucian influence on the social, political, and economic life of the East Asian peoples. It might take some time before we will have that, and our task here is to demonstrate the characteristics of Confucian influence in the two Koreas very briefly.

When Confucian influence in East Asian modernization is discussed, some of the items most often mentioned include familism or high value placed on family relations, importance of education, status-seeking tendencies, respect for authority and the elderly, hierarchical authoritarianism, collectivism over individualism, mobilizational political culture or the active role of and unusual deference rendered to the state, industriousness, discipline in everyday conduct, perseverance, and the like. (MacFarquhar, 1980; Tu, 1996; Kim, 1988; 1994).

---

[2] Some notable examples of such works include Krieger and Trauzettel (eds.) (1991); Kim (1994; 1996); and Tu (ed.) (1996).

Whether such an argument is correct or not, it is true that those items certainly are prevalent among the Korean people in their day-to-day social life, even today. We need to examine some of these items in some detail.

Above all, in many respects, North Korean society may be said to have maintained Confucian characteristics to a larger extent than the South, mainly due to its relatively lengthy closure and isolation vis-à-vis the outside world. Since no survey data or any reliable accounts of direct observations of North Korean society are available, we have to rely upon various publications, including novels, magazines, and newspaper articles, and the reports of defectors from the North. According to these sources, we shall summarize some of the most starkly Confucian legacies, together with the probable influence of other factors so that a historical perspective may be gained in elucidating the experience of modernization in the two Koreas (Lee, 1988; 1993).

2. Material-Technical Aspect of Culture

Before we discuss the cultural features of modernization of the Two Koreas, let us briefly examine the material-technical aspect of the process. Geographically, North Korea is a very mountainous country relatively rich in mineral resources. Therefore, while its incipient rapid industrialization might be partly attributable to this factor, agricultural development has been more difficult. The main source of technical-managerial know-how needed to modernize the economy came first from the colonial experience, but after liberation, the Soviet Union became the major supplier of such knowledge, and communist China became a significant role model as well.

Both industries and farms were collectivized based on the models of the Russian *kolkhoz* and the Chinese people's communes. Although productive activities were controlled by technical staff, these economic communities were also operated as political organizations closely supervised and commanded by party cadres. Such a strategy had worked effectively for mobilizational purposes initially, but soon North Korea encountered the problem of socialist inefficiency with its command principles of economic operation and political intervention. And naturally economic performance began to slow down.

Since the late 1960s when the *Juche* ideology was invented, for internal political and external diplomatic reasons, self-reliance even in research and development became the central tenet of North Korean modernization. Self-reliance turning into autarky has prevented the society from importing necessary and useful information and know-how from outside, eventually leaving the country way behind the world community in science and engineering needed for further economic modernization. When you read the novels and stories published in North Korea during this period, the picture of scientists and engineers struggling to develop techniques for improving industrial and agricultural production on their own, with very little input from outside, clinging to the teachings of the Great Leader and the Dear Leader, is almost pathetic (Lee, 1988; 1993).

Beginning in the 1980s, North Korea has been showing some signs of opening up, in a very restrained manner. Still with the gradual influx of North Korean expatriates living in the United States, for instance, technical information must have been seeping into the society bit by bit. And in very restricted areas like missile development, and more recently, computer software technology, the North has even exported some products. However, the material base, in the meantime, has been deteriorating. Mineral resources for energy generation like coal which was rather abundant have been exhausted, and the rich mountains have gradually become barren, caused in part by agricultural failure over a consecutive number of years and in part by flooding and drought. The rest of the story of tragic famine and poverty is well known. Thus, in a very unique way in North Korea, even the technical aspect of modernization has largely been determined by the non-material political culture.

South Korea, in contrast, is geographically less mountainous and hence less blessed with mineral resources but more richly endowed with larger arable land than the North, and hence was an agrarian society with minimal industries at the time of liberation. It had remained fairly much so until the early 1960s. During this period of rapid economic development, the main body of technical-managerial culture of industrialism was introduced directly from the United States. Nevertheless, it was to be mixed with whatever lingered on from the colonial economic culture of the immediate past and the traditional elements before that. In fact, the influence of Japanese economic culture continued to be felt after South Korea embarked on industrialization, mainly because Japan became the closest economic partner even during the phase of economic take-off and afterwards.

In short, the acculturation in the material-technical aspect involved the impact both from the United States and Japan in the post-war economic development of South Korea.[3]

In this sense, therefore, it would be interesting to note that South Korea's managerial philosophy and practices and industrial relations culture are an odd mixture of traditional patriarchal, patrimonial, and paternalistic Korean and Japanese culture with modernized Japanese and American culture. One example would be that while many enterprises in South Korea adopted a sort of life-time employment system, labour force turnover in Korean firms is much higher than in Japan but lower than in the United States. In a way, one could characterize this cultural mix as a form of capitalist economy directly adopted from the United States operating in the context of traditional Korean culture, modified by Japanese colonial and post-colonial filtration.

3. Patriarchal Familism

Emphasis on the importance of family relations in Confucian teachings and practices thereof arouses virtually no counterargument.[4]

Which aspect then of familism has survived?

In the incipient phase of socialist reforms, the North Korean regime adopted the Leninist pledge to liberate women from the slavery of household chores, recognizing equality of gender in principle. This gibed nicely with the need for the extensive mobilization of the female work force to compensate the shortage of human resources in industry and agriculture which were collectivized rather early on in the process of reforms. Nurseries for children left behind by their working mothers were extensively set up and even some collectives built "factories" for rice and *kimchi* (the famous fermented vegetable preserved Korean style). The proportion of women in all sorts of professional jobs and traditionally male dominant occupations increased substantially, comparatively much higher in the North than in the South (Lee, 1988; 1993).

Under the circumstances, one would expect a rather drastic change in family life. Contrary to that expectation, however, content analysis

---

[3] Evidence of this can be found in our own study of the elite in Korean society. See Kim and Lee (1983; 1987).

[4] On the Korean family, see Lee (1997).

of the materials mentioned above strongly suggests that the traditional patriarchal familistic tendencies have not shown any sign of substantial decline. Almost regardless of whether or not the woman in the family works outside the home, the authoritarian pattern of relationship between the man and wife, parent and child, and male-female siblings has remained intact, to a large extent. Moreover, complaints have been registered to the effect that women are doubly burdened with work outside the home and gruelling household labour which is almost completely left with women.

Familism, in principle, places great emphasis on the importance of family and blood relations. Although the relative weight of extended families may have been reduced for various demographic and economic reasons including housing shortages, the nature of social relations has not been fundamentally altered. Interestingly, this patriarchal familism has been most prominently demonstrated in the political sphere, climaxing in the succession of power from Kim the father to Kim the eldest son. Evidence strongly reflects the familistic connectionism in the composition of the core elite corps of the North Korean regime. One could easily identify that the most important positions in the party, army, and government offices are filled either by Kim Il-Sung's relatives by blood and marriage or by the family members and the descendants of his old buddies in the guerrilla movement during the colonial days.

Not only that, as the regime was cooking up the succession scheme, the ideologues came to formulate new ideologies of "loyalty and filial piety through generations," towards the Supreme Leader, the father, and the Dear Leader, the son. This ideology and slogans to indoctrinate the general populace leave a curious sense of the old Confucian teaching. Thus, one might be even tempted to claim that North Korea may be the most Confucian society existing in the whole world today, though in a restricted sense of the term.

The Japanese were not particularly interested in discouraging patriarchal familism among the Korean people, for it was seen as a useful means to maintain order in the colony which showed unusually strong resistance against colonial rule. Christianity was also introduced in the 19th century, but this did not affect the familistic tradition either. And the socialist reforms, ideologically criticizing some elements of the traditional family system, apparently have not had sufficient impact on the actual loosening of the familistic tradition.

As a matter of fact, it was to be used by the Kim regime for their political purposes, as can be evidenced in all kinds of political exhortations and pronouncements emphasizing the importance of the family, including the Constitution itself. Kim Il Sung, in his effort to consolidate his power and personality cult, even used to proclaim that the whole nation was "a big family" (Lee, 1988; 1993). In a very curious way, he was identified not merely as the benevolent Father but also as the Parent of the people. In the Korean language there is a special term referring to the inclusive parental status, both father and mother at once, and he used to be called both as the Father and the Parent in this sense. After the elder Kim passed away, the junior Kim did not inherit the status of Father or Parent. These have been reserved for his late father. The Juche ideology has very conveniently proclaimed that Kim lives on in spirit among the people, still looking after them. Kim Jong Il has obviously benefited from the halo effect of his late father.

The traditional element of familism remains to affect social life in South Korea, too. Above all, familism within the family has turned into what is widely labelled in this country as family-centred "collective egotism" or a tendency of selfishness of the family as a group. People would do anything to protect and promote family interest at the expense of the collective interest of the larger society or immediate community. Naturally, this has contributed to the general social disintegration of the entire society. This, we surmise, may be a unique hybrid of old familism infected by Western individualism introduced with the democratic political ideology and capitalist economic system. This tendency of familism has been extended into the domains outside the family, like business, private schools, and other nonprofit social organizations. In the case of large corporations, what is known as *Jaebol*, or Korean-style conglomerates, it has become patrimonialism.

The patriarchal orientations are still prevalent in the area of male-female relations, despite the professed ideology and legal provisions of equal rights for women. Discrimination against women is widespread in education, labour force, marriage, and even in the form of "son preference" for birth. In the elementary school classrooms, for instance, the sex ratio has gone up to 110 in the lower grades. This is said to be caused by the practice of abortion in the case of female fetus detected by certain devices used by obstetricians. Such a phenomenon of gender discrimination against women is also related to authoritarianism that we shall touch upon shortly.

4. Patrimonialism

In old China and Korea, the predominant political culture could be characterized as what Weber called "patrimonialism" (Weber, 1951; Jacobs, 1985). Essentially, it is a form of patriarchal familism transplanted into political culture. The ruler is the patriarch who owns virtually the state itself, the whole property and the entire population of the country. Members are obligated to obey the ruler who in turn is expected to look after the subjects like the father of the family. All the subjects then are forced by circumstance to compete for the special favours and mercy of the king, by showing almost absolute loyalty to the ruler.

In the status system of Korea and China of the old days, the gentry class or the learned Confucian scholar-officials formed the elite stratum of aristocracy. Recruitment into the elite positions was done through civil service examinations conducted by the state or the ruler himself, which was virtually the only official channel through which one could attain the status of a scholar-bureaucrat and high social status. These tests assessed the extent of learning and mastery of the Confucian classics. Thus, the gentry class became the sole source of authority and legitimacy in state affairs and was the moral-intellectual elite in society.

Familism also had a hand in this political culture. The male offspring in the family and the clan were socialized to achieve high status in Confucian officialdom, whereby they were expected to rise in the world and gain fame, not merely for themselves but eventually for the glory of the family and the entire kinship group. Since, however, the official positions available were limited in number, competition was severe and connections based on family relationship played a very important part in attaining a higher hand in the process. This has often resulted in serious factional strife among the elite.

The fact that the Kims in the North Korean regime have ruled like kings in absolute monarchy, the elite corps is composed mainly of Kim's family members, their cliques and their relations, and factional strife that was rather rampant in the process of consolidation of power can be said to reflect the patrimonial tradition of Korean society. Again, Japanese colonists found in this patrimonial tradition a very useful political culture for their own purposes. On account of this, one could say that North Korea probably maintains the purest form of patrimonial political culture in the 21st century world.

They have even created a new set of ideology nicely replacing the old, apparently outdated Confucianism. In place of the gentry, party cadres monopolize the moral-intellectual legitimacy that used to be enjoyed by the Confucian scholar-officials.

One could thus conclude that the North Korean regime was quite adept in adopting the Soviet-type proletarian dictatorship in which the strong party leader ruled like a king with his communist party cadres and recreating a political system in the mould of old patrimonial political culture. The intervening Japanese influence was in the direction of buttressing rather than suppressing such tradition.

As a modified form of patriarchal familism, the patrimonial tendency is found even in the South, most starkly in the political parties and business corporations, followed by universities, schools, religious institutions, media, and other nonprofit, nongovernmental social organizations, wherever family influence may be exerted. Of course, public institutions are supposedly immune from such intervention. Political parties are formed not exactly around ideological and policy orientations but more or less around cliques with a boss who plays the role of patriarch and ruler, who has to provide political funds and political positions for his men. The owner of a business firm or the CEO with the largest share of stocks in corporations gone public would also rule the enterprise like patriarch and king, looking after his subjects. In return, he expects them to obey and pay absolute loyalty to him, in politics, business, or other social organizations.

Again, with the introduction of democratic ideas and practices directly from the West, this tendency has become a target of criticism and is hence less popular in South Korea. Nonetheless, it is unlikely to be discarded over night, until some new forms and principles of social organization are created or found.

5. Authoritarianism
Respect for the authority of the father or parent, ruler, elders, male, superior, and the like was stressed in old Confucian teachings, mainly for the sake of establishing and maintaining social order, which was one of the central goals sought after by orthodox Confucian advocates. This authoritarian emphasis had often been abused by secular rulers of China and Korea throughout history. The basic Confucian tenet, however, was benevolent authority of the patriarch or ruler, not exactly autocratic dictatorship of absolute monarchy. If any hint of autocratic dictatorial authoritarian tendency is detected in the

political culture of either North or South Korea, we contend this was primarily due to the Japanese influence during the colonial period.[5]

The Japanese brought in their own version of autocratic militaristic bureaucratic authoritarianism to enforce strong colonial rule in Korea. They were rather fortunate enough in this respect, for Korean culture had already inherited the Confucian version of authoritarianism. Their version in itself was already an amalgam of the traditional feudalistic political culture of warriors, requiring absolute loyalty to the lord, the modernized form of emperor-worship, and the Prussian version of absolute monarchy manned with modern bureaucracy, plus the iron rule of dictatorial military statesmen. Liberation in 1945 did not help ameliorate this tendency in the North because this time the Soviets imposed totalitarian control over the population.

The authoritarian tendency among the Koreans is not confined to such political culture alone. The unique type of hierarchical authoritarianism is embedded in the language itself. In Korean language, like in Japanese and a few others, there are peculiar expressions of honorific deference. Depending on the relative social, demographic status of the person in conversation, you have to use the terminologies and expressions precisely appropriate to the relative position of the addressee and the social interaction situation, otherwise you run the risk of seriously offending the other person. Since human consciousness is constituted in language and consciousness, in turn, constitutes social relations, the hierarchical differentiation in language usages is naturally reflected in social interaction in an authoritarian manner. And the political culture mentioned above has only reinforced this tendency.

For this reason, socialist ideology and reforms intending to realize it in terms of social equality of all members of society, men and women, elders and youth, parents and children, and so forth, apparently have had little impact on easing the hierarchical authoritarian culture of the Koreans, even in the North, in their everyday life. Evidence to this effect is abundant in various fictional and non-fictional writings of North Korea (Lee, 1988; 1993).

---

[5] For discussion of authoritarianism and other subsequent traits mentioned in this work, see Kim (1988).

Authoritarian human relations and organizations are also prevalent in the South. It is true that democratic experience in political life and inculcation of the ideology of democratic society through the educational system has generally weakened the authoritarian tendency. But the authoritarian governments of Rhee Syng Man whose political career started in the last days of the old dynasty, the ex-military leaders of the 1960s like Pak Chung Hee who had been trained as a teacher and army cadet under the Japanese and other soldier politicians of the 1980s who were much more directly influenced by the authoritarian culture of the military itself, have not helped to ameliorate the situation. Interestingly enough, however, the more recent presidents who came to power—one of them even became a Nobel laureate—on account of their lifetime struggle for democracy are not necessarily non-authoritarian, either, in their consciousness, everyday conduct and interaction with others.

In daily life, too, Koreans must show due respect to those who are in a superior position, by age, gender, kinship relations, school class, occupational status, and what have you. Such are the intensity and extensiveness of the authoritarian inclinations among the Korean people, both in the South and North. Embedded in the language and consciousness of the people, it would be difficult to expect them to disappear soon. Modernization has only touched the very superficial level of Korean consciousness as far as authoritarianism is concerned.

6. Status-Orientation

Related to authoritarianism is the strong status orientation that also affects the social life of the Koreans. Unusually strong yearnings for education and social positions in Korean culture, as discussed in relation to patrimonialism, for example, were also reinforced during the colonial days. By closing the channels of education and status mobility for the Koreans, the colonists in fact stimulated able Korean youths to seek better education by putting their utmost effort to join the Japanese on the ladder of upward status attainment. Reflecting the Confucian preference for intellectual-bureaucratic occupations, Korean youngsters worked hard to choose professions, such as teaching, law, medicine, journalism, and so on, bureaucratic positions in the colonial government, or other white-collar jobs. Commerce and industry were relatively looked down upon. Opportunities, however, were extremely limited and job openings for the Koreans were scarce.

The more restrictive and discriminatory such channels were to the Koreans, the stronger became the aspirations to seek those values.

When Korea was liberated, the North Korean regime adopted socialist programmes of free universal education and this opened up the door of upward mobility for the general populace. Practically speaking, even in North Korea, education has become an effective channel for upward social mobility, making it easy to understand why everybody in the North places a high value on education. Under the communist political system, however, joining the party became an important status achievement. Since the economy seriously shrank in the 1980s and 1990s, the military has become an attractive place for the North Korean youth to seek employment. This is because Kim Jong Il has come to depend heavily on the support of the military and he has, in return, provided disproportionate social and economic favours to military personnel under a new policy called the "Military First Policy." In short, even under the socialist economic system where the wage differentials have become virtually meaningless, it is ironic that the political and prestige-wise significance of an occupation has become much more practically important because it is accompanied by subtle discrimination in privileges.

The same status orientation has distorted the whole educational system so severely that these days, everyone in South Korea complains about how bad education has become. The logic runs like this. Every mother (and father, but more so with the mother) wants to see her son (particularly son, not necessarily daughter) go to a better school, a first-class university in a most promising field of study, like law, management, medicine, obtain a more prestigious job, get promoted to the top level, and enjoy the enormous amount of privileges attached to such top status positions. The mother usually does anything to help her son to accomplish this (a typical example of familism), often pouring unbelievable amounts of money into private education outside the school system needed to help him reach the goal (in fact, her goal, not necessarily her son's).

In various institutions, one is expected to attain some high status, otherwise one is not going to be treated as somebody of importance in the organization and in society at large. So, in the university, for example, a professor is not given due respect unless he/she becomes a dean or president, or better yet a cabinet minister or national assemblyman in the government. Everybody who would like to be reckoned as somebody carries a name card in this country. If you do not have one you are virtually nobody. Modernization has only expanded the scope of such status-seeking activity.

7. Personality Cult

North Korea's personality cult is not matched by any such practice in any country in human history. Some believe that this might be a reflection of its Confucian legacy, but it is much more complicated than this requiring more careful analysis.

In his lifetime, Kim Il Sung was worshipped like a god and the Juche ideology provided very crudely formulated ideas justifying divinity of the political leader. He was not only praised as the most brilliant genius in the history of human civilization, but he was also thought to be immortal, and is still thought to be living among the people even after his physical demise. Let us try to account for this phenomenon from the viewpoint of our modernization theory.

When the Soviet army landed on the northern part of divided Korea at the end of the Pacific War, they were intent upon setting up a Soviet state in the peninsula as the bridgehead for their advance into the Far East. Since this was the incipient phase of the Cold War era, they were looking for an appropriate leader for the new nation. As has been described earlier, there were respected nationalist leaders who fought for independence during the colonial era and local communist elite intellectuals available as potential political leaders. Nevertheless, they were uneasy figures to handle for the Soviet military authorities with a mission to accomplish. In fact, most of them were opposed to the rule by external forces from the beginning. Because the time span of Soviet involvement in the Far Eastern theatre was short, and because Siberia was a difficult place to wage guerrilla warfare with the Japanese, there were an inadequate number of candidates with potential and with direct Soviet connections among the prominent Korean figures.

Given the circumstances, Kim Il Sung who happened to be a major in the Soviet army towards the end of the war, virtually fled to Far Eastern Soviet Russia in his guerrilla effort to fight the Japanese army. With this very slight connection, he was almost handpicked by the Soviet authorities to be the new leader of the emerging nation. He was still a very young man in his early thirties when he was introduced to the public for the first time as the country's new leader. The Soviet military needed to blow his image up to put him on stage as the rising leader. Personality cult, which was already a familiar practice with the Soviets under Stalin's rule, was employed to build Kim's image as the legitimate independence movement leader to lead the new nation. Such was the beginning of the personality cult of Kim Il Sung in North Korea as the act of none other than the Soviets, the foreign forces who occupied the country.

Although the road to consolidate power for Kim was not exactly smooth and easy, for he had to wage a series of political purges, he managed to stay in power and became one of the longest ruling leader among contemporary political figures until his death in 1994. During this half a century of totalitarian rule, he gradually built himself up as a divine leader of the North Korean people, by developing a crudely interesting ideology called Juche.

Curiously enough, this ideology and his personality cult are based on a mixture of a few extremely opposing traditions: the Confucian tradition of ancestor worship transformed into the Japanese style emperor worship or the nationalistic religion of Shintoism in form, modified by the Stalin and Mao cult, and even an element of Christian doctrine in a very limited sense. When the Japanese left after their defeat, North Korea's door to the outside world was immediately closed, except to Russia and communist China. As has already been pointed out, the personality cult was swiftly introduced from the Soviet Union. But as the image building continued, however, Kim apparently came to realize that the Korean people were still not free from the Japanese legacy of emperor worship which used to be practised before 1945.

In addition, in the course of consolidating his personality cult, Kim also introduced a small part of the Christian faith into this idolatry. In one part of the Juche ideology, for example, the idea of eternal life was inserted especially towards the end of his life and at the stage when his succession drama was almost completed. Loyalty and filial piety through generations was urged, not only to the original Great leader, the Father, but also to the young Dear Leader, the Son. In this context, it is claimed that the Great Leader is immortal, and everybody in North Korea would live forever in his grace. It is said that Kim Il Sung, in his youth before he became a guerrilla leader, was raised in a Christian family and he has some ministers and devout Christians among his close relations.

Our point here is that the case of Kim's personality cult is a cultural mixture, a product of adaptive change in the process of modernization. In contrast to the North, in South Korea there has not been anything that even comes close to what we have seen in the North. Only President Rhee Syng Man, or his stooges to be more precise, once tried to build some kind of personality cult, but this never worked in the South.

Nevertheless, one should not be deceived by the apparent lack of such a cult in South Korean society on the surface. The patriarchs in politics, business, religion, media, schools and universities, and other NPOs [in full?] and NGOs (non-governmental organizations), yes, they are being treated almost like kings within their own circles. Even the presidents well known for having been democracy fighters are no exception. This kind of practice may not be considered as personality cult, but certainly they are not anything you would expect in a genuinely democratic society.

8. Collectivism and Connectionism

Collectivism can be practised in various ways. The Confucian version of collectivism is basically familistic in nature. It is family-centred, emphasizing the importance of blood relations above all other forms of relationships in society. Also, the rural cluster village life was amenable to inculcating a strong sense of community, another form of collectivism. This general collectivistic orientation was further reinforced during the colonial period because Japanese society, too, is basically collectivistic, although her version is not identical. When the collectivistic orientation is extended beyond and outside the immediate family and kinship context, it can easily turn to patrimonialism in politics, paternalism in business, or all sorts of "connectionism" or a tendency to try to establish family-like or pseudo-family relations with anybody with some connections such as the same local origin, identical school background, military, or working experience. Thus, collectivism and connectionism often go together.

We have already touched upon various aspects of this tendency in the above discussion. To recount briefly, this collectivistic background might have been a cultural feature that has made it feasible for the North Korean people to absorb and adapt to the collectivistic ideology and institutions of socialism after liberation. At an early phase of reform, they collectivized agriculture and industrial enterprises without much resistance. Furthermore, the North Korean elite corps is composed of people with various connections, and status mobility in the society, in general, is largely affected by these connections; the better connected you are, the greater opportunities for status attainment. This is important especially in a society like Korea where such a great weight is placed on status-achievement, as has been discussed above.

Collectivism in the South Korean context takes two major forms. One is the type of familism or family-centred collectivism that we have described above, and the other is factionalism in virtually all the institutional sectors of the society. Both are a sort of expression of group selfishness. Factions are particularly rampant in the political arena and are causes of social divisiveness.

Traditionally, Confucian politics in the Choson Dynasty was marred with fierce factional strife that was at once political and intellectual-moral in nature. Towards the end of the dynasty, it turned into a sheer power struggle, causing its eventual demise. During the colonial period, the Japanese adopted the typical divide-and-rule policy towards the Korean people, which created division and disjuncture in society. Coupled with the traditionally collectivist orientation, this divisiveness took on the form of factionalism. Even after liberation, the nation was divided and a fratricidal war was fought. This experience certainly did not help ameliorate the situation. Ever since then, Korean society has not been able to overcome this problem of factionalism.

There are few things more amenable than the existing connections that provide the basis for factionalism. Individuals and groups connected by some relationship constitute natural components of collectivism and when these collectivities are divided into factions, people with different connections are divided into different factions. In a society where status positions are filled with privileges, competition for such positions is keen and tight. In the process of competition, factional strife becomes rife. And in the course of modernization, the imported market economy encouraging competition has reinforced this factional struggle.

When the South Korean economy crumbled in the late 1990s and required an IMF (International Monetary Fund) bailout, many observers pointed a finger at what is dubbed "cronyism" as one of the crucial villains of the financial crisis. This phenomenon is supposedly a product of what we are dealing with here as connectionism, collectivism, and factionalism, encouraging favouritism, nepotism, and other forms of depravity in business practice. This line of argument has been rebuffed by others who try to view such practices as having been conducive to the earlier growth of the economy, in the context of Korean development. Globalization is going to affect this tendency in the future. To observe how South Korea adapts to the process and the consequences of such an adaptation would be quite interesting.

9. Mobilizational Principle of Organization

One could hardly help being amazed at the sight of mass games of enormous scale and precision staged by North Korean youth and children during festive occasions. This is only one small sign of how effective North Korean society can be in mobilizing the masses for specific purposes. Their early socialist reforms and industrialization were all successful owing to this ability to mobilize social and human resources. Where does this come from culturally?

During the dynastic era, the masses were mobilized extensively for military service, other labour purposes, or in times of disaster. This, however, should not be immediately identified as a Confucian trait. Confucianism as such does not necessarily impart ideas encouraging rulers to mobilize people and people to unconditionally obey the order to participate en masse. Rather, it was the officials, particularly local magistrates, who would take advantage of the generally patrimonial authority of the state to easily order people around and mobilize them massively whenever needed.

Still, our interpretation is that this political culture of mobilization and the principle of mobilizational social organization were much more affected by the Japanese influence than the old Confucian tradition. Japanese colonists badly needed to mobilize the Koreans whenever possible to build up the infrastructure for their economic exploitation of the colony. Particularly, during the war in the Pacific, the principle of war-time mobilization of resources, human and otherwise then was much more urgently utilized for the conduct of war. And then, the Koreans had gone through another war in the early 1950s, during which time, as well, mobilization was frequent and extensive.

In North Korea, this political culture of mobilization has been constantly reinforced by the unceasing indoctrination of Juche and other political ideologies to back up the Kim cult, to push economic programmes, and to bring order in society in difficult times. When the North Korean economy started to dwindle beginning in the 1980s, for instance, the young Kim would be put in a role to become the vanguard of mobilizational programmes to revitalize the economy.

The general populace have become familiarized with this type of political culture through incessant indoctrination sessions held everyday and extensive military training.

In the fall of 1997, the South Korean government, announcing the decision to agree to the bailout programme of the IMF to overcome its foreign exchange and financial crisis, pleaded with the people to voluntarily donate or sell their gold valuables so that U.S. dollars could be purchased to bolster South Korea's dwindling foreign exchange holdings. The Korean people flocked to the banks with gold rings, bracelets, necklaces, hairpins, keys of luck, turtles symbolizing longevity, and whatever was made of gold. The event culminated in a collection of gold stuff worth millions of dollars almost overnight, surprising many peoples around the world. This we call a mobilizational society.

Thus far, people have usually responded to the call for mobilization of resources for some national cause. The strong nationalistic sentiment among the Koreans, both in the North and South, has been the driving force behind this kind of move. While the North Korean regime may still take advantage of this inclination for their mobilizational purposes, in South Korea the causes for mobilization are becoming more divergent. Various interest groups mushroomed in the course of democratization and they can now instigate the people's participation in mass mobilization in pursuit of some group self-interest.

Or, as in the case of the 2002 Korea-Japan FIFA World Cup Football matches, millions of people were mobilized just overnight to gather in any city plazas or squares to support the Korean soccer team. This time, the mechanism of mass mobilization happened to be the internet and mobile phones, which we never have had a chance to utilize for this kind of purpose. In other words, the modernization process has yielded a phenomenon of the old *modus operandi* cleverly utilized for new causes and purposes.

10. Other Individual Traits

As far as such traits as perseverance, discipline, diligence, and hard work, are concerned, Koreans both in the North and the South must stand out as extraordinary exemplars hardly paralleled by any other peoples around the world. This obviously originates from the traditional values of the old Confucian ethics. Nonetheless, we had better be careful in this respect, not to attribute everything to Confucianism.

Even in traditional times, other religions including Buddhism all used to emphasize those values, and in the process of modernization, as well, foreign religions like Christianity and secular ethics taught at school have also promoted such values.

We might, therefore, want to look into the historical circumstances in which those individual traits have been inculcated in the psyche of the Korean people. During the Choson Dynasty, the common folks suffered a great deal under strict Confucian normative order and exploitative patrimonial political culture. They had to learn to obey, to contain their own emotions and complaints, work hard, and endure whatever hardships they encountered. The colonial period has not eased this kind of suppression at all; rather it has strengthened it. The two wars within a span of less than ten years have further reinforced this tendency. And then, the drive for rehabilitation after the war, under severe chronic poverty way into the 1960s and 1970s, has not left any leeway for the North Korean people to loosen up their tight belt. Particularly in North Korea, socialist control and ideological indoctrination have kept the people in constant vigilance. No wonder, these people are used to perseverance, discipline and diligence. And when you are put in a situation of terrible famine and unbearably inhumane poverty, you have no choice left but to do whatever you can to survive.

The same virtues have contributed to economic development in the South, as well. In more recent years, however, people have begun to show much less eagerness to endure, work hard, and behave, especially the younger generation. This may be partly due to the rise in the cost of living and partly affected by the influx of mass culture inciting the people to a more relaxed and luxurious lifestyle. If this trend continues, then, it may become less feasible for the society to mobilize resources than in the past.

Epilogue

To reiterate our central idea, modernization is the dialectical interplay of international acculturation and adaptive change of indigenization, resulting in a set of cultural mixtures emerging in the process. Societies must meet the tide of modernization with whatever cultural resources they have inherited, and keep making adjustments and creating new institutions and practices. The process as a whole, therefore, is one of mixing the old and new, domestic and international, local and imported, and so on—it is an ongoing effort to indigenize the change. Though limited, we have tried to summarize the most salient cases of such cultural mixtures in the two Koreas as they have sailed the sea of modernization in the past century or so.

Now we shall briefly ponder upon the potential impact of globalization on the future development of modernization in the two Koreas. One of the most significant divergent features of modernization in the two Koreas is the degree and nature of exposure to the outside world. Extreme isolation of the North has caused the society to run into enormous hardships for the people and the regime, whereas the extensive openness of the South has been the source of both success and failure. At the present moment, both parts are facing the challenge of globalization with different tasks and burdens ahead of them. The future of both Koreas is heavily dependent upon how they fare in meeting this challenge.

The most difficult dilemma faced by the regime in the North is to eat and have its cake at the same time or to catch two rabbits at once. It is most urgent for them to rehabilitate North Korea's dilapidated economy as quickly as possible. In order to do so, they must open up to the outside world without their old communist allies to protect them from the pernicious infection of the capitalist world system. This poses two extremely difficult problems for them. On the one hand, the North has to be able to meet global standards, notably in economic transactions and diplomatic conduct. Opening up can mean a simultaneously fast disintegration of the system in the North.

One of the most formidable forces that can create cracks in and eventually cause the downfall of the tightly controlled patrimonial system of the North would be the free inflow of information from outside. This information of the outside world can not only help stimulate the people to form in their minds certain dreams to become like others in the outside world, but also reveal that the regime has been a deceptive one all along. The god-like image of the elder and junior Kims would be shattered with all of the hundreds of statues of Kim Il Sung still standing in every corner of the society. Kim Jong Il, too, would have to fear for his life.

Globalization, indeed, is a pain in the neck but a necessary evil, too, for North Korea. Since the June meeting of the two Kims in

2000, there are signs that Kim in the North may be very cautiously testing the water to see if it is possible for him to follow a path of Chinese reform. So far, Kim has been selling the idea that he would open a few select spots for capitalist development to lure investment from outside, but in order to make those projects successful he has to make many difficult adjustments internally and be able to show clear evidence to the world that his intentions are genuine and his system will make the necessary changes to accommodate global participation. In the summer of 2002, he seemed to have experimented with some programmes of market economy, terminating the food and other ration programmes, liberalizing prices for goods on the market, raising salaries for the workers, and the like. The real effect of these measures on the overall economy is yet to be seen, and many observers outside North Korea are not hesitant in expressing their grave doubts about the real impact of—and the real motive behind—such programmes.

At any rate, Kim desperately needs to obtain economic and technical assistance quickly, not only from the South but also from both Japan and the United States. Normalization of diplomatic relations with these countries is an important first step towards this goal. Things, however, have worsened in this regard since the terrorist incident of September 11th in the United States. George W. Bush included North Korea in his "axis of evil," and North Korea has reacted with a confession that it has been developing a nuclear weapons programme all along, even after the Geneva Agreement banning such effort on the part of North Korea in exchange for the construction of nuclear power plants in the North. The international community, including the United Nations, has come out condemning North Korea and is insisting that it should immediately and unconditionally stop the nuclear and other programmes involving weapons of massive destruction and dismantle all the relevant facilities. Some economic sanctions have already been implemented against the North. It seems, therefore, that unless North Korea cooperates with the international community in this respect, its prospect to modernize its economy by adapting to the tide of globalization is enormously dim.

In the meantime, Kim Jong Il is still playing with the obsolete tactics of indoctrinating the people with self-reliant, our-own-way style Juche ideology. Time seems to be running out on him because people are dying of starvation and disease every day and there is very little he can do to ameliorate the situation quickly. In short, there is a long and rough road ahead for him to proceed with successful modernization and effectively meeting the challenge of globalization.

It sounds rather ludicrous to constantly refer to the person of Kim Jong Il even in our own discussion, but it reflects the reality of North Korea where this man alone is virtually running the whole system. He owns the entire society. And this fact in itself is a pathetic phenomenon demonstrating the unique nature of the society. As long as this remains true, it would be very difficult for the society to change in the direction where it can reap the fruit of globalization.

Globalization is a thorn in the flesh for South Korea as well. A rather interesting characteristic of South Korean society in this connection is that while it has been taking an open stance towards the outside world, it has also been showing unusually strong nationalistic sentiments against globalization forces. Either out of pure nationalistic fervor or from the vantage point of sheer political, economic interest, there are forces within South Korea among intellectuals, civil society groups, and the labour movement that resist the trend of globalization adamantly.

Since the IMF bailout of the late 1990s, South Korean society has been going through some fundamental alterations in the system, trying to get rid of some of the most obnoxious elements from traditional legacies, with a view to creating a system amenable to global standards. The future destiny of the society seems to hinge upon the success of this painful process of restructuring the entire system. Here, too, the most difficult obstacle to overcome seems to be political. The sticky collusion between politics and business has been one of the central reasons for the financial failure of the past decades. But reform and restructuring most needed in politics are still far away, and they keep blocking the progress of even the urgent reforms in the economic sector.

Whether you like it or not, globalization is irreversible. Modernization of the two Koreas, therefore, would not be completed before they succeed in meeting the challenge of globalization and come out as competitive and resilient as they can. North Korea faces a much greater challenge, but the task is not at all easy for the South, either. Perhaps, a unified Korea, or even the two Koreas working closely together under an umbrella of peace and security, might be a more useful path to take in the journey of modernization ahead.

One final thought. If and when the two Koreas are reunified through non-violent processes involving a series of dialogues and exchanges and by means of a carefully and methodically built institutional-legal framework to eventually establish an entirely new, qualitatively different social, economic, and political system, dialectically synthesizing the two divergent systems, we might be able to claim that the Korean nation accomplished something historic, indigenous and ingenious in nature. This would be a laudable achievement perhaps contributing to the emergence of new civilizations in this new millennium.

References

An, Tai Sung (1983) *North Korea in Transition: From Dictatorship to Dynasty*. West Port, Conn: Greenwood Press.

Bunge, F.M. (ed.) (1981) *North Korea: A Country Study* (3rd ed.), Washington, D.C.: Department of Army.

Dirlik, Arif (1999) "Culture against history?: The politics of East Asian identity." *Development and Society* 28(2):167–90.

Foster-Carter, A. (1977) "North Korea: Development and Self-Reliance: A critical appraisal." *Bulletin of Concerned Asian Scholars* 9 (Jan.–Mar.): 45–57.

—— (1987) "Standing up: The two Korean states and the dependency debate— A bipartisan approach." In Kyong-Dong Kim (ed.), *Dependency Issues in Korean Development: Comparative Perspectives*. Seoul: Seoul National University Press. pp. 229–69.

—— (1990) "Still waiting for change." Letters, *Far Eastern Economic Review* (6 September): 7.

Halliday, J. (1989) "The Democratic People's Republic of Korea: Is it democratic and is it even a republic?" Paper presented at the Conference on "Marxism and the New Global Society." 25–27 October. Seoul: Institute for Far Eastern Studies, Kyungnam University.

Jacobs, N. (1985) *The Korean Road to Modernization and Development*. Urbana, IL: University of Illinois Press.

Kim, C.I.E. and B.C. Koh (eds.) (1983) *Journey to North Korea: Personal Perspectives*. Berkeley, CA: Institute of East Asian Studies, University of California.

Kim Kyong-Dong (1985) *Rethinking Development: Theories and Experiences*. Seoul: Seoul National University Press.

—— (1988) "The distinctive features of South Korea's development." In P.L. Berger and H.H.M. Hsiao (eds.), *In Search of an East Asian Development Model*. New Brunswick and Oxford: Transaction Books. pp. 197–219.

—— (1994) "Confucianism and capitalist development in East Asia." In L. Sklair (ed.), *Capitalism and Development*. London and New York: Routledge. pp. 87–106.

—— (1996) "Confucianism and modernization in East Asia: Theoretical explorations". In J. Kreiner (ed.), *The Impact of Traditional Thought on Present-Day Japan*. Munchen: Iudicium-Verlag. pp. 49–69.

—— (ed.) (1987) *Dependency Issues in Korean Development: Comparative Perspectives*. Seoul: Seoul National University Press.

Kim Kyong-Dong and Lee On-Jook (1983) "The U.S. educated among the Korean politico-bureaucratic elite: An aspect of American socio-cultural influence." *American Studies* 6:53–69.

—— (1987) "Educational background of the Korean elite: The influence of the United States and Japan." In Kyong-Dong Kim (ed.), *Dependency Issues in Korean Development: Comparative Perspectives*. Seoul: Seoul National University Press. pp. 434–58.

—— (2000) "System *versus* lifeworld discrepancies in Two-Korea relations." Paper presented at the International Conference on "The Reshaping of Inter-Korean Relations: Peace, Economic Development, and Unification." 14 December. Seoul National University.

Krieger, S., and R. Trauzettel (eds.) (1991). *Confucianism and the Modernization of China*. Mainz: v. Hase & Koehler Verlang.

Lee Kwang-kyu (1997) *Korean Family and Kinship*. Seoul: Jipmoondang.

Lee On-Jook (1988) *Bukhansahoe Yongu* (A Study of North Korean Society). Seoul: Seoul National University Press (in Korean).

—— (1993) *Bukhansahoe ui Cheje wa Saenghwal* (System and Lifeworld in North Korean Society). Seoul: Seoul National University Press (in Korean).

Macdonald, D.S. (1988) *The Koreans: Contemporary Politics and Society*. Boulder, CO: Westview Press.

MacFarquhar, R. (1980) "The post-Confucian challenge." *The Economist* (Feb): 67–72.

Moore, W.M. (1963) *Social Change*. Englewood Cliffs, NJ:Prentice-Hall.

Savada, A.M., and W. Shaw (1992) *South Korea: A Country Study*. Washington, D.C.: Library of Congress.

Tu Weiming (ed.) (1996) *Confucian Tradition in East Asian Modernity: Moral Education and Economic Culture in Japan and the Four Mini-Dragons*. Cambridge, MA: Harvard University Press.

Weber, M. (1951) *The Religion of China*. Translated and edited by H.H. Girth. New York: Free Press.

FROM DEVELOPMENTAL LIBERALISM TO NEO-LIBERALISM: GLOBALIZATION, DEPENDENT REFLEXIVITY AND SOCIAL POLICY IN SOUTH KOREA

Chang Kyung-Sup
Seoul National University

Introduction

When warnings from overseas and domestic sources pronounced the possibility of a national financial collapse in 1997, South Korean officials in charge of economic affairs downplayed it by pointing out the supposedly sound "economic fundamentals" of the country. Macroeconomic indicators concerning economic growth, trade, and inflation seemed to ratify an optimistic appraisal of the economic situation. However, when the balance-of-payment crisis broke out, economic fundamentals turned out to be full of bubbles (i.e., over-investment, overproduction, overemployment, excessive corporate borrowing, and so forth). Even more menacing was the fact that what may be called *social fundamentals* were in total disarray. Neither public institutions and programmes nor private families and individuals were prepared to deal with massive unemployment and poverty ensuing from the economic crisis. Structural reforms pursued by the Kim Dae-Jung administration, which had been inaugurated in just a few months after "the South Korean surrender" to the International Monetary Fund (IMF), seemed to quickly gain positive signals for economic recovery. Indicators of production, trade, and inflation were stabilizing. By contrast, there was every indication that social fundamentals were even further pulverized by the neo-liberal policies.

Recent studies and media reports reveal several distressing trends in South Korean society. First, job security evaporated for a majority of South Korean workers. For the first time since industrialization, the proportion of temporary and daily workers surpassed that of regular workers. Under the euphemism of labour market flexibility, almost all of those entering and reentering the labour market were forced to accept the status of transitory labourer. Besides, those giving up job search itself increased explosively. Unfamiliar and painful problems were concealed behind the impressive decrease in unemployment since 1999. Second, income disparities due to massive layoffs, widening wage differentials, and swelling capital incomes reshaped South Korea into a "growth with inequity society". Most of the rich people almost completely recovered their pre-crisis income level, but a majority of poor people still struggled with incomes far below the pre-crisis level. Third and relatedly, there was a shocking increase in the number of households below the absolute poverty line set by the government. More disturbing was the observation that the prospect for overcoming such poverty is extremely dim for most of these poor households.[1] Their poverty appeared to be structurally built in the new economic system arising in the post-crisis period. Fourth, the rapid degradation of living conditions and environments was apparent as policy regression in the areas of environmental protection, public safety and health, and education and culture were coerced as an exigency of swift economic recovery. Deregulation and commercialization were the core principles governing these matters.[2] Finally, cultural inferiority complex was widespread. Westernization was elevated from a means to an end of national development. The government, business corporations, and media were loudly asking South Koreans to live by global (in practice, American) standards.[3] As these social predicaments of neo-liberal reforms coalesced, South Korea was instantly transforming into a dual society in which grassroots people in rapidly increasing numbers were being disenfranchised from the mainstream social and economic system. Just as observed in the United States and many other countries under neo-liberal rule, there

---

[1] This pessimistic condition was reflected in the sharp increases in the number of suicides caused by poverty. The so-called "IMF economic crisis" was directly responsible for the shocking increase of suicides from 9,109 in 1997 to 12,458 in 1998 (*Pressian*, 1 September 2003). Amid gradual economic recovery, the number decreased slightly to 11,713 in 1999 and 11,794 in 2000. However, it rebounded to 12,277 in 2001 and 13,055 in 2002. Most of these fluctuations are suspected to have resulted from economic difficulties.

[2] Progressive civil movement organizations harshly criticized Kim Dae-Jung, a president who had been elected with their strong political support, for neglecting these social policy concerns so badly.

[3] Some even insisted that English should be the common language. *Chosunilbo*, the largest newspaper, once staged a noisy campaign for English proficiency. SK, the rising *chaebol* group, thanks to its prosperous communication industry, decided to use English in the regular meetings of top executives. Seoul National University, the top institution of high education and research, once reportedly considered using English in the interview of undergraduate applicants.

was an inverse relationship being established between economic growth and grassroots life condition.

The South Korean situation was particularly distressing owing to her particular developmental history. The economic miracle under Park Chung-Hee in the 1960s and 1970s had been achieved through what may be called *developmental liberalism*. Following the economic theory that maximum investment leads to maximum economic growth, most of the public budget and borrowings were spent on industrial projects and corporate subsidies. Thus, public expenditure on social policy matters—such as social welfare, labour rights, environmental protection, public health and safety, and cultural life—was practically negligible. If there was any coherent policy line concerning these matters, it was the sacrificing of labour rights, welfare, environment, health, safety, and culture for maximum economic growth. The ideology of "*seonseongjang hubunbae*" (growth first, distribution later) was propagated to justify the extremely conservative approach to social policy. This ideology, nonetheless, accepted a future imperative of distribution (or, more broadly, a serious social policy regime).

Perhaps the early 1990s were an unavoidable timing for the transition from growth to distribution. However, conservative bureaucrats and politicians, under the open praise from *chaebol*, decided to maintain the developmentalist policy line and forego the pursuit of active social policies. It was at this moment that Western neo-liberalism, with its strong anti-welfare state orientation, was brought in to South Korea in full scale.[4] Neo-liberalism succeeded developmental liberalism as the core ideology for legitimitizing the conservative developmentalist approach. But, as far as social policies were concerned, its applicability to the South Korean context was extremely limited. It was nothing but an utterly irreflexive policy option in a society already characterized by tenacious conservatism in social policies.

With the exception of labour rights, which had improved impressively thanks to the forceful political challenge of the government and business by strongly organized trade unions since the mid-1980s, other social policy matters—, such as welfare, environment, health, safety, education, and culture—suffered stagnation and, in some cases, even regression. The cost of disregarding and sacrificing these social

---

[4] Neo-liberal ideology and theory were already recognized in policy discussions from the mid-1980s. But the political situation since 1987 prevented them from producing aggressive neo-liberal policies, in particular, social matters.

concerns became evident in the mid-1990s as the South Koreans' celebration of the GNP 10,000 US dollars era was almost completely overshadowed by internationally headline-making environmental disasters, safety accidents, and violent social discontent. It became even more evident when the national financial collapse in late 1997 drove both poor and middle classes out of work and income without any effective social safety net providing buffers or shelters.

To make matters worse, a more intense version of neo-liberalism was encouraged by the IMF and Western leaders and adopted by the Kim Dae-Jung administration, hopefully, as a quick solution for the economic crisis. The cause for the crisis was prescribed as its remedy. As neo-liberal reforms practically necessitated social extortions—be they jobs, incomes or hopes—a majority of grassroots South Koreans had to go through utmost difficulty in making a living. Further and further conservative turns in social policy have inevitably pulverized *social fundamentals*. Even if the South Korean economy showed an impressively quick recovery, the rapidly deteriorating social conditions of grassroots life brewed a possibility of major social disenchantment or upheaval. The possibility was real so that the new president, Roh Moo-Hyun, has spent most of his first year in presidency pacifying angry workers, farmers, and youth on the street. South Korean development was no magic in the sense that the protracted neglect of social conditions of grassroots life was destined to decapitate her potential for sustained development.

The socially catastrophic tenacity of conservative developmentalism is hinged on the interplay of the limited nature of South Korean democracy and the haphazard pursuit of economic globalization. South Koreans may well take great pride in their arduous struggle against military dictatorship and achievement of stable democratic procedures. However, the democratically elected state leaderships have failed to show sufficient democratic capacity for solving major social problems. It is extremely ironic that two civilian presidents, Kim Young-Sam and Kim Dae-Jung, turned to the same conservative bureaucracy as had been relied on by Park Chung-Hee to analyse social and economic conditions, set regime goals, and prescribe policy measures. Political parties and the parliament have been practically pushed aside in shaping the direction and content of public policy. Critical media and intellectuals, not to mention grassroots citizens, have rarely been reckoned with.

The government bureaucracy has in practice functioned as a public policy monopoly that sets the agenda of state work, decides the governing ideology, promulgates necessary laws and policies, and, of course, implements such laws and policies. Economic developmentalism, of course, has continued to be the core ideology of government bureaucrats despite its neo-liberal modification since the late 1980s. As in former socialist countries, the concentrated authority in bureaucracy tends to cause repeated crises of social reflexivity. When they do not have to be accountable to grassroots citizens or parliamentary representatives—that is, when they should cater to the particular interest and inclination of the individual state leader only— government bureaucrats tend to turn a deaf ear to critical voices of reflexive citizens and intellectuals.

The state bureaucracy has equated neo-liberal reform with globalization in order to silence critical voices concerning the domestic social and economic conditions. In their preaching, the exigency of economic globalization makes it inevitable to ignore grassroots demands for labour rights and redistribution. They have tried to reinvent themselves into the crusaders for global standards and practices. In this way, the bureaucracy has successfully sustained its dominating position in national politics with full support from the civilian presidents. However, their cause does not constitute anything global but has led to uncritical acceptance of Western neo-liberal reforms and demands. This is how neo-liberalism, a flatly irreflexive line of ideology in the South Korean context, can exert such power as to override the demand and opinion of grassroots citizens and intellectuals.

Catching-up Politics, Crisis Politics, and Dependent Reflexivity

Throughout the latter half of the 12th century, the predominating ideology in national politics in South Korea was "catching-up". Under American pressure and advice, the Republic of Korea adopted a political system premised upon social pluralism, i.e., the American model. However, the Cold War did not allow South Korean society to remain or become pluralist. In the post-liberation period of the 1940s, left-bent social groups were brutally cracked down on by the allied forces of the US occupation army and the right-wing South Korean government. Even many middle-path political leaders were assassinated or politically emasculated. The Korean War made both South and North Korea even further mono-ideological. Leftist intellectuals and politicians fled to the North; rightist ones fled to the South. In the process of growing out of war debris, physical and material survival became the only viable goal of national development. Such physical and material survival, in the judgment of South Koreans, required rapid catching-up with Japan and the West, at least in economic terms. Rapid capitalist industrialization became an indisputable catchphrase for national development no matter which political group took charge of power. North Koreans also engaged in their own version of economic catching-up under a state-socialist regime. The continuing competition and conflict between South and North Korea intensified this politics of economic catching-up.

The politics of economic catching-up in South Korea culminated under Park Chung-Hee's reign for two decades (cf. Amsden, 1989). While there is intense debate over the historical origin of Park's programmes of industrialization and export promotion (e.g. Kohli, 1999), he had a clear mode of political rule. He tried to mobilize South Koreans into an effort at compressive industrial build-up so that the country might become a "*seonjinguk*" (advanced country) within the shortest time possible. Economic development was equated with "*minjokjungheung*" (national revival). He officially evaluated the performance of his government against numerical economic targets, i.e., certain levels of per capita income, national product, export volume, and so forth. Reaching the targeted levels of economic indicators was possible, usually within shorter periods than planned originally. Park hoped this economic achievement would override public criticism and resistance against his political dictatorship.

Park's political heirs from the military, Chun Doo-Hwan and Roh Tae-Woo, and also Park's political rival, Kim Young-Sam, perpetuated the politics of catching-up, albeit, in slightly modified versions. After two decades of miraculous economic development and amid continuing economic growth, these political leaders insisted that South Korea was or would be in a state of economic crisis. Such insistence was always seconded by the business elite and conservative media. South Korean officials, industrialists, and journalists coalesced to *invent economic crisis* in public mind. "*Gyeongjereul sallija*" (let us rescue economy) became a forceful public slogan.[5] The miraculous suc-

---

[5] This slogan was even satirized in a popular television comedy show in which a desperate mother shouted "Please save our Gyeongje!". Gyeongje was the name of her wounded son, not the economy. But when she shouted (without her son appearing as yet), viewers were intentionally misled to think of the economy.

cess of export promotion inevitably made the South Korean economy extremely dependent on foreign trade and thus unusually vulnerable to international economic vicissitudes. Even casual indicators of international economic changes were often exaggerated as symptoms of an impending crisis. Since the country was supposedly under economic crisis, the government maintained its conservative pro-business economic policy, usually in an authoritarian manner. The official prescription for economic recovery was not much different from that for economic development. Since it was just an excuse for maintaining the developmentalist policy line against various critical voices, the supposed economic crisis did not lead to any serious effort at structural reforms of the economy.

The succession of catching-up politics by crisis politics had crucial ramifications for social policy concerns. Since economic catching-up supposedly required maximum mobilization of economic and social resources in the production process, the Park Chung-Hee administration minimized public investment in social matters, such as welfare provision, labour protection, environmental management, safety enforcement, health promotion, educational service, and cultural development. As illustrated by the slogan of *"seonseongjang hubunbae"* (growth first, distribution later), the project of catching up with Western countries and Japan in economic strength supposedly necessitated deferred gratification. Under what may be called *developmental liberalism*, the successive administrations suppressed grassroots demands and rights concerning the humane quality of life and exhausted public financial resources to finance industrial projects and corporate subsidies. The need for redistribution and balanced development was acknowledged as early as in the 1970s as the government changed its five-year economic development plan into five-year economic *and* social development plan. But no serious action was taken for the policy transition under Park Chung-Hee. While the 1980s indicated that these plans were behind schedule, the political discourse on economic crisis served as another obstacle to the establishment of a serious social policy regime. Sometimes even more conservative actions were taken in the areas of welfare, labour, environment, safety, health, education, and culture in order to overcome the supposed economic crisis. The powerful political challenge of labour unions and progressive civil activists in the late 1980s forced the government to pay attention briefly to social matters. However, it soon dumped such social burdens to individual companies, only a handful of which were actually able to provide welfare and other social benefits (Song, 1995). Social, not economic, crisis was actually deepening.

It was under Kim Young-Sam in the early 1990s that Western neo-liberalism, with its regressive social policy orientation, fully materialized. At a time when various serious policy measures were required in order to stabilize dangerous situations in social, cultural, and ecological aspects of grassroots life, South Korean politicians and bureaucrats turned a deaf ear to concrete social realities. Instead, they subscribed eagerly to the Western ideology derived from the particular historical situation of the West. The South Korean government adopted Western neo-liberalism as a core remedy for the economic crisis they had invented. Neo-liberalism, an outcome of Westerners' (conservative) reflexivity on their social democratic past, turned out recklessly irreflexive in the South Korean context. During neo-liberal reform in the early and mid-1990s, South Koreans had to go through globally headline-making accidents, disasters, and uproars. Among others, mass urban poverty, housing shortage, educational crisis, environmental disasters, and safety accidents put South Koreans into collective panic. All these social costs were coerced even before a real economic crisis of 1987 would require South Koreans to confront unprecedented experiences of mass unemployment and poverty.

The *transition from developmental liberalism to neo-liberalism* throws a crucial question on the nature of modernity South Koreans have been constructing (cf. Chang, 1999a). It is often pointed out that the exceptional educational zeal of South Koreans has been a core factor for the economic success of South Korea. It is true that South Korean people, if not their government, have invested intensively in education in order to build a competent industrial labour force. But this does not mean that serious investment has been made in developing an autonomous knowledge production system (Chang, 1998). Neither building an independent basis for knowledge production nor creating distinct theories, ideologies, and technologies autonomously has been a top priority in national development. In emulating the West and Japan, the best knowledge seemed to reside in the West and Japan (Amsden, 1989). South Korea became one of the largest importers of international knowledge trade.[6]

---

[6] The export-import ratio in international technology trade was only 0.06 in 1980 and then fell even further to 0.02 in 1990 (NSO, 2000:333). Later the ratio recovered but still fluctuated around the level of more than two decades ago.

Knowledge dependency may be interpreted as part of the "advantage of late development." It is undeniable that late developers can save time and money in national development by learning and utilizing the abundant pool of modern knowledge and technology prepared by advanced countries. Nonetheless, late developers should at least have an independent capacity for appraising their particular social and economic situations, setting the appropriate goals of development, and selecting knowledge and technology suitable for such situations and goals. This independent capacity may not have been particularly weak in South Korea. However, the extent of knowledge dependency was so excessive that many catastrophic side-effects arose.

The most problematic aspect of knowledge dependency in South Korea has been the irreflexivity of political, economic, and academic elite concerning their current historical status and future developmental direction (cf. Beck, Giddens, and Lash, 1994). As no indigenous theory or ideology provides a persuasive and influential diagnosis of the long-term developmental status of South Korea, whatever prevails in the West enters the centre stage of the South Korean political and intellectual world (Chang, 1999a). Neo-liberalism, in its anti-welfare state version, was noisily imported into a society where social welfare had always remained at an extremely weak level. Social ramifications of such dependent (ir)reflexivity turned out extremely disastrous, particularly on the eve of an impending national economic collapse.

From Developmental Liberalism to Neo-Liberalism: Backward Reforms in Social Policy

Like other aspects of South Korean society, public welfare (or, more broadly, social policy) has been shaped by the interplay of long historical traditions and various external influences. In every dynastic state since almost three millennia ago, various public relief programmes for poor and starving people and those afflicted by natural disaster, epidemic, and war were implemented as a core mechanism for political rule.[7] Even land tenure was basically an entitlement

---

[7] The confirmed history of public welfare in the Korean peninsular dates back to almost three millennia ago (Nam and Cho, 1995:84–85). In 843 BC, a poverty relief law called Yunhwanbeop was established in Gijajoseon. In 675 BC, a public institution called Jeyangwon was established to support "the four deprived" (i.e., widowers, widows, orphans, and the childless elderly).

system designed to satisfy grassroots subsistence needs in an egalitarian manner. In grassroots communities, various forms of mutual support and relief have been found in every historical period including the present day. On the other hand, as the Koreans' own effort at national transition to modernity had been frustrated by internal political conflict and foreign invasion, the Japanese colonial government instituted the first modern form of public welfare (Nam and Cho, 1995). This was designed to legitimitize the Japanese imperial rule, prevent Koreans' anti-Japanese rebellion, and transform Koreans adaptable to colonial capitalism. Another line of foreign influence was exercised by the United States when war-torn Koreans had to turn to American aid and missionary charity and social work in the post-Korean War period. As state-provided welfare was extremely limited in the colonial and the immediate post-war periods, grassroots people relied frequently and heavily on communal mutual assistance and extended family support.

In launching the ambitious industrialization project, the military regime of Park Chung-Hee had two mutually contradictory goals concerning public welfare. On the one hand, Park had to mobilize political support from various social groups (including civil servants and the military in particular) by providing welfare benefits. On the other hand, the exigency of catching-up industrialization necessitated minimal state spending on public welfare. This contradiction was resolved in a deceptive manner. A comprehensive range of social security laws and regulations were instituted in the 1960s and 1970s, however, with extremely limited benefits provided in practice. Actual state expenditure on public welfare, in terms of budget proportion, remained stagnant. Welfare and health expenditure merely fluctuated around the 6 per cent of the state budget for two and a half decades since the early 1960s. Comparatively, South Korea has remained as a country where the government spends extravagantly on economic affairs vis-à-vis welfare matters. In this way, there emerged an on-paper social policy state having some elementary forms of social insurance, poverty relief, and welfare service (Nam and Cho, 1995: 92–94). Since both Park Chung-Hee and the people felt that the *raison d'être* of the Park administration was rapid industrialization and economic growth, such futile welfare programmes and policies did not create any major political crisis.

When another military regime was established by Chun Doo-Hwan through a *coup d'état* in 1980, the social and political environment had changed dramatically. South Koreans were not content with modicum income increases in exchange for political oppression and social control. They also learned that they should—and could—express anger and launch resistance when their life was affected by unjust policies and activities by ruling groups. Thus, the Chun regime could not rely on economic development alone for political justification of unlawful political leadership and thus sought other complementary legitimation mechanisms. In this context, laws were made and revised in order to expand welfare benefits for labour and needy social groups (such as children, elderly, and the handicapped). However, social welfare was still considered a negative element to economic development and thus minimized whenever possible. Moreover, since Chun relied much more on physical coercion than on material concession, a serious social policy state had yet to be established.

It was during another ex-general, Roh Tae-Woo's presidency that more progressive slogans were pronounced and more active programmes were pursued concerning social welfare (Nam and Cho, 1995). His administration, set up by the normal procedure of direct presidential election, was much softer politically and relied more on material concessionary policies. Also, the political strengthening of organized labour exerted remarkable pressure for the improvement in social policy. For the first time in history, the establishment of the welfare state was declared as a long-term political goal. New and revised laws were prepared to expand the range of social groups under welfare protection and stabilize grassroots living conditions through insurance and pension programmes. Ironically, it was at this moment that neo-liberalism began to influence politicians, bureaucrats as well as businessmen as a sort of counter-ideology. The big and/or interventionist state was condemned as something critically harmful to sustained economic development. The main objective was to liberalize and reduce the economic role of the state, but a suspicious and pessimist view spread concerning social welfare as well. Despite slight increases in the proportion of welfare expenditure, the general neglect of social policy was maintained by the state. However, the political rise of organized labour led to a situation where the government had to shift gradually to a neutral position in labour-capital conflict. Consequently, workers were able to win higher wages and various welfare benefits from their employers (Song, 1995). Another significant social change consisted of people's rapidly enlarging awareness and demand about non-material interests, such as environment,

health, education, and culture (Lim, Lee, and Chang, 1998). With
state elite remaining passive and narrow-sighted, their distance from
vibrant civil society concerning social policy grew critically.

The dysfunctional outcomes of neo-liberalism grew full scale during the rule of a civilian president, Kim Young-Sam. His administration pursued the "*Singyeongje*" (New Economy) policy intended to
boost the already overheated economy. Concerning social policy,
even the previously instituted policies and programmes of the state
were scaled down whereas the substitutive roles of market, family,
private organizations, and local governments were emphasized under
what may be called "welfare pluralism" (Nam and Cho, 1995:97;
Chang, 1997). In particular, the privatization of welfare services and
social insurance programmes was strongly recommended as an alternative welfare strategy (Committee for Appraising Social Welfare
Policy, 1994). In the latter half of Kim Young-Sam's presidency,
some of his aides proposed what was called "the globalization of the
quality of life" (The National Welfare Planning Commission, 1995).
But most of the governmental and political elites were not cooper-
ative in making this proposal into a serious social policy line with
sufficient financial backup. His administration also pursued neo-liberal labour reform for the sake of labour market flexibility, leaving
many workers and managers unemployed and labour unions indig-
nant. But the collusive relationship between the government and *chaebol* remained unchanged and, in some cases, grew stronger, so that
a national financial fiasco was destined to break out due to excessive corporate borrowings and suicidal investments. On the economic
front, the Kim Young-Sam government remained too shy in the
(neo-liberal) reform of *chaebol* whereas financial deregulation and liberalization were hastily pursued to the liking of both Wall Street and
the *chaebol*. A degenerated version of the developmental state in economic policy combined with a neo-liberal regime in social policy
drove the country into an unprecedented economic crisis against
which no social protection mechanisms were prepared. Kim Young-
Sam's presidency ended leaving his country in a state of economic
collapse without any meaningful safety net.

The Cause as Remedy? The 1997 Crisis and Neo-Liberal Responses

A decade of lavish governmental spending on mega-size public projects and unconstrained corporate investment in heavy industries was followed by an instant collapse of the South Korean economy in late 1997. The more immediate cause was, of course, the irresponsible rush and flight of speculative international financial capital. The economic crisis came at a moment social conditions of grassroots life were extremely unstable due to the outright neglect of social policy by the previous administrations. Even without an economic crisis, grassroots South Koreans may have had experienced unbearably hurtful living conditions. The economic crisis fell on a social crisis that had already been aggravated to a critical level. There were no social buffering mechanisms against this unprecedented economic breakdown. A *societal crisis* was in order as massive unemployment due to corporate bankruptcies and structural adjustments was added to the already long list of deleterious conditions of everyday grassroots life.

A blunter version of neo-liberalism was adopted by the Kim Dae-Jung administration as a quick remedy for the economic crisis (Chang, 1999b). As discussed above, neo-liberalism had influenced the preceding two administrations so that the establishment of a serious social policy regime was prevented. As the developmental liberalist ideology had lost its appeal by the mid-1980s, bureaucracy and business coalesced to insist that the national economy was under a crisis and that redistributive and welfarist policies should not be in the way of sustained economic growth. As neo-liberals in the West preached that welfare expansion supposedly led to the weakening of the economic growth potential, the developmentalist coalition of South Korean bureaucracy and business gladly converted to neo-liberalism in the 1990s. Thereby an opportunity for redressing the developmental strategy into a socially sustainable one was lost. Less than a decade after the ideological conversion to neo-liberalism, a *real* economic crisis broke out and the intensification of the neo-liberal policy line was determined as the crisis management strategy. Kim Dae-Jung and the International Monetary Fund concurred on the structural causes and basic solutions of the economic crisis. Severe austerity and unconstrained lay-offs were immediately forced on middle and poor classes whereas financial and organizational restructuring was demanded of the *chaebol*, however, with little leeway for disobedience.

As they had revived from war ruins, grassroots South Koreans were accustomed to the austere mode of living. As far as someone in their family earned income, family members would engage in various strategies for collective survival. In the near absence of social assistance and insurance programmes for ordinary people, paid or self-employed work was the only universally available mechanism for physical survival. However, the abrupt and massive unemployment came to displace the precondition for such collective survival of grassroots families (Chang, 1999b). Families with no income at all increased dramatically, and a widespread dissolution of families was inevitable. Even austere living was no option when material resources totally ran out. Kin network for emergency mutual assistance functioned to rescue some people, but generous kin members themselves came to lose their jobs and incomes. To many families and individuals, unemployment meant nothing other than a free fall to the ground. For most of the laid-off workers and bankrupt businessmen and merchants, state programmes for unemployment relief were unheard of or ineffective at best. Unemployment insurance was instituted in a hurry, but its effect has yet to be realized.

It was rather obvious that workers would risk their lives to prevent the structural reforms that would sacrifice their jobs and threaten their sheer survival. In addition, labour activism was nothing new in this contentious society. Experienced and militant South Korean unions would not endure the neo-liberal reforms targeted asymmetrically at their members. Without any effective material and institutional resources to pacify the anger of immiserated workers, political persuasion and compromise were the last resort for the state leadership. Fortunately, Kim Dae-Jung was the best candidate to undertake the heavily demanding work of resolving these crucial issues. The Labor-Employer-Government Committee (Nosajeongwiweonhoe) was constituted to reach agreement on the terms of structural reforms concerning labour, business, and the public sector (Nosajeongwiweonhoe, 1998). Kim's core objective behind this seemingly corporatist political arrangement, of course, was to exhort labour to accept massive lay-offs as the key condition for corporate survival and, ultimately, for national economic survival. Labour leaders accepted the pact expecting that the government and business would engage in sincere reforms on their part. However, the government and business accepted the utility of the tripartite committee only when labour reforms were necessary. This sly tactic angered workers bitterly so that unions repeatedly pulled out of the tripartite committee (Chang, 1999b).

Nonetheless, the government came to realize the true cost of lacking a sound social security system. If an economic crisis of any sort immediately threatens the sheer survival of ordinary people, economic development is not socially sustainable anymore. Structural reforms cannot acquire legitimacy when they lead to the total alienation and impoverishment of weak social groups with no reliable public rescue programmes. This was realized by conservative officials only after the financial crisis had led to a societal crisis. The business community also shared this understanding. In the opinion of international advisors (such as the I.M.F., the World Bank, the O.E.C.D.) and Western lenders, the near absence of social security programmes in South Korea was a serious obstacle to the neo-liberal economic reforms they were encouraging South Korean officials, industrialists, and workers to adopt. In this context, a social safety net became a serious political catchword for public policy for the first time in history.

However, the administrative effort has been confined to the unemployment issue (Chang, 1999b). Government officials have refused to accept the need for a serious social policy regime programme and instead focused on unemployment as an economic issue. They have been dealing with labourers as economic input, not citizens with social rights. Their insistence that the public budget should be spent "productively" for those programmes which could redeploy unemployed labourers led to the neglect of protecting the immediate living conditions. Widespread waste and virtual embezzlement of the emergency public funds in those *economic* programmes set up for the unemployed were reported while most of the laid-off and bankrupt people complained that they had not benefited from—and were not aware of—public relief programmes of any sort (Chang, 1999b). At the same time, more general welfare concerns received rather diminished governmental commitment. At one point, the government even planned to reduce welfare expenditure while the structural adjustment of various social insurance programmes required workers to pay substantially higher premiums.

Despite these problems, South Korea made a remarkable recovery economically. The South Korean economy recorded an astonishing 10.7 per cent growth of GDP in 1999 after a 6.7 per cent decline in 1998. However, caution against the possible "overheating" of the economy was pronounced. But it was also clear that "growth with equity" was not a Korean phenomenon anymore. On the contrary, abrupt employment destabilization, wide inequality, and rampant poverty served as the primary foundations for economic recovery (Chang, 1999b). The social pulverization under neo-liberalism transformed South Korea into a society distinctly different from even her immediate past.

In September 1999, according to the National Statistical Office, the proportion of non-regular workers (i.e. temporary workers and daily workers) surpassed that of regular workers for the first time in history by 53 per cent vs. 47 per cent (*Hankyoreh*, 16 Nov. 1999). The Korean Labor Research Institute estimated that 92 per cent of the newly employed workers in the first half of 1999 were either temporary or daily workers (*Hankyoreh*, 16 Nov. 1999). Those who were excluded from unemployment statistics because they had given up job search may have numbered as many as two-thirds of the unemployed (*Hankyoreh*, 22 Nov. 1999). Thus, the gradual decline in the overall unemployment rate since March 1999 was highly deceptive (cf. Kim Yu-Seon, 2003). However, the misery of these workers had an ironic effect / outcome. In early 2003, *Forbes* (30 January 2003) indicated that South Korea ranked third (after the United States and Canada) in labour market flexibility among all OECD (Organisation for Economic Cooperation and Development) member countries.

The widening of income disparities and the increase in the number of those below the poverty line are no less worrisome (see Table 3). Before the economic crisis, according to official statistics of the National Statistical Office, the richest 10 per cent of the urban worker households used to earn six to seven times as much as the poorest 10 per cent. After the economic crisis, however, this ratio surged to frequently surpass 9 per cent. If statistics including non-worker households as well are examined, the income gap may be much bigger. The expansion of absolute poverty was alarming. The national economic crisis and instant recovery turned out to be a financial bonanza to the richest group as they garnered huge incomes from the IMF-forced high interest rate in 1998 and the overheating of the stock market in 1999. In a research report delivered to the United Nations Development Plan (UNDP), by contrast, Chamyeoyeondae (Participation Alliance) estimated the size of the population below the poverty line during the first quarter of 1999 as 10.3 million (*Hankyoreh*, 11

Nov. 1999). The corresponding figure was 9.2 million for the first quarter of 1998 and 7.6 million for the first quarter of 1996. Obviously, economic recovery failed to alleviate the destitution of the poor.[8] As a more conservative appraisal, a study by the government-affiliated Korea Development Institute estimated that the absolutely poor households increased from 8.8 per cent in 1994 to 11.7 per cent in 1998 and 12.0 per cent in 2001 (*Yonhapnews*, 16 February 2003).

The changing structure of taxation also dampened economic inequality. The necessity of the expanded government spending for economic structural adjustment at a time of economic depression led to the sharp increase of indirect taxes vis-à-vis direct taxes. The impoverishment of future taxpayers, i.e., the young people, is also a serious social problem. The year-end total state debt was predicted to be 109 trillion won (or 23.0 per cent of GDP) in 1999 (*Hankyoreh*, 14 Dec. 1999). The corresponding figure was only 49.7 trillion won (or 11.9 per cent of GDP) in 1996, 65.6 trillion won (or 14.5 per cent of GDP) in 1997, and 87.6 trillion won (or 19.5 per cent of GDP) in 1998. If debt repayment guaranteed by the government had also been included, the state debt would have doubled. Most of the expanded debt was used to rescue defunct financial institutions, and yet more public spending was needed to complete the reform of financial industries. Such heavy indebtedness of the state was unprecedented in the South Korean context and would inevitably require future taxpayers' grave sacrifice.

Besides these social and economic concerns, neo-liberal retreat and encroachment in the areas of environmental protection, public safety and health, high education, and cultural life were also condemned by intellectuals, civil activists as well as professionals. Environmental disasters, safety accidents, and educational conflicts were taking place at grave levels. Policy statements on these matters, if any, called for deregulation, commercialization, liberalization, globalization, and so

---

[8] This study flew in the face of the Kim Dae-Jung administration which was in a self-congratulatory mood amid rapid economic recovery. Officials expressed doubt about the validity of the study on the grounds that its reliance on consumption data could be misleading because of people's tendency to reduce consumption under economic difficulty (*Hankyoreh*, 19 Nov. 1999). However, since consumption can be considered a measurement of the actually realized quality of life, the conclusion of the study does not appear seriously incongruous. On the other hand, officials tried to pressure a paragovernmental research institute to lower the official level of the minimum living expenses below which households are classified as absolutely poor (*Hankyoreh*, 23 Nov. 1999).

forth. They were dealt with primarily from the economic point of
view and by economic policy.

Democracy, Globalization, and Reflexive Development

Until the day of the financial breakdown, explosive economic growth
over three decades had made South Koreans confident and optimistic about their indulgence in rapid material expansion. In particular, technocrats and industrialists seemed to believe that their
developmental growth was infallible. The unreserved praise of the
South Korean economic achievement by Western politicians, scholars, and media reinforced such self-perception. In particular, liberals praised that the supposed adherence of South Korea to free
market and free trade had made the economic miracle possible. They
even tried to share the credit for the South Korean economic success by insisting that they had advised South Korea to pursue economic development through free market and free trade. South Koreans
had rarely looked back on the steps they had taken.

However, the financial collapse of South Korea turned around the
situation all at once. South Koreans were rebuked for having distorted the economic system through excessive government intervention, government-business collusion, lax economic discipline, and so
forth. South Koreans suddenly became crony capitalists (Palat, 1999).
As people who supposedly lack the capacity for understanding their
own structural problems, South Koreans were advised to listen carefully to what was being said about themselves by Western specialists, journalists, and credit appraisal companies.[9] Having lost confidence
in the plausibility of their economic development project, South
Koreans eagerly subscribed to the appraisal and advice by Westerners.
Newspapers and television programmes were full of reports by Western
credit appraisal companies, remarks by Western political leaders and
economic specialists, and suggestions from international economic
agencies. On the other hand, the failure of self-monitoring became
a crucial subject for academic and political debate. South Koreans
wondered how or why signals of the impending economic break-

---

[9] Just as the crisis of social sciences was pronounced in Western academia after
the sudden collapse of Soviet-bloc socialist countries, many South Korean intellectuals deplored their incapacity to diagnose the national economic breakdown of
1997.

down had not been detected or communicated. Was it the deficient capacity for self-monitoring or the political and bureaucratic distortion of communication that caused the governmental inaction about the impending financial collapse?

The South Korean crisis broke out not because South Koreans ignored Westerners' thought and advice but because they adopted such thought and advice without reckoning their particular social and economic conditions carefully. First of all, the financial mess was created almost overnight after the reckless liberalization of the financial sectors was carried out under the tenacious urge of Western neo-liberals since the late 1980s. Financial liberalization may not be a source of economic jeopardy in itself, but its combination with the lack of the governmental monitoring capacity, the propensity of South Korean business for excessive borrowing and indiscreet investment as well as the speculative behaviour of international "hot money" led to a financial runaway situation. More broadly, the loss of an apt timing for the implementation of active social policies was caused by the blind subscription of South Koreans to the Western neo-liberal criticism of the welfare state. The utility of neo-liberal reforms, if any, presupposes a long experience or experimentation with the Keynesian welfare state. However, what had been experienced in South Korea for decades was an excessively conservative policy line about welfare, health, environment, education, and so forth. As far as social policy was concerned, South Korea had virtually nothing reformed or liberalize. In this context, the function of the neo-liberal ideology was only to preempt the possibility of a serious social policy regime. Since there was no persuasive reason that South Korea would enjoy sustained development while forgoing serious social policies, the neo-liberal influence was highly perilous.

The economic and social crises attested to the limited nature of South Korean democracy and its vicious interplay with neo-liberal globalism. Neither the government nor the parliament was meaningfully accountable to citizens. Once democratically elected state leaders were sworn in, they rarely challenged the bureaucratic monopoly of the state policy line. Political parties did not represent social classes or ideologies but served the individual political interest of their leaders. Thus, political parties and parliamentary members rarely exercised serious influence on the government bureaucracy. In practice, South Korea was ruled by the dictatorship of a *bureaucratic party* entrusted with presidential authority. Ironically, even Kim Young-Sam and Kim Dae-Jung, the chief critics of Park's bureaucratic authoritarian rule, came to repeat what they had criticized resolutely.

Bureaucratic offices and officials, in turn, remained beholden to the ideological and intellectual dominance of the West. Since the mid-1980s, neo-liberalism was all the more acceptable because they judged that their ideology and prestige, centred on economic developmentalism, might be preserved in the process of exercising strong authority to reform business and labour. Their subscription to foreign ideas and ideologies went hand in hand with the authoritarian suppression of reflexive voices by critical specialists, intellectuals, and citizens. The blind pursuit of neo-liberal goals required undemocratic control of social demands, expert advice, and academic judgments.[10] The broad and loud call for the establishment of a serious social policy regime did not generate any tangible repercussion on the part of the developmentalist bureaucracy imbued with neo-liberalism.

The state bureaucracy equated neo-liberal reform with globalization in order to silence critical voices concerning the domestic social and economic conditions. In their preaching, the exigency of economic globalization makes it inevitable to ignore grassroots demands for labour rights and redistribution. They tried to reinvent themselves as the crusaders for global standards and practices. In this way, the bureaucracy successfully sustained its dominating position in national politics with full support from the civilian presidents. However, their cause did not constitute anything global but led to uncritical acceptance of Western neo-liberal reforms and demands. This was how neo-liberalism, a flatly irreflexive line of ideology in the South Korean context, exerted such power as to override the demand and opinion of grassroots citizens and intellectuals.

Unfortunately, Kim Dae-Jung's emphasis on democracy and market economy did not seem to derive from recognition of the centrality of democratic reflexivity in national development. His argument that the authoritarianism of his political predecessors had been responsible for state-business collusion, bureaucratic corruption, and distortion of the financial sector was not mistaken (*Hankyoreh*, 27 Feb. 1999). But his self-declared mission of completing democracy and

---

[10] For this reason, many scholars and civilian specialists refuse to accept positions on governmental advisory bodies.

market economy was more in line with the demand of Western neo-liberals. Thus his strong appeal to Western political and economic leadership was quite understandable. On the other hand, his neo-liberal reforms did not reflect democratically mobilized voices from domestic citizens, intellectuals, and experts. On too many occasions, his administrative staff were determined to maintain: control over workers and other needy social groups who felt neo-liberal reforms threatening their sheer survival and thus staged various acts of resistance. Even the Labor-Employer-Government Committee lost its function. That was why Kim's popularity fell to a dismal level after all his fiat in debt renewal and economic recovery. Politically, Kim seemed to think that his own presidency was full evidence of democracy. However, political reform was not pursued in any meaningful manner or degree until the eruption of activist civil organizations against political corruption and irresponsibility. Paradoxically, neo-liberal reforms led to another line of political authoritarianism, of which social reflexivity was no significant element.

Conclusion and Prospects

"Economic miracle" in South Korea did not take place without equally consequential social costs. The so-called development state under Park Chung-Hee and his military successors was renowned for their intrusive entrepreneurial role in industrialization and export promotion, but its interest and commitment to social policy matters were extremely low-keyed and, at best, bluntly conservative. Under what may be called *developmental liberalism*, the successive administrations suppressed grassroots demands and rights concerning social citizenship and exhausted public financial resources to finance industrial projects and corporate assistance. As illustrated by the slogan of *seonseongjang hubunbae* (growth first, distribution later), the national project of catching up with Western countries and Japan in economic strength supposedly necessitated deferred gratification. Inevitably, various risky social conditions in welfare, environment, safety, health, education, and other social matters were accumulating behind the eye-catching process of unprecedented rapid economic growth.

In the early 1990s, Western neo-liberalism (with its regressive social policy orientation) was formally accepted exactly at a time when various serious policy measures were required to stabilize dangerous situations in social, cultural, and ecological aspects of grassroots life. Even after three decades of splendid economic development, South Korean officials, industrialists, and journalists coalesced to *invent an economic crisis* in public mind and adopted Western neo-liberalism as a core remedy, thereby intensifying the pro-business doctrine. The succession of catching-up politics by crisis politics and its ideological legitimation by neo-liberalism generated a crucial obstacle to the establishment of a serious social policy regime in South Korea.

Neo-liberalism, an outcome of Westerners' conservative reflexivity on their social democratic past, turned out recklessly irreflexive in the South Korean context. During the neo-liberal reform years of the early to mid-1990s, South Koreans had to go through globally headline-making accidents, disasters, and uproar. Among others, mass urban poverty, the housing crisis, environmental and safety disasters, and educational conflicts created collective panic among the South Koreans. To make matters worse, the prime beneficiary of neo-liberalism—i.e. *chaebol*—drove the country into national bankruptcy after several years of suicidal expansionist drive using short-term foreign loans as well as government policy loans.

The state bureaucracy equated neo-liberal reform with globalization in order to silence critical voices concerning domestic social and economic conditions. In their preaching, the exigency of economic globalization supposedly made it inevitable to ignore grassroots demands for labour rights and redistribution. They tried to reinvent themselves into the crusaders for global standards and practices. In this way, the bureaucracy successfully sustained its dominating position in national politics with full support from the civilian presidents. However, their cause did not constitute anything global but led to uncritical acceptance of Western neo-liberal reforms and demands. This was how neo-liberalism, a flatly irreflexive line of ideology in the South Korean context, came to exert such power as to override the demand and opinion of grassroots citizens and intellectuals.

The emergency reform measures of the Kim Dae-Jung administration, sharing the neo-liberal doctrine with the American-controlled International Monetary Fund, seemed to produce some market-disciplinary pressure on lax industrialists, but their dysfunctional impacts on social policy concerns brewed potentially explosive social conditions. As far as grassroots social conditions were concerned, his neo-liberal strategy for crisis management was self-contradictory and irreflexive.

He presented the cause as the remedy. A truly reflexive line of reform seems to require democratic mobilization of critical intellectual resources, which most South Koreans are not yet optimistic about. Neo-liberalism was destined to become a grave failure not only as a social policy but also as a political project. The establishment of a serious social policy regime may lead to the deepening of democracy by which social reflexivity is actively developed and incorporated by political leaders and public administrators.

References

Amsden, Alice (1989) *Asia's Next Giant: South Korea and Late Industrialization*. New York: Oxford University Press.

Beck, Ulrich, Anthony Giddens, and Scott Lash (1994) *Reflexive Modernization: Politics, Tradition and Aesthetics in the Modern Social Order*. Stanford: Stanford University Press.

Chang Kyung-Sup (1997) "The Neo-Confucian Right and Family Politics in South Korea: The Nuclear Family as an Ideological Construct". *Economy and Society* 26(1):22–42.

—— (1998) "Knowledge Production and Reflexivity Ritual in the Making of Compressed Modernity: Reflections on the South Korean Experience." Paper presented at the First International Conference of Asia Scholars (ICAS), Noordwijkerhout, the Netherlands, 25–28 June 1998.

—— (1999a) "Compressed Modernity and Its Discontents: South Korean Society in Transition". *Economy and Society* 28(1):30–55.

—— (1999b) "Social Ramifications of South Korea's Economic Fall: Neo-Liberal Antidote to Compressed Capitalist Industrialization?" *Development and Society* 28(1):49–91.

Forbes 30 January 2003.

Giddens, Anthony (1990) *The Consequences of Modernity*. Stanford: Stanford University Press.

Hankyoreh (various issues).

Kim Yu-Seon (2003) "*Hanguk Nosagwangyeui Gaehyeok Banghyang*" (in Korean; The Direction of Reform in Labor Relations in South Korea). Paper presented at the Symposium on "The New Search for South Korean Labor Relations and the Implication of European Models". 5 September 2003.

Kohli, Atul (1999) "Where Do High-Growth Political Economies Come From? The Japanese Lineage of Korea's 'Developmental State'". In Meredith Woo-Cumings (ed.), The Developmental State. Ithaca: Cornell University Press. pp. 93–136.

Koo, Hagen (1993) "The State, Minjung, and the Working Class in South Korea". In Hagen Koo (ed.), *State and Society in Contemporary Korea*. Ithaca: Cornell University Press. pp. 131–62.

Lim Hyun-Chin, Lee Se-Yong, and Chang Kyung-Sup (eds.) (1998) *Hangukinui Salmui Jil: Sinchejeok, Simrijeok Anjeon* (in Korean; Koreans' Quality of Life: Physical and Psychological Safety). Seoul: Seoul National University.

Nam Sae-Jin, and Cho Heung-Seek (1995) *Hanguksahoebokjiron* (in Korean; Social Welfare in Korea). Seoul: Nanam.

Nosajeongwiweonhoe (Labor-Business-Government Committee) (1998) "*Nosajeong Gongdong Seoneonmun*" (in Korean; Nosajeong Co-Declaration). 20 January 1998.

Palat, Ravi (1999) "Miracles of the Day Before?: The Great Asian Meltdown and the Changing World-Economy". *Development and Society* 28(1):1–48.

Pressian (www.pressian.com).

Republic of Korea, Committee for Appraising Social Welfare Policy (1994) *The Development Direction for Social Welfare Policy* (in Korean).

Republic of Korea, National Statistical Office (NSO) (2000) *Tonggyero Bon Hangugui Moseup* (in Korean; The Appearance of the Republic of Korea Seen through Statistics).

Republic of Korea, National Welfare Planning Commission (1995) *'Salmui Jil' Segyehwareul Uihan Gukminbokji Gobongusang* (in Korean; The Basic Plan of National Welfare for the Globalization of 'the Quality of Life').

Song Ho-Keun (1995) *Hangugui Gieopbokji Yeongu* (in Korean; Korea's Company Welfare: An Empirical Research). Seoul: Korea Labor Institute.

Yonhapnews (www.yonhapnews.co.kr).

VIETNAMESE WOMEN IN TRANSITION AND GLOBALIZATION

Le Thi Quy
Research Center for Gender and Development

Vietnam is one of the poorest and most densely populated countries in the world. It has an area of about 311,113 sq km, three-fourths of which are mountains and highlands. By the year 2000, Vietnam had a population of over 76 million, 51 per cent of whom were women.[1] In 1986, Vietnam obtained an annual GDP growth rate of 8 per cent. Although Vietnam was also affected by the regional financial crisis in 1998 and suffered a setback: its per capita GDP increased to US$330 during the period 1999–2000.[2]

In 1986, the State announced the *Doi Moi* (economic renewal) policy, shifting the national economy from a centrally run to socialist-oriented market economy. Thus policy has created major changes in all spheres of the social economy and added new dynamism to production and people's lives.[3]

According to some foreign experts, although there is much to do Vietnam's economic renewal policy has brought about encouraging results, helping to improve people's lives. In 1996, Vietnam was the second biggest rice exporter in the world. To date 90 per cent of Vietnamese people are literate, the mortality rate of new-born is 34 per cent, 98 per cent of children have sufficient immunization.

Vietnamese Government Policy Relating to Women's Issues

Marxism-Leninism has been the leading ideology in Vietnam in the contemporary and modern time. It has initiated and supported gender equality. The Political Thesis of the Communist Party of Vietnam issued in 1930 asserted three tasks of the Vietnamese revolution, namely national liberation, class liberation and women emancipation.

---

[1] According to the 1999 Population Censuses.
[2] Data released by the World Bank in Vietnam.
[3] See socio-economic development indicators in Annexes.

These three tasks have been done simultaneously and assisted one another in the common struggle. The August 1945 Revolution and then the socialist construction in North Vietnam (from 1954 to 1975) were an illustration of the ideology. Immediately after the liberation of northern Vietnam in 1954, the new administration declared "equality between men and women". Before 1954, Vietnam had experienced nearly 2,000 years of feudal regime and nearly 100 years of both colonial and feudal regime. In the later period, Vietnam was under some influence of Western culture on socio-political issues including women's issues, but this influence was rather weak. Confucianism remained the leading ideology of the Vietnamese society.

From a gender viewpoint, Confucianism robs the women of their human rights in both family and society. Confucian principles and criteria such as the three principles of obedience, the four virtues, polygamy and virginity tied the women's lives and spirit to the patriarchal regime.[4] These concepts were still very strict even in early 20th century. Women who committed adultery or became pregnant outside marriage were severely punished. They would have their nape shaven and smeared with lime, or they were led around the village to be exposed to shame or they may even face execution where they were put on a raft and then left to float in the river. That is why it was a persuasive revolution when the new government issued timely and practical policies eradicating backward customs and habits such as polygamy, underaged marriage, husbands beating wives, and eradicating parents' complete rights to decide their children's marriage. The new government asserted women's rights to participate in social activities, their right to go to school and be free to choose their lover. Many laws and codes have been issued, among which the Law on Marriage and the Family affirms the status, responsibilities and rights of women in relation to men in their family and society. It is safe to say that government policies in this period laid a foundation for the women's emancipation movement in Vietnam, helping improve their status from slavery to freedom and helping them get out of the solitary confinement of their own houses to take part in social activities on equal terms as

---

[4] The three "obediences" obedience to father before marriage, obedience to husband after marriage and obedience to son after the death of the husband. The four virtues: doing good housework, beautify herself to please her husband, tender and obedient speech and keeping virtue and virginity for her husband.

men. For this reason, the August 1945 revolution was different from the previous ones. It was not only a social revolution but also a revolution in the family for the emancipation of women.

Gender equality remains a major target of the Vietnamese government. It is not only an effective continuation of the initial aims of the Vietnamese revolution, but is also suited to the current world viewpoint on civilization and development. It can be seen not only in legal documents but also in social life. Compared with many other countries in the world, Vietnam has a rather good legal system with more than 40 Laws and Codes, more than 120 Ordinances and over 850 legal documents issued by the government and Prime Minister. The Vietnamese government has ratified and participated in 13 international treaties on human rights. Progressive policies relating to gender issues have been acknowledged in many laws such as the Law on Marriage and the family (issued in 1959 and revised in 1986), the 1980 Constitution, the Law on Nationalities, the Labour Code, the Law on Inheritance and the Penal Code. The State acknowledges equality between men and women both in the family and society. Men and women have equal rights to vote and to stand for election and have the same opportunities to learn and to progress. They are equal at work and should be given the same working conditions and the same payment for the same job that they do. The State recognizes and protects monogamy. Men and women have equal rights to inheritance, to bring up their children and receive property after divorce. In addition, the government also issued special policies on women based on their reproductive function. For example, priority is given to women not to take on heavy and hazardous work such as working in the mines, on high scaffolding or contacting hazardous chemicals. Female government employees are entitled to a four-month maternity leave. Vietnam is one of the countries to ratify the Convention on the Elimination of any Discrimination against Women (CEDAW) very early for two major reasons: the articles of the Convention are in conformity with Vietnam's policies; and Vietnam is able to implement this Convention.[5]

Although gender equality was already included in government policies and implemented in some spheres of social life and social movements, so far no profound and serious studies were conducted,

---

[5] The Convention was issued on 18 Dec., 1979 and came into force on 3 September, 1981. It was verified by Vietnam on 19 March, 1982.

particularly in social sciences and the humanities. This gap was bridged only after gender science was introduced into Vietnam with its pioneer as the Centre for Women Studies established in 1987.[6] The centre greatly supported the women's emancipation movement in Vietnam with their studies. However, it does not mean that the road to equality of the Vietnamese women is shorter and simpler than those in other countries.

We would like to quote here the 1999 report of the Ministry of Science, Technology and Environment at the workshop reviewing 20 years of implementing the Convention on Elimination of any Discrimination Against Women (CEDAW) in Vietnam held by the National Committee for the Advancement of Women which says that as a CEDAW participating country, the Vietnamese Party and State have issued many resolutions, policies, and decisions and many specific measures to ensure full development and progress of the Vietnamese women, so that they will be able to realize and enjoy fundamental human rights and freedom on the basis of quality between men and women. However, awareness and reality on gender and actual equality between men and women remain an urgent issue.[7]

Women in Vietnam's Economic Renewal Process

Labour and Employment

As early as in the mid-1950s, on the basis of government policies, the attack on the "thinking highly of men and belittling women" has been strongly launched in all spheres from the family to the society in northern Vietnam, causing changes to economic structure, concepts of morality, customs and habits and particularly changes to the women's status and position in comparison with the feudal times. Nowadays women are able to participate in almost all productive and servicing activities. They are economically independent and their status in the family has improved. During the war, Vietnamese women have played an important role in production and serving the war.

The economic renewal policy (Doi Moi) has removed many ties in production and business. In addition to the state-owned and col-

---

[6] It is now called the Center for Family and Women Studies—Author.
[7] Ministry of Science, Technology and Environment Report—1999.

lective economic sectors (the main economic sectors of the past), the government has assisted the private sector and joint-ventures with foreign countries to develop. It not only leads to competition among companies and enterprises, generating a gap between the rich and the poor, but it also creates a change in labour division and labour forces.

Currently, women play an important role in the national work-force. Women now make up 52 per cent of the total 38 million in the national workforce. At present, women account for 70 per cent in the textile and garment industry, 60 per cent in the food pro-cessing industry, 60 per cent of the workforce in the health sector and 70 per cent in general education. Women account for 53.3 per cent of the workforce in agriculture with nearly 10 million farmer households and 27 million farmhands, and 45 per cent of the labour force in industry.[8]

Women are very capable in production and business. Hundreds of state-owned, private and joint-venture companies are successfully run by females directors and general directors. Under their man-agement, these companies have made profits and gain credit in Vietnamese and international markets. Many women have received high awards from the government and foreign countries. In many branches of activities, women employees have been acknowledged as being highly skilled and professional.

However, one of the great disadvantages facing women in the market economy is employment. The unemployment rate in the whole country is now 7.4 per cent, women account for half of this figure. It is difficult for women to compete with men who are stronger, have more access to education and are free from human reproduc-tion. Among the new graduates, men have more job opportunities than women. Unemployment forces women to accept heavy, low-paid and unstable jobs. For example, in order to get a job, many women in the central provinces have to sign contracts with foreign owners which are disadvantageous to them. They have to commit not to get married or bear a child in five years, not to go home during the holidays, and work extra time without payment. Meanwhile, some female workers in state-owned enterprises opted for a four-month maternity leave instead of six months so that they can go

---

[8] Statistics released by the Ministry of Labour, Invalids and Social Affairs.

back to work earlier and receive higher payment from the piece-work system. Unemployment also forces quite a few rural women to migrate to the cities, to participate in the non-formal economic sector and lead a disadvantaged and poor life, accepting any job to earn their living even as a prostitute or be involved in drug trafficking.

Vietnam is an agricultural country. More than 80 per cent of its population live in rural areas. Since the introduction of the Doi Moi (renewal policy), Vietnam's agriculture has made great progress. In the mid-1980s, the country was still threatened by hunger. But since mid-1990s, Vietnam has become one of the largest rice exporters in the world. However, in the market economy, the gap in living standards and income between rural and urban areas caused mainly by the shortage of farm land and cheap prices of farm produce has led to many complicated socio-economic issues, such as migration from rural to urban areas, poverty, rapid growth in pollution, and imbalance in healthcare and education. So sustainable rural development is one of Vietnam's important strategies.

Land use right is very important in agriculture. At the start of the Doi Moi, farm land was allocated equally by number of household members and labourers (within villages and communes). However, this situation has changed much now. In the past, it was completely forbidden to buy and sell or transfer land use right. Now these moves occur in many localities after a short period of polarization between the rich and the poor. Many poor farmers, after a short period of time after the allocation of farm land, had to sell it away and then work for hire for richer households. In cases where both spouses are farmers, the woman has no right to have her name written on the land use right certificate. However, in Vietnam it does not mean that the women have no right in production and doing business on the piece of land allocated to their household. Even when the husband wants to sell the right to use that piece of land, he has to discuss with his wife.

Changes in the form of land use right also lead to changes in labour division. In the past labour division was done in the agricultural cooperatives. Now it is done in the households and household economies. In many localities, particularly poor localities, the breadwinners of the households have to migrate to the cities or other areas to earn their living. In these households, women have to bear the brunt of all farm work. They have to do the ploughing, harrowing, sowing, transplanting, weeding, fertilizing, spraying of pesticide and harvesting. It means that when the men are working far from home, the women have to do their share of the work. Moreover, these women have to work for hire for other households in rice transplanting and harvesting.

Besides working in the field, many women are also involved in other occupations such as producing noodles and small trade. They work very hard in the hope of earning enough for their family, build a small house and send their children to school. Meanwhile, they still have to take care of housework. This situation leads to the fact that female farmers are now very active and dynamic but their labour intensity and long working hours reach an alarming level. Obviously, female farmers play an important role in the production of rice and other food, but compared to male farmers, they are the most disadvantaged in terms of enjoying social policies and welfare.

In the development process, the number of women having positions in political and economic leadership has increased in both quality and quantity. Although the proportion of female deputies to the National Assembly has decreased in the previous terms: 32 per cent (1971–1976); 27 per cent (1975–1981); 22 per cent (1981 1987); 18 per cent (1987–1992); 18.5 per cent (1992–1997), it increased to 26.22 per cent (118/450) in the 1997–2002 term. The calibre of the women representation has obviously increased. The proportion of female representatives to the People's Councils at all levels was 12 per cent (1989–1992) and is currently more than 22 per cent. Vietnam ranks second in the Asia-Pacific and ninth among 135 countries in the World Inter-Parliamentary Alliance vis-à-vis the proportion of women in the National Assembly.[9]

Science is one of the key aspects in the national economy and it is considered a hard job for women. In the feudal and colonial times, there were hardly any women participating in scientific activities. Over the last 50 years, the number of female intellectuals in all science sectors of Vietnam has increased in both quantity and calibre. However, if we compare the proportion of women in the national population (51 per cent) and the proportion of women in the labour force (52 per cent) and their actual capacity, we can say that the number of female intellectuals remains very modest. Currently, women account for 37 per cent of the total number of college and university

---

[9] Data released by the National Committee for the Advancement of Women.

graduates out of which 132 of them are professors and assistant professors (or 6.7 per cent) and 1,635 have received Ph.D. (or 19.9 per cent).[10]

Over the last few years, many female scientists have brought into play their initiative, combining scientific research with practical service in people's lives. However, the number of female scientists participating in state management at all levels remains low and the higher the level is, the lower the women participation. Almost no women participated in the leadership of ministries on science and very few participated in the leadership at institute level. There are no women in the board of directors as well as female directors in the institutes under the National Centre for Natural Sciences and Technologies and the National Centre for Social Sciences and Humanities, the two biggest science centres in Vietnam. In the ten research institutes under the Ministry of Health, there are only one director and three deputy directors. In the six research institutes under the Ministry of Construction, there is only one deputy director. Even in the education and training sector where women account for more than 70 per cent, they only make up 29 per cent of the total number of directors and deputy directors of provincial and district departments and 19 per cent of the total number of directors and deputy directors of the ministry's departments.[11]

Currently the number of women having degrees and ranks has reached 18,000 but the number of directors of science and technology projects at all levels, particularly at state level, is very low. During the 1991–1995 period, Vietnam had more than 500 projects in 31 key national science and technology programmes. However, there were only 21 female project directors (less than 4 per cent). During the 1996–2000 period, although the number of female project conductors increased to 10 per cent, the figure is still very low and does not correctly reflect their capacity and contributions to important national scientific and technological tasks.[12] It is very common now that most researchers participating in national projects are women (sometimes they play the key role in research work) but project directors are men. In many cases, it is a paradox that the capacity and knowledge of the participating female researchers are higher than their male managers.

---

[10] Ministry of Science, Technology and Environment, Report—1999.
[11] Ministry of Science, Technology and Environment, Report—1999.
[12] Magazine, *Women of Vietnam*, issued on 25 Oct. 1999.

Family and Culture

Currently in many countries, particularly those in the Orient, there remains the view that it is a "function", an "inclination", a "sacrifice, self-denial" and "feminity" of women to serve unconditionally their own husbands and children in particular and men in general. This viewpoint also stems from patriarchal ideology. It has mingled in social lives for centuries now in the name of a social "morality" and traditional customs and habits. It has become a strong iron curtain covering the patriarchal ideology when gender inequality is likely to be exposed. To a different extent, this viewpoint has assigned women with major heavy tasks in human reproduction to fulfil all productive activities as men. Meanwhile their enjoyment and entertainment are considered secondary, or even not taken into account.

Statistics show that on average, a woman works from 16 to 19 hours a day while a man only works from 8 to 10 hours.[13] Women are thus very busy and have little time to rest, study and have entertainment. As they work too hard, many women's health is affected and even worse, they have not spent time with their family which lead to their husbands getting involved in adultery or with prostitutes which then result in broken families.

The Women of Vietnam magazine in its 25 October 1999 issue carried a story entitled "Women in my home village—the hidden lives" written by Duong Phuong Toai. The story goes:

> . . . Women in my homeland of Yen Hung, Quang Ninh province still live a disadvantaged life as stunted flowers for lack of sunlight. In many villages, hard work and disadvantages seem to haunt many of them for life. Under-aged marriage, no birth spacing, lack of education, low knowledge strive many communes, particularly those in remote and out-of-the way areas. There is a woman aged about 39 or 40 but has as many as 9 children. As she gave birth to only daughters, she is not allowed to stop. Even some girls can not sign their names on their marriage certificate as they live on fishing boats all year round and their parents forgot about their education.

Feudal practices return. While the husband is having a bottle of alcohol and food, his wife and children are cooking to serve him and they will eat later. If he is not pleased, he immediately beats her. There exist two types of diets in such a small family. Ms Nguyen

---

[13] National Committee for the Advancement of Women—UNDP Gender Statistics in Vietnam, November 1999.

Thi B., over the last twelve years, has often gone to the deep for-
est to fell bamboo and wood illegally, to sell them in the market for
money. But she still cannot earn enough to pay for her husband's
alcohol consumption.

During a recent rice transplanting season, I had a chance to pass
through a field in Phong Hai commune. I saw some women working very hard to transplant rice in the blazing sun. I was curious to
remove the conical hat covering their meals. Under a layer of banana
and lotus leaves is white rice (very lucky that the rice is no longer
mixed with cassava roots or sweet potatoes as in the past), some
boiled vegetables and some spiced salt they bought in the market.
It is the lunch of those women who "sell their back to the heaven
and place the seeds of hope in the earth"! Some women after transplanting rice on their own land go hastily to work for hire in other
fields. They work from morning till evening to earn about VND
15,000 a day (a little more than US$1). Then the following morn-
ing, she has to spend one-third of that sum to buy alcohol for her
"fat horn and large neck" husband.

On a ferry across Chanh River, I met a woman wearing a blue
shirt which looked new but wrinkled, surely it had been put in the
box for a long time. Her new shirt cannot hide her emaciation. She
carried a three-year-old child to the hospital, followed by a girl of
about ten years wearing shabby clothes. The small child had been
having diarrhoea for some days. Her family was poor and had no
support. The woman took the two children to the hospital herself.
The motorbike taxi driver took them to Lien Vi, 15 km away. He
felt so much pity for her, he did not ask for payment. But where
was her husband, the father of her two children? He was busy gambling and drinking. She said, on the verge of tears, "This time after
my child recovers; I might have to sell early rice to have money to
pay the debt . . ."

Poverty is closely linked with low education. The lower women's
education is, the more they try to avoid taking part in socio-cultural
activities. They have a greater inferiority complex and are wrapped
up in working only.[14] Conversely, if they do not participate in socio-
cultural activities, they have no chance of improving their cultural
standards. It creates a vicious circle which ties women to the fam-

---

[14] Ministry of Science, Technology and Environment, Report—1999.

ily chain for their whole life. In a study on domestic violence, I consider that women working too hard are a type of "*invisible domestic violence*". Nowadays while many husbands love their wives and share with them the family burden, quite a few remain indifferent or leave all the family responsibilities to their wives. In these families, the wife has to look after everything, including earning a living and managing housework such as shopping, cooking, washing clothes, taking care of old members of the family, and bringing up and educating their children. While the wife is busy from dawn to dusk, the "king" of the family is idle and carefree, loitering about karaoke rooms or drinking to "relieve his sorrow".

Asked about domestic violence, Mrs. Nguyen Thi T., 58 from Dong village, Co Nhue commune says that her husband is very good-natured. She affirms that she has never been beaten by her husband, they live in harmony and she has the right to decide important matters of her family. However, she always complains that an invisible pressure has forced her to work to the utmost, no joy, no rest and no entertainment for her whole life. Mrs. T told us: "His mother, then his father died when he was 13. He is illiterate, having no skill no job. But my family is happy because we never quarrel, one speaks and the other listens, we can work together and easily let pass other's mistakes. Anything we can tolerate we tolerated. I think we are happier than others because no one in my family involve in drinking, gambling and using drugs" (Case 6—indepth interview).

Such a viewpoint on family happiness makes Ms. T. sacrifices her whole life for a husband who is good for nothing.[15]

Another case, also in Co Nhue is that of Ms. Cao Thi T. village 9:

"Q: You have to work to earn your family's living. How do you think about it?

A: I think it is my responsibility. As a wife, I have to work to feed my family and bring up my children. In general, a woman is required to handle family affairs.
Q: What does a husband do?
A: A husband should handle big affairs, love his wife and children, and is not indulged in plays and drugs.
Q: So what is "big affairs" of a husband?
A: Keeping himself good to make an example for his children.

---

[15] Study conducted by Dr Le Thi Quy and her project staff on "Domestic Violence" in Co Nhue commune, on the outskirts of Hanoi, in 1999.

Q: That is all?
A: Yes, that is all. However, not many husbands can do so".

Cao Thi T. from Village 9, Co Nhue commune (Case 5—indepth interview)[16]

A major cause greatly affecting labour division without taking into account gender sensitivity at present is the *lack of knowledge about gender* of both women and men. People of both sexes still consider it is the women's responsibility and function to support a family. Domestic labour division in general reflects and is affected by social labour division. In a society where labour division between men and women is rather equal, then domestic labour division is also the same. Meanwhile in a society of "thinking highly of men and belittling women" where men often have well-paid jobs, they will become the master and have final authority in their families and control all members.

Many families now pay more attention to economic activities while neglecting their moral responsibilities and the need to ensure that their children receive education. The role of individuals is heightened while the need to respond to the community or to exist in terms of a community is reduced. Money has shown its positive and negative sides not only in the society but also in the family. Over the last few years, studies on gender issues have pointed out a big contradiction in labour division between men and women in the family. They found out the reasons for these inequalities and recommended solutions to them. Some scientists have proposed the building of a new type of family where all members are ensured an equal life both physically and morally.

In population development, there remain many problems relating to the right to reproduction and women's reproductive health. That rural women give birth to too many children is closely related to the lower socio-economic development in these localities. Women are under pressure of old customs and habits to wish to have many children, and the preference for male children to continue their legacy. So women have to give birth to many children without family planning when they are both materially and morally poor. Rural

---

[16] Study conducted by Dr Le Thi Quy and her project staff on "Domestic Violence" in Co Nhue commune, on the outskirts of Hanoi, in 1999.

women have little chances to access health service due to a lack of medical doctors and nurses or medical fees are so high that they cannot afford them. Currently, women are still the main target of family planning programmes with or without men sharing responsibilities. There are a rather large number of women facing pregnancy and delivery complications and children suffering from malnutrition and other diseases.

Another noteworthy issue is that in some rural and mountainous areas, men and women still have unequal access to information and education. Women, particularly female children, are the most disadvantaged. They have less access to education because of economic reasons. In a poor family when the parents cannot afford sending all their children to school, very often girls have to give up the chance to study to their brothers. They stay home to take care of housework, work to earn their living or get married very early. Social reasons are also found. Outdated views and practices have returned in some rural areas, maintaining that girls do not need much education—it is enough for them to know how to read and write and if they want to learn, they should learn farm work, cooking and taking care of their small brothers and sisters. When the girls grow up, they will work in the field, do housework and take care of the family. It is not necessary to invest in girls as they will soon become "daughters of others". In some other cases, girls (even boys) cannot attend school as the schools are too far from their houses (10 km away or more). They include children in remote rural and mountainous areas or fishing villages.

Women and Social Issues

Many complicated social issues have appeared in the current globalization process and women are often the victims. They are victims of many social evils, such as violence including social and domestic violence, rape, sex coercion and exploitation, and trafficking in women and children for labour and sex exploitation.

According to incomplete statistics provided by 18 provinces and cities, over the last 8 years, 11,630 cases of domestic violence have occurred in their localities which required the intervention of the authorities and law-keeping forces to settle the problem. Among them 515 cases occurred in Ba Ria-Vung Tau; 819 cases in Khanh Hoa; 1,123 cases in Thai Binh; 1,484 cases in Ha Tay, 967 cases in Ninh

Thuan and 2,002 cases in Kien Giang.[17] Most of these cases involved husbands beating wives or adults maltreating children. The remaining cases involved the maltreatment of old parents by grown-up children, and between brothers and sisters; parents-in-law and daughters-in-law. However, these figures are only the tip of the iceberg. They are based on administrative reports and the cases which were already seen and settled by the public. Meanwhile domestic violence is sensitive by nature and often kept in the dark as many victims do not denounce it for various reasons.

While the number of domestic violence is on the increase, the scope of violence is also widened. Domestic violence has even appeared among highly educated and intellectual families who are working in social and humanitarian fields. It is a major worry for the women's emancipation movement.

Early in the 1990s, a special concern for the trafficking of women and children was highlighted. It is estimated that about tens of thousands of Vietnamese women and children have been smuggled or taken to foreign countries through two major roads, namely the border with China in the north and the border with Cambodia in the southwest. As an extension to this, marriage intermediary services, which are very popular in the south, have become a means by which the trafficked women are often forced to be wives of men in China and some other countries, or become prostitutes in Cambodia, China, Thailand and Hong Kong.

Trafficking in women in Vietnam is closely linked with migration, poverty and sex imbalance in Vietnam and China. It is a complicated phenomenon which has been strongly condemned in Vietnam.

Women Empowerment in Sustainable Development

Women empowerment is one of Vietnam's development strategies. This strategy is included in state laws and government policies and has been gradually implemented.

As mentioned earlier, women empowerment in Vietnam has already appeared in major campaigns and movements, and government policies. Now reality has proved that a combination of efforts between people and state and between bottom-up and top-down groups will be more efficient. For example, a policy should be made on the

---

[17] Data provided by the People's Supreme Court, in 1999.

basis of the people's needs and implemented using people's initiative and creativity to meet its final objective of serving the people. A policy on women empowerment is no exception. To do this, first of all, researchers, policy makers and social activists should investigate to comprehend women's capacity, the use of that capacity in society and women's needs of empowerment. In this respect, we are required to answer the following questions: What is women empowerment? Why does it need to empower women? Which groups of women should be given priority to be empowered? Who will help with women empowerment, the state, the society or the women themselves? How can we promote women empowerment?

First of all, it is awareness. Changes in social awareness on some gender and women-related issues will have a direct impact on guiding activities to change the situation. In this respect, communication on equality between women and men and gender issues could be disseminated through the mass media (including the radio, TV, newspaper and magazines). Besides, many training courses on gender have been held from national to grassroots levels for different target groups including intellectuals, staff of women's union, policy makers, managers, social activists and the women themselves. Many field researches relating to gender issues have been developed and contributed initial results to improving social awareness.

In the Vietnamese society, farmers have an unstable life because they run short of farm land, farm produce are cheaper than industrial goods, and production depends completely on nature. Therefore, farmers' income is the lowest in the society. Poverty has led to poor living conditions and less access to education, cultural activities and information and knowledge in general and information and knowledge about markets in particular. Female farmers are in a weaker position than their male counterparts, so they are the most disadvantaged social group when it concerns improving their lives and empowerment. Like male farmers, female farmers have to work very hard to earn their living. Besides, they also have to shoulder the bulk of the housework and suffer the most when backward feudal practices return. In many localities, women seem to be robbed of their basic human rights: many women have to accept illegal polygamy, underaged marriage, giving birth to many children, discrimination in participation in village affairs, total dependence on husband and the in-law family and domestic violence. The wish to have a better life and their sufferng nature which encourage them to work hard cause them to deny themselves for their husband and children and to refuse to take part in those activities which they think do not relate to or benefit their family, including socio-cultural activities for empowerment. However, when they do not take part in social activities and have no access to information, they cannot improve their knowledge about human rights and their rights and responsibilities. So it is not an easy task to attract this group to activities relating to women empowerment.

Over the last few years, in addition to macro activities, women empowerment, particularly that of female farmers, has been included in specific projects which meet actual needs and the needs of gender strategy. These specific projects place men and women on equal terms in terms of needs, capacity, contribution and enjoyment with attention paid to characteristics of each sex and to women who are most vulnerable and the most disadvantaged social group. Experience shows that this has brought about effective results which help improve not only the lives of the beneficiaries but also their activeness and capacity, particularly women. A number of projects have been evaluated as successful, including projects on poverty reduction, development of household economies, rural clean water, loans for poor rural women, reproductive health, literacy, and trafficking in women.

The research project on trafficking in women conducted by the Youth Research Institute, for example, works in co-ordination with the Center for Family while Women's Studies is aimed at helping women reintegrate into the community.[18] The projects formulated, according to some women's groups, have changed their lives. The groups operate on a voluntary basis and work on the principles of building self-confidence and self-reliance. Women involved in the programmes would have access to loans in the "Gramin Bank" formula; the group will act as their guarantor. The loans were small but they discussed and helped each other to effectively use them in their economic activities. After a short period of time, their income and living standards improved. More importantly was that they became aware of their responsibilities and interest in society. Gradually, their inferiority complex disappeared and they reintegrated into the community. As a result, their domestic and social status improved and they were more empowered to help themselves. Group activi-

---

[18] Youth Research Institute: Project on Trafficking in Women in the Mekong Delta (1996–1998).

ties have helped local authorities change their outlook, thinking and way of working to solve this issue.

Another form of activity to empower women is the pilot campaign for women in the elections to the People's Councils at all levels in year 2000. The National Committee for the Advancement of Women has coordinated with the Vietnam Women's Union to generate opportunities for female candidates to meet and talk with voters. They have organized training courses for female candidates and advocated people to vote for women. These activities have obtained initial results: the number and calibre of the women who won the elections were better than before. This model will be studied and replicated in the coming period.

Studies and research have dug up specific issues of social life and made new recommendations relating to women and gender issues. These have laid the foundation for policy and law makers to formulate policies and laws closer to reality. By doing so, scientists have contributed to solving many problems relating to gender equality. Gender theories have been taught in universities in order to provide students with basic knowledge and research methodologies so that they can join this new field of research. However there are just initial activities. Gender inequality remains serious in all social spheres. Challenges and difficulties stem mainly from the viewpoint "thinking highly of men and belittling women" of both men and women, poverty and insufficient government policies.

Some Comments

The globalization process has a profound impact on the people's lives in general and women in particular. While globalization has generated new development opportunities for women, it has also brought them new challenges as well as disadvantages.

Some Advantages

• Like the men, women have enjoyed the fruits of scientific and economic development, including information technology. Scientific development has helped improve the people's physical and social lives and reduced the burden of housework and other manual work. Women now have more time to study, take part in social activities and spend more quality time with their family.

- Domestic and international co-operation has provided women a chance to improve their knowledge in all fields, helping them consolidate their status in the family and society and facilitating the struggle for gender equality.

Some Disadvantages

- Rapid technological changes and fierce competition have caused regular changes to the labour market. These have a negative impact on poor countries and women. Men and women have different job opportunities because women are not physically as strong as men, women have the human reproductive function and in many countries with backward thinking, women still have to shoulder the bulk of the housework. Women are more likely to lose their jobs than men or to undertake low pay, high risk and heavy work. Currently, inequality remains in women and men's wages in many countries. Besides, women remain the major force in unpaid jobs, namely housework. So we can see that at present, women's work time and intensity of work are too high and contradictory to their payment.
- Women are victims of some regional or global social evils, such as drugs, rape, sex exploitation, trafficking in women and children, and violence including domestic and social violence.

It is a very difficult and long-term struggle to overcome gender inequality. Gender equality can only be obtained in a fair and civilized society with sustainable economic, cultural, educational and human resources development. This is the target of the Vietnamese society.

RELIGIONS AND OTHER WORLD VALUES

FROM THEOLOGY TO ANTHROPOLOGY OF RELIGIONS: HOW TO ANALYSE THE ROLE OF RELIGIOUS TRADITION IN A GLOBALIZED WORLD?

Jan Hjärpe
University of Lund, Sweden

There are three ideas that we find rather often as more or less subconscious premises in the discussions on the role of religions—especially Islam—in the contemporary conflict ridden world. They are occurring perhaps less in scholarly and scientific analyses as they are so evidently contrary to empirical facts, but they are very much to be found in popular debate, in political discourses, and in media reporting.

The first one is the concept that a religion or a religious tradition is a *constant* entity, unchanging, recognizable during the centuries, at least essentially the same always. The second is that religious belonging is a *determinant* factor, decisive for the choice of behaviour of the individual. The third that what religious *leaders* and functionaries say is representative of people's beliefs, norms and behaviours.

All three are contradicted by empirical evidence. Religions and norm systems are not permanent entities, they change—the selection from tradition becomes different due to changing situations. We find continuing reinterpretations, changes in what is regarded as the focus. The actual societal functions of rituals, narratives, jargons, change over time, and sometimes in a very short period of time. And, above all, people do not do as religious functionaries and leaders say. Leaders preach, make their pronouncements, write books and pamphlets, just because people *do not* behave as they are supposed to do.

Italy and Spain are the two countries in Western Europe with the lowest birth rate. Most Italians and Spaniards are Catholics. The Catholic church (i.e. the functionaries, the hierarchy) proclaims contraception as religiously illegitimate. Nevertheless, nativity is low. Catholics, in Spain and Italy, evidently do not apply the norms of the church. They use contraceptives. Still, they are Catholics, but the fact is that they choose other things from the Catholic tradition than the sexual norm code of the church.

The *verbalized* norm, which we can find in official texts, in the doctrines, in the pronouncements of religious functionaries, and sometimes in the expressions of common people too, has evidently very little (if anything) to do with the *real* norm, i.e. what people actually do. This means that (holy/official) texts and formulated doctrines are of low *prognostic* value. They cannot be taken as *descriptions* of people's actual religiosity and religious praxis, and choice of behaviour.

We can see that much of what people actually make use of from the religious tradition can be characterized as *entertainment*. In all the world's great religious traditions we can find exciting narratives, engaging eloquence, beautiful music, art and architecture, perfumes and incense, festivals and solemnities, attractive rituals, game and drama, celebrations in family life—in short: entertainment. This is very much in the centre of actual religious praxis. New media have today made this kind of experiences more available. The individual is no more dependent on a local religious community and its leadership in order to get them. One can enjoy them independently of a formal belonging to a specific religious community. I can go to a shop and buy me a CD with *qawwali* music and enjoy it at home. I do not need to be a Muslim and a Sufi to have access to the religious songs of Nusrat Fateh Ali Khan.[1] I do not need to be a Christian in order to appreciate *The Messaiah* by Handel. Religion as entertainment and emotional experience is neither bound to individual nor collective communitarian belonging.—It is sometimes rather a part of a global culture; a youth culture and its World music.[2]

What we can see today is a globalization of the immense store of material for emotional experiences from the religions, rather than any "clash of civilizations". The material is available through parabolas, cassettes, videos, and the Web. Media development has diminished the role of conventional religious leaders and hierarchies and

---

[1] Qawwali is a common traditional form of the Islamic Sufi *samāʿ* in the Indian subcontinent and in central Asia. Nusrat Fatih represents an interesting synthesis of jazz and qawwali. We find his music in Martin Scorsese's film, *Last Temptation of Christ*. He has cooperated with Jan Garbarek, Bruce Springsteen, and Eddie Vedder. Joan Osborne has taken singing lessons from him. His voice can be heard in the film *Natural Born Killers*, and he has gained world status through some of his songs. His concerts drew huge audiences in Europe. His connection with Peter Gabriel's WOMAD has been of special importance. Cf. Rick Glanvill's presentation in the booklet to the CD *Rapture Nusrat Fateh Ali Khan* (NSCD 013; 1997).

[2] Cf. Jan Hjärpe (2003), "Entangled Music", in *Orientalia Suecana*, Vols. LI–LII (2002–2003), Uppsala, pp. 189–97.

their authority in other ways too. We have access to a huge multitude of religious opinions, debates, arguments—and all the texts—on the Web. For the interested one, there is only need to pick and choose.

Even the *palliative* function of religion is today less dependent on religious specificity. This is important, as we well know that the "consumption" of religion increases in trying situations, death, illness, sorrow, accidents, catastrophes, wars, tribulations and afflictions.

One example—among several possible ones—is the spontaneous cult community that developed after a disastrous conflagration during a disco session in a building in Gothenburg, Sweden, in 1998, where more than 60 young people, of various religious and ethnic background, were killed.[3] A spontaneous ritualization of the expressions of sorrow and despair took place: candles were lit in the street outside the building, flowers were placed there, as well as teddy bears and toy animals. Young people wrote letters to the dead comrades and glued them to the walls and fences, likewise pictures of them. People assembled in a church in the neighbourhood, finding affinity and communion in sorrow, in the common experience. The classmates and friends participated in the funerals of the deceased comrades, regardless of religious affiliation (many were Muslims). This spontaneous community still functions five years after the catastrophe. People meet, and the graves in the cemetary have been connected with each other with chains—as far as I know a new ritualized expression for community/communion.

We can compare this example with another incident, the funeral of a young woman of Kurdish descent, Fadima Sahindal, murdered, in Uppsala in Sweden, "for honour's sake" by her father. The event made a huge impression on society and provoked an intensive and ongoing debate in both Swedish media and in the political establishment. To distinguish from the case just mentioned, this funeral got, due to the attention it aroused, a very official character. The ritual was performed in the national cathedral of Uppsala, with its dean officiating, in the presence of representatives of the government and the royal family. But the deceased was not Christian, and the rituals were "religious" in character but neither "Christian" nor "Muslim", they were without specific confessional doctrinal traits.

---

[3] A report on the event was compiled by the Board for Psychological Defence: *Göteborgsbranden 1998, SPF rapport 179* (Stockholm 2000).

And included were more or less spontaneous, *ad hoc* features that we recognize from the global youth culture.[4]

These two examples are not in any way unique; we have to take into account that the formal religious affiliation today has not the same role and importance as the case mentioned earlier in the function of religions. The change is most visible on the individual level. People neither behave nor believe as the doctrines say—although they "consume" religious palliatives and entertainment. Thus, we cannot conclude how the individual experiences and interprets his/her existence, or how he/she will act, from the normative texts, official pronouncements or theological systems a group is supposed to embrace.

There is a tendency to exaggerate the role of formal religious affiliation. For most people this is not the most important belonging. The individual has simultaneously many "identities" or belongings (family, clan, tribe, ethnicity, nationality, professional community, interest groups, political idelogy or party and so forth). A characteristic for modernity is that these "identities" are differentiated, less intertwined with each other than was the case before. Which one of all these belongings is the most important one in a given situation? When will all these loyalties change their order in the hierarchy of norm systems that are simultaneously existing in the cognitive universe of the individual human being?

We meet the assumption that a religion, confession or religious tradition is characterized by certain traits (or doctrines) that are essential for it, traits or doctrines which are constitutive and central. But this assumption is a rather dubious one. The assertion is either stipulative or a generalization of that which is common in a number of instances. But the idea of "essence" blurs the borderline between a *description* and a *normative* statement.

Formulated creeds say nothing as to personal religious experiences, religious emotions, or individual behaviour. Creeds, doctrines, theological systems, have other functions, functions that are possible to analyse in sociological terms rather than ideological. Creeds are tools of power: they are the words that you have to pronounce (or at least not to deny) in order to be counted as a member of the community. Observances (clothing, dietary rules, specific behaviours) have very much the same social function, as markers of group belonging.

---

[4] The act was recorded and sent to the national TV channels.

But all communities/groups, religious or profane, have such markers of belonging in the form of words (jargon, creeds, vocabulary), clothing, consumption, ritual behaviour, be it a pentecostal congregation, the Muslim Brethren, Hell's Angels, Rotary or a football club.

The historian of religions can easily point out that what has been seen as central or essential in a religion (or religious tradition) can vary and fluctuate considerably as to time or place. What does a radical pentecostal in the north of Sweden, a liberation theologian in Latin America, a Catholic mafioso in Sicily, president George W. Bush and Mother Theresa have in common? All are "Christian". Some words are in common, some narratives. But have these words any common cognitive significance or similar emotional effect at all? Do they lead to similar behaviour? We can possibly maintain that they all in one way or other relate to these words/narratives, but the prognostic value of that assertion is very limited.

Now we will have to ask the question *why*. Why do we meet the tendency to *essentialism* when we discuss the role of religion? Why do we so often encounter the idea that religious belonging is determinant, that religion is a constant, the idea that religious functionaries are representative for their communities, and likewise the idea that religious behaviour, rituals, norms are specific for each religion, when the empirical fact is that religious functions are changing, and that they are syncretistic in character?

My thesis is that it has to do with the fact that religious studies and research have for a long time been related to theological study, not only in Sweden or in Europe, but in general, all over the world. This means that certain premises and preferences connected with theological formulations of the problematic in regard to how religions function have been taken more or less for granted. Even when the studies have been within a framework of humanities and social and political studies of religion, some of the structuring, the categorizations and questions asked, can be seen as "survivals" from the structuring and premises of theological study.

A look into how the actual condition and circumstances have changed during 20th-century Sweden can give us a rather interesting example. In the beginning of the 20th century, the purpose of religous studies at the Swedish universities was *production of ideology* for the society. State and church constituted one and the same entity. Christianity was supposed to represent the foundation of the norms of a citizen in society. The system of education in the country and the church of the state was under the same state administration (the Ecclesiastical Department). The head of the state was simultaneously the head of the national Church. Thus, the theological faculties of the state universities (two at that time) were supposed to produce ideology relevant for the state and its citizens. For that reason, they were theological, not institutions for *"Religionswissenschaft"*, i.e. secular religious studies. There were differences and conflicts as to the *content* of the ideology, "old" or "new" theology, fundamentalist-Biblicist standpoints against historical-critical "liberal" theology. But as to the very function, there was a consensus: the need for norms for the citizens, simultaneously being the doctrine and preaching of the national Church. The theological faculties were regularily asked to give their opinions on questions of morality, norms and legislation.

However, with the 20th century came changes in society. The state sector was secularized. The industrial development, constituting a profane sector with another ideological basis, became the economical foundaton of society. Popular mandate—democracy, not religion—became the legitimation of political power. Religious education in schools changed from training in Lutheran Christianity to information about religions and worldviews. Lutheran Christianity ceased to be the official national marker of the State.

Within this a problematic within the epistemological conditions for scholarly and scientific work presented itself : could production of ideology (= theology) be regarded as scientific? There came a demand for empirism, an empirical basis for the studies, as well as research about religion(s). The value nihilism of the very influencial Uppsala school of philosophy[5] denied the possibility of an objective validity of moral norms. The alternative to theology was then "Religionswissenschaft", the secular and empirical study of the history of religions and of religious phenomena.

The faculties of theology continued nevertheless to regard themselves (in a way) as producers of ideology, or at least as producers of what could be used normatively, but now to a successively smaller section of society, namely the Christian churches and denominations, not for the society/the State. One became "oecumenical", multi-confessional, but still with a purpose to produce Christian theology, or the basis

---

[5] This school was connected especially with the leading teachers of philosophy at Uppsala University, Axel Hägerström, Magnus Phalén, and later on with Ingmar Hedenius.

for such a theology, "creative theology", at least to a certain degree. This was evidently a process of their marginalization in society. The demand for empirical facts resulted (especially after a conflict in the 1950s)[6] in a concentration on history, historical studies of churches, denominations, doctrines and texts. The strictly observed historical source criticism and historical methods gave the necessary scientific legitimacy. But this concentration on historical investigation meant that the consumers, the churches and denominations did not get the ideological studies they wanted.

It was possible to meet that demand by applying a more *essentialistic* approach to the study of religions. In Sweden, but also internationally, the role of the theologian-philosopher Anders Nygren was important in this respect.[7] He maintained that specific religions and confessions were characterized and constituted by certain "*Leitmotifs*", which could be studied objectively, detected, and discerned scientifically in the research on the history of ideas. By this "motif research" approach, it was possible to conduct theological research on a theoretical foundation that made it possible to use the results normatively in the preaching of the churches. It was so to speak possible to see (quasi-) objectively what was "authentic" and what could be seen as "deviations" in the history of the specific religion or denomination.

For the society outside the churches and the believers, the results were of very limited interest. But the very fact that churches and denominations were regarded as the main consumers of religious studies had consequences for the *structuring* of the studies at the faculties and institutions, not only in Sweden and Europe, but globally, in the university systems, with a considerable influence on the idea of "religion" in the general debate. It is important to try to detect that influence and its premises.

The most common structuring of the theological study can perhaps be called "the Schleiermacher model".[8] When it was developed in the 19th century, it had at that time the self evident premise that

---

[6] The so-called Hedenius' debate, cf. Johan Lundberg, *När ateismen erövrade Sverige: Ingemar Hedenius och debatten kring tro och vetande* (2002), Nya Doxa: Nora.

[7] His approach was to find certain "Leitmotifs" as constitutional for specific religions and confessions. This is exemplified in his most famous book, *Den kristna kärlekstanken genom tiderna: Eros och agape*, published in many editions and translated into many languages, including Chinese. Cf. his *Filosofi och motivforskning* (Stockholm 1940).

[8] So named after the very influential theologian F. Schleiermacher 1768–1834.

the goal for education was to give the student theoretically well-founded tools for his future task as a preacher and religious counsellor, priest or pastor. Even if the studies were confessionally free and with a theoretically irreproachable scientific methodology, churches and denominations were considered to be the users. The model can be found, to this very day, in theological faculties and Divinity schools all over the world.

In this system, the studies start with "fundamental theology", i.e. a certain orientation in the general history of religions and religious phenomena, often called Comparative Religion, a certain philosophical orientation, and the study of relevant languages (Hebrew, Greek, Latin) in order to give the student an ability to read the normative texts. The purpose of Comparative Religion is then to reach the normative, in the meaning that one can discern "the specific", either in the respective religion in comparison with others, or to find the essence in the very phenomenon of religion as general concept. Essentialism is a characteristic of the study, i.e. the idea that "religion" can exist independently of the actual human beings, that is, it can be objectivated.

Then comes the study of the normative texts of Christianity, Biblical exegesis. One reads the texts and apply theoretically founded methods of interpretation. After that follows the study of "historical theology", i.e. church history and the historical development of doctrinal systems. This leads to the next step, systematic theology and Christian ethics, intended to give the student the ability to apply the religion in a philosophically founded thought system. At last follows the actual application: practical theology, and the training for church service.

There is no doubt that this is a well functioning model if the purpose is to give a good foundation for service in the church. But it is a fact that the same structural model has been influencing, and is applied, for the study of non-Christian religions and for the history of religions in general. We can see this in almost all more established handbooks in the history of religions and comparative religion during the 20th century. Each religion has its own chapter, and this chapter is structured according to the "Schleiermacher model". First comes an orientation on the texts/holybook(s) of the specific religion, so its history, its doctrinal development in different "schools" or sects, and its practical application in rituals, rules, and institutions, as they are described and regulated by religious leaders and the official texts. This means that the study is strucured, even if shortly, as if the student were to become a [quasi-] functionary in the specific religion. The confessional approach has structured the description. The leaders and the official texts and hierarchies are regarded as the very centre of the religion.

We can notice the very similar structuring that is to be found in other confessional educational systems, where the goal is to produce competent religious functionaries. We can look, e.g., at the Islamic tradition of *usûl ad-dîn* at the Sharia faculties of Muslim universities or at traditional *madrasa* institutions. One may begin (nowadays) with a course in *muqâranat al-adyân* (Comparative Religion). But first and foremost, the student should learn the language of the texts (i.e. Arabic), and get an education in *tafsîr al-Qur'ân* (Qur'an exegesis), and then in *hadîth* and hadith criticism (i.e. "historical theology": the traditions on the Prophet and his sayings, and the early Islam), then in *mantiq* (logic/philosophy) and *kalâm* (systematic theology) leading to the application: *fiqh*, the jurisprudence, the rule system, and *da'wa*, the "call", the preaching.

What we have to question is if this "Schleiermacher model" is a relevant structuring also of the secular empirical studies and research on religions. I would say that the use of such a model has favoured essentialistic ideas, premises leading to a tendency to regard religions as determinants, constant entities, and to regard the institutions, hierarchies and religious functionaries as representative for the actual function of religious elements in society. I would maintain that the very structuring (and its perhaps unconscious premises) contribute to a lack of analyses of religious phenomena more relevant to the realities of the contemporary world, a lack of relevant religious studies, research and competence in the secular society.

We need studies, empirical research and analyses of the actual functions of religions and religious elements in society, in the world, and in the global processes that we meet. This means that we should accept a shift from "production of ideology", and the essentialist perspective, to what we can label an *anthropology of religions*; from the focus on established institutions, hierarchies, doctrines, to research on the actual function of religious experiences, narratives, rituals and observances among human beings, the role of religious phenomena in social and political occurrences. Our task is to show and analyse how religions actually function, and the relations between the phenomena of *religiosity* and the many *profane* functions that religions and religious institutions actually have.

At the Chinese Academy of Social Sciences in Beijing there is an institute for the study of "World Religions and Atheism". There is one department or section for each one of the more important world religions. But this too is a kind of "Schleiermacher model", as it presupposes specificity, each religion is seen as a separate entity. But it is an empirical fact that actual religious praxis is "syncretistic", mixed. Neither do the actual conflict borders in religious life follow the borderlines between specific religions. "Liberals" stand against "fundamentalists" regardless of religion. New interpretation methods stand against old ones, regardless of religion. The consumption of religious material does not follow from the specific belonging. Thus a model having as its very basis the idea of specificity, of "motif research", obstructs and blurs the study of religion and religiosity as empirical phenomena.

What Model Then?

It has to be said that we cannot deprive us of the history of ideas and the historical perspective. But then I would like to suggest that the study be otherwise structured according to three perspectives:

a) A psychological perspective, with the focus on the phenomenon of religiosity in relation to the function of our brain and our psyche. What role have religious rituals, narratives, categorizations and observances for our perceptions, how we interpret and arrange our experiences? What role do they have as palliatives, as consolation, giving meaning to the vicissitudes of life? What is their function as a factor giving a feeling of security? Finally, what is their role as entertainment?

b) A sociological perspective. How do various religious communities, groups and cults actually function? What is the relation to other kinds of belonging, the whole set-up of identities that an individual has to cope with in contemporary society? How does the group function as a network for security, for transmitting and transforming the tradition? How about the "cults", i.e. the spontaneous communion around specific experiences?

c) A politological perspective. Which are the elements from religious tradition in political life? How do they function in propaganda, in mobilizing opinions? When do they legitimize political power, and when and how do they function as expressions of opposition and protest? What is their relation to legislation and societal norm systems? How do they contribute to the legitimation of *change*? What is the relation between verbalized norms and real norms?

More general problems of a philosophical nature would include how the phenomenon of religious experiences relates to language, cultural patterns, to social structures, to intellectual life. Text studies are still relevant, certainly, but the texts as sources that tell us about human religiosity in the past; and we can study the functions of the texts in rituals and other contexts. The three perspectives, psychology/the individual, sociology/the group, politology/society and state can be applied as well in relation to texts as to the anthropological field study.

In order to illustrate how this can be done, I would like to present, very shortly, some rather recent dissertations and monographs where such perspectives have been applied and developed theoretically. With the exception of the ones mentioned first, I have chosen studies belonging to my own field, Islamology, but we could easily find examples from other specializations too.

A common trait in such empirical studies of the functions of religions in the contemporary world, is a special interest in the processes of *change*. What changes can we see in the use of elements from religious tradition, in different specific religions, and in religious life in general? What kind of processes can we see in the selection, use, and actual function of elements from the huge material of rituals, narratives, historiographies, categorizations, terminologies and observances which are to be found in the world religions and in religious life?[9]

They are treating the problematic of what is going on in the area between religious tradition and the changes in economic, societal, and political structures and conditions, this area constituting the borderland where the re-selections and reinterpretations take place. As examples of this we can mention:

Eva Hellman, *Political Hinduism: The Challenge of the Visva Hindu Parisad* (Uppsala 1993), is a treatise on the new Hindu-nationalist

---

[9] Cf. J. Hjärpe (1997), "What will be chosen from the Islamic Basket?", in *European Review*, volume 5:3, July, pp. 267–74; and "Historiography and Islamic Vocabulary in War and Peace", in D.P. Fry and K. Björkqvist (eds.) (1997), *Cultural Variation in Conflict Resolution: Alternatives to Violence*, Mahwah NJ: Lawrence Earlbaum Associates Publishers, pp. 115–22.

and extremist movements, and Mattias Gardell, *Countdown to Armageddon: Minister Farrakhan and the Nation of Islam in the Latter Days* (Stockholm 1995) provides a very thorough analysis of the Nation of Islam movement and its development in relation to changing conditions in the USA. Especially interesting is Gardell's analyses of the changes in ideological outlook and mythology due to the social effects of the norms developed in the movement. We can learn a lot from this study on dialectic processes between ideology and social conditions.

Ola Hammer, *Claiming Knowledge: Strategies of Epistemology from Theosophy to the New Age* (2000), treats the phenomena within religious movements and constellations connected with what is usually called "New Age" phenomena. These in themselves are examples of contemporary "syncretistic" religious beliefs and praxis. In this connection, he also treats the role of secularization and globalization.[10]

We may also mention an ongoing research project regarding a new religious movement in Indonesia—centred around a prophetess [Lia Aminuddin] regarded by her adherents as Maryam reborn and with revelations from the Archangel Jibril. Her preaching is a very interesting example of syncretism combining what we can call fantasy literature elements and New Age attitudes with Islamic, Christian and Hindu-Buddhist traditional elements, using recent information technology and music styles in rituals and propaganda.[11]

In her thesis on *Tarbiya*, "Islamic education"[12] Anne Sofie Roald analyses the tension between theory (or perhaps rather ideology) and practice. The Islamist movements like the Muslim Brethren, or the JIM and ABIM in Malaysia have ideas on education: in what ways the religious tradition can be applied and transmitted to future generations in such a manner that it is regarded as relevant under contemporary conditions. This theorization on education is evidently influenced by ideas and terminologies in debates on the global level. But the social structures and ideological conditions are very different in the two chosen countries, Jordan and Malaysia, although both are under the impact of global processes in the economic field and in the field of information technology. She was able to show the

---

[10] P. 23ff.

[11] Cf. Frida Mebius, "*Är du galen, Lia? Ärkeängeln Gabriels uppenbarelse i det postmoderna Indonesien*" ["Are you mad, Lia? The Archangel Gabriel's revelation in post-modern Indonesia"], in *Svensk Religionshistorisk Årsskrift 1999*, pp. 163–95.

[12] Anne Sofie Roald (1994), *Tarbiya: Education and Politics in Islamic Movements in Jordan and Malaysia*, Lund Studies in History of Religions.

tension between theory and practice. On the organizational level, there was a verbalized emphasis on intellectual development and an intellectual interiorization of the elements of religious tradition, but the actual practice consisted of traditional memorizing and recipient learning. She then analysed the *responses* to change of conditions. Her conclusion was that the Islamic movements, in spite of the common normative sources and traditions, were "heterogeneous and a product of environments, linked to economical, political and psychological conditions". The ideas of ideologists like Hasan al-Banna, Sayyid Qutb, Abu al-A'la Mawdudi, spread widely all around the globe. They were greatly appreciated in Islamic circles, and were adapted to the local environments. Here the comparison between Jordan and Malaysia proved very relevant as the social structures are so clearly different.

Modernity as a global phenomenon includes evidently the idea of modern natural science, science as a secular, a profane way of perceiving and understanding nature and the surrounding world. The relation between religion and science has been since the time of the Enlightenment a field of controversy, debate, and intellectual considerations, as it includes very fundamental epistemological questions. The "solutions" have been many, from very simplistic apologetics to deep philosophical debate, and the process of intellectual "negotiation" goes on. In his dissertation,[13] Leif Stenberg analyses four positions in the Muslim debate on "islamization of science" and some very well-known exponents of these positions. The choice of the exponents had to do with their impact on the global level. They are all part of a socially rather homogeneous "jet set" of individuals, who are found, either in person, as participants in conferences, or represented by their books, all over the world: Maurice Boucaille, as exponent of the more simplistic kind of apologetics, Seyyid Hossein Nasr, as a proponent of a more "hermetical" approach, Ziauddin Sardar and Ismail Faruqi and those inspired by them within a certain Muslim elite (in the USA). The subtitle of Stenberg's thesis is significant: these four are of interest as they are part of a process "Developing an Islamic Modernity". The key concept in his analysis is *discourse*, "denoting the practice that shapes different statements, a practice concerned with power". He sees the different positions as

---

[13] Leif Stenberg (1996), *The Islamization of Science: Four Muslim Positions Developing an Islamic Modernity*, Lund Studies in History of Religions.

part of a struggle where the winner is in the position that will be regarded as the Islam, i.e.—for the time being—the established tradition, until it is challenged by another trend. But there is no winner in the long run. There are always different groups, opinions, trends contending for influence or trying to exclude what is regarded as heretic. The theoretical influence of Michel Foucault is obvious in this thesis, and perhaps even more in those that follow.

Roald combined in her research the analysis of the "discourse" on education within the Islamist movements with an anthropological approach with participant observation within the movements and their local institutions. Stenberg's study was mainly on the texts of the proponents of the four positions and their followers, but combined with a special kind of field work. He had conducted interviews with the persons he studied, asking for their comments on his preliminary analyses of their texts. This functioned very well (with the exception of Maurice Boucaille who refused to meet or to discuss with the researcher).

The thesis by Garbi Schmidt on the development among Muslim youth in Chicago[14] is founded mainly on research in the field, i.e. she collected her material as much as possible in direct contact with the persons and groups that she was studying. What interested her most was the activists within the Sunni Muslim communities in Chicago. What happens, within the different social groups, and different generations, when "Islam" so to speak was negotiated in a situation of minority position and social marginalization? She studied Muslim Sunday schools, other kinds of educational institutions, colleges, students' associations, Muslim centres and so on, and their actual function, in this period of the late 1990s. Her problematic is in a way similar to that of Stenberg: "knowledge" production. What is meant with "knowledge" and how is it objectified? Who are considered able to present "authoritative" interpretations of Islam, and how do they obtain this status? Here too the aspect of *power* comes in, as well as the idea of "knowledge production", in the sense that has been established in the tradition of Peter Berger and Thomas Luckmann. Two perspectives are to be learned from her investigation. Firstly, the role of *age* in the processes of change in the interpretation and actual practice of religion: the differences between the

---

[14] Garbi Schmidt (1998), *American Medina: A Study of the Sunni Muslim Immigrant Communities in Chicago*, Lund Studies in History of Religions.

generations, and thereby the change in the cognitive universe of the individual. Secondly, the role of the successful *professional* in the process of gaining authority. The professional becomes a religious authority by his (or her) success as an engineer, teacher, scientist or physician—or as a specialist in computer science. Religious authority comes from a professional, non-religious, career.

Garbi Schmidt later made a number of small studies on "Islam on the web", i.e. the knowledge production in the new global media of information. This is evidently a vast field for future research.

The thesis by Jonas Otterbeck analysing the successive presentation of the religion in a Muslim magazine in Swedish[15] has a very clear orientation to the problematic of interaction between global flows of information and local application. Here also is the key term discourse. In a way, his study corroborates with the results that Garbi Schmidt got from Chicago. These articles in this local magazine in Sweden were mainly female Swedish converts with professional education and careers, but without formal traditional religious education. Much of the material in the magazine were translations or adaptations of material, mainly in English, from organizations and centres like the Islamic Foundation in Leicester (with connections to the Jamaat-i Islami in Pakistan and the "Mawdudist" interpretation of Islam). Again the sociology of knowledge in the tradition of Peter Berger and Luckmann is combined with perspectives of power, the struggle for influence. There is a successful attempt to combine these Foucault-Bourdieu perspectives with theories of globalization and religion (Roland Robertson, Peter Beyer, Ali Mazrui, Armando Salvatore, Robert Schreiter and so forth). One of the points in the investigation is the changes in attitudes, from the start of the magazine 1986 to the end of the century. May I quote from Otterbeck's own abstract of the thesis: "Three globally spread discourses are identified as important in the genealogy of *Salaam*'s discourse: the *da'wa* of the Islamic movement; the Western European and North American modernity; and globalization, especially a group of specific global flows that are connected to certain key values in . . . modernity" (Otterbeck, 2000).

---

[15] Jonas Otterbeck (2000), *Islam på svenska: Tidskriften Salaam och islams globalisering* ["Islam in Swedish: The Magazine Salaam and the Globalization of Islam"], Lund Studies in History of Religions.

Torsten Janson, in a report to the Swedish Board for Coordination of Research, analyses the changes over time in the content and tendencies of the publications from the "main source" of the magazine *Salaam*, i.e. the Islamic Foundation in Leicester (U.K.). The report shows the interrelation between these tendencies and the changes in the social position of the group behind the organization, and the responses to global processes.

One of the "key values", on the agenda very much on the global level, is the question of women's rights, women's conditions, women's liberation, and therefore as a consequence the question of women's relation to religious tradition. These questions are posed to every specific religious community, denomination or normative system. Jonas Svenssons' thesis,[16] "Women's Human Rights and Islam", has a method similar to the one in Leif Stenberg's on the islamization of science. He has chosen to analyse three positions and three exponents: Riffat Hassan, Fatima Mernissi, and Abdullahi Ahmad an-Na'im. The UN's Declaration of Human Rights, and the later international conventions and human rights' documents are very much part of a global flow, with an immense impact on what questions must be asked. The three exponents are likewise very much a part of an international group of jet setting participants in the debate. All three can be seen as accommodists, i.e. they seek, in different ways, to accommodate these international legal instruments, and the values and norms they are promoting, and interpretations of Islam that—in each case—are proposed as more correct, better and more genuine than the traditional ones. Svensson analyses in what ways, and with what methods, the normative sources are used, the Qur'an, the Hadith literature, but also the historiography, the reinterpretations of the narratives of the religious tradition. These new interpretations compete with others—in a way similar to what we have seen as to the "islamization of science", a struggle to reach the status of the "true" interpretation of what Islam is. He also points out the differences in argumentation, when intended for different audiences, and he sees the social function of the argumentations within the debate (the power perspective again).

---

[16] Jonas Svensson (2000), *Women's Human Rights and Islam: A Study of Three Attempts at Accommodation*, Lund Studies in History of Religions.

A thesis written by Philip Halldén[17] analyses four sermons on cassettes. These sermons were given by famous and influential Saudi Arabian preachers, in opposition to the regime in the country, two by Ahmad al-Qattan, one by Isma'il Hamidi, and one by Salman al-'Auda. His main interest is not so much the content of the four sermons, but their rhetoric. In what ways do the rhetorical methods and rhetorical styles change in relation to the tradition of Islamic homiletics, the rhetorical tradition both modern and ancient in the Muslim world? In what way does the fact that these sermons spread with the help of a new medium, the sound cassettes, influence their rhetorical style? The very fact is that what was previously a local activity (the sermon in front of a specific local audience) now becomes globalized—spread all over the world. Does this fact lead to changes in the ways of preaching? Obviously that is an important question as very much of today's communication, not least in the field of religious proclamation, is with the help of the new media: video, sound cassettes, satellite TV, and the Web.

Halldén's thesis is in this respect innovative, and differs from the previously mentioned ones, but nevertheless, all these studies, Halldén's included, have some theoretical traits in common: The theories regarding *knowledge* as a social construction, the idea of a *discourse* as a power struggle between different interests, the search for key persons, "*exponents*" of specific positions within the debate on a global level, the idea of global "*flows*" of information and ideas, and the *accommodation* or local application to specific audiences. A common trait too, of course, is that being dissertations in the field of Islamology, the material is taken from the Muslim debate and in relation to Islamic tradition and its sources. We could do the same kind of studies for the Christian tradition or whatever religion we might choose.

But there is another aspect to the relationship between religion and globalization, which transcends the role of the specific religion. The local cults and religious traditions are no more taken for granted. Even the eager adherent today is aware of the fact that there are alternatives, that the norms, ideas, and observances on the local level are not the only ones in existence. The idea of common values, be it human rights, democracy, the rights of the citizen and so forth,

---

[17] Philip Halldén (2001), *Islamisk predikan på ljudkassett: En studie i retorik och fonogramologi* ["Islamic sermons on cassettes: A study in rhetorics and phonogramology"], Lund Studies in History of Religions.

are regarded as globally valid, or at least as part of a debate on a global level. It is not possible for that reason to relate them only to one religious tradition, confession or local community.[18] And so we see the phenomenon of Parliaments of World Religions discussing the possible foundation for "global ethics". When we try to see the possible relation between ethics, norms, human rights, on the global level to the religious tradition and to religious affiliations locally, we must consider the following: the religious community, and the individual's affiliation to it can have many different functions, not necessarily related to personal piety or individual religious experiences. We have to make a distinction between "religion" as institution and "religiosity" as a human personal experience. We must try to distinguish the actual functions. When do the observances and norms have the function of being markers of belonging, of affiliation to a specific group, ethnicity or nationality, and when are they expressions of personal piety? The analyses of "political religion", as the one by Eva Hellman on Hindu political nationalist movements, has to do with this distinction. Creeds, theologies, observances, have a connection with power and power struggle, the power to exclude those who are not wanted. But they are not necessarily connected with personal piety and religious experience. The aspect of power is quite evident when the argument for "cultural authenticity" is used in the political rhetorics to argue against the idea of universal human rights. The idea of cultural relativism has to be analysed from the point of view of power struggle: "cultural authenticity" in whose favour?

Religious communities can have a number of profane functions: religion as entertainment, religious community as a social and economic network, a network for education, including professional contacts; they can have the function of entities within a jurisdictional system (personal law, family law, law of inheritance); the religious community can form a part of the institutional structure of a state, and so on. When the state and its institutions are weak or inadequate, the religious community can take over some of its functions. The religious affiliation, and the religious community, is then not necessarily an expression of personal belief, but has to be analysed with

---

[18] Cf. Jan Hjärpe (2002), "Religious affiliation as a problem for universal ethics", in Göran Bexell and Dan-Erik Andersson (ed.), *Universal Ethics: Perspectives and Proposals from Scandinavian Scholars*, The Raoul Wallenberg Institute Human Rights Library, Vol. 11, The Hague/London/New York: Martinus Nijhoff Publishers, pp. 119–28.

the help of sociological and politological theories. Is it possible to argue for universal ethics, globally valid norms with religious arguments? We know that this is done, these "parliaments of world religions" being one of the examples. The goal is to find a common platform, and the goal creates the means. But the question is: What is the actual function of these endeavours? Has it an instrumental function and value, the intention being to get a local (and confessional) acceptance of the international documents as the UN Declaration and Conventions, so they can be seen as legitimate from the point of view of the specific religious tradition? Or is the purpose mainly apologetical? Modernity and globalization are secular phenomena, not related to any specific religious tradition. In front of these secular flows, there is perhaps a need to show, by reinterpretations, the relevance, not only of the specific religion but the societal and political relevance of "religion" in general; a response to the actual secularization of the concept of ethics, due to globalization. The problem is that universalism is the opposite to communalism, that "community" (if not including the entire humanity) is an exclusivist concept, and that globalization in the long run has to be combined with an idea of a common human nature rather than with religious specificity.

So the change of perspective from a theological to an anthropological analysis of religious phenomena can be seen as having practical political consequences too.

RELIGIOUS DIVERSITY AND HUMAN RIGHTS: CLASHES AND CONVERGENCES IN ASIAN-EUROPEAN DIALOGUES

Elisabeth Gerle
Center of Theology and Religion
Lund University

Are human rights universal or not? Or are they a Euro-American notion? In the ongoing debate on human rights and universality, Europe and Asia are often set up against each other as having opposing views. While Europe and the United States seem preoccupied with rights of the individual, Asia is said to have an understanding of life built upon a collective way of living. Family, local community, religious identity and nation shape the life and role of the individual. His or her position is given in a fixed system.

The question in this paper is, however, whether this dichotomy is optimal for the very complex relationships between cultures and human rights due to religious, historical and socio-economic diversities? Late modernity and several features of globalization highlight diversities and asymmetries not only between civilizations and regions but also within nations and various religious traditions.[1] This has an impact also in relation to which dimensions of human rights are emphasized. My argument in this paper is that Asian and European religious traditions have the potential to collaborate around important human rights issues. Today the most visible alliances between religions emerge as resistance to certain human rights.[2] A collaboration to support and advance human rights may reveal that certain

---

[1] See e.g. Thomas Hylland Eriksson, 2002, *Ethnicity and Nationalism;Anthropological Perspectives*, and Elisabeth Gerle (2002), (1999) *Mångkulturalism för vem?* (Multiculturalism for whom?) Nya Doxa: Nora.

[2] See e.g. Ann Elizabeth Mayor, "Religious Reservations to the Convention on the Elimination of All Forms of Discrimination Against Women: What do they really mean?" pp. 105–66 in Courtney W. Howland (ed.), (1999), *Religious Fundamentalism and the Human Rights of Women*, London; and Elissavet Stamatopolou, "Women's Rights and the United Nations" pp. 36–48 in Julie Peters, Andrea Wolper (eds.), (1995), *Women Rights, Human Rights, International Feminist Perspectives*, New York, London: Routledge.

aspects of human rights are associated with modernization processes more than with specific cultural aspects.

Pre-modern societies, in varying degrees, all have some kind of respect for human rights and human dignity. My thesis in this paper is, however, that such respect for human rights are different from what we today mean by human rights. In pre-modernity, human rights were mainly understood in relation to social position, age and sex. Slaves, workers, non-philosophers and women were not considered to be real citizens in ancient Greece. Democracy and human rights were the entitlements of free, independent, male citizens. Women were not seen as legal subjects or as citizens in Palestine at the time of Jesus the Nazaree. This is why his way of treating women with full respect for them as persons was considered revolutionary by his contemporaries.

Also today there are some real tensions around human rights within traditions as well as between them that need to be acknowledged. As the title indicates I want to reflect upon clashes as well as on convergences in the dialogue between Europe and Asia.

These clashes and convergences will be discussed in a context where postmodern thought is challenging the rights discourse for being unaware of its cultural biases. "Rights" are seen as emerging out of natural law perspectives and a belief that there is a fundamental nature or human essence. It is argued that the understanding of human beings as bearers of rights is connected to the Enlightenment tradition in the West and its focus on autonomy and egalitarian values. Autonomy came to be associated with the individual man, understood as first of all a mind and as an island. Modern pursuits of egalitarian values have therefore, often made the white, European male a prototype of the human being. Everybody else was supposed to become similar. Coloured women and men, white women, everybody was supposed to become the same as the white, heterosexual man valuing independence, autonomy and freedom. The egalitarian emphasis came to be "sameness", not respecting "difference" or "alterity". Hence, postmodern key words are "difference" and "asymmetry".

This challenge and critique against a European hegemonic discourse has been liberating and made at least some European intellectuals aware of cultural biases. The critique in itself can, however, easily side with cultural and ethical relativism undermining all forms of emancipatory ambitions. Difference and asymmetry can be launched in defence of inequality and injustice as well as against European or

American blindness and preoccupation of self. Hence, sensitivity of cultural preconditions and assumptions need to be combined with a continued discussion and recognition of core values. Values need to be understood in their context and often renegotiated. If a postmodern critique of sameness could lead to ethical relativism and to the undermining of egalitarian values as such it appears important to highlight contradictory trends.

While many philosophers and politicians in Europe seem to abandon the value of egalitarianism and equality as a societal vision, social movements in various parts of Asia are pursuing justice based on egalitarian values between cultures but also within cultures. Some draw on ancient Asian philosophers to underline that the value of the person is integral and indigenous in Asia.

In my view a radical scepticism against egalitarianism can only be to the disadvantage of marginalized groups.[3] Neither women nor people of the Global South or in the so-called two-third society that is spreading as part of globalization will benefit from the undermining of the rights discourse by postmodernism. It is like an ironic gesture of fate that when people in Africa and Asia are invoking principles of equality, non-discrimination and rights and are using them against their former rulers, new philosophical teachers emerge in Europe undermining the basis of argumentation for women and for people in poorer countries. Resistance to equality and defence of authoritarianism has deep roots as well in Europe. In the 18th century, counter-revolutionary philosophers argued, in the name of religion, against the Enlightenment and "the philosophers of the Encyclopedia". Similar values emerged in the anti-modern fascism in Europe and in contemporary populist right-wing movements in Europe and United States, defending the patriarchal family as the centre of a hierarchical society. As part of globalization such values are now quite central in Indian Hindu-nationalism and in militant political Islamism. Resistance to modernity and to human rights is a modern phenomenon.

However, other theoretical underpinnings of a rights discourse have emerged among the critics of modernity in Europe. Explorations into how the human being is constituted and which forces shape the

---

[3] See e.g. Seyla Benhabib (1992), *Situating the Self, Gender, Community and Postmodernism in Contemporary Ethics*, Cambridge: Polity Press, especially the chapter "Feminism and the Question of Postmodernism", s. 209, 217ff.

life of the individual is a preoccupation of many philosophers and sociologists concerned with critical constructivist theory. One theme is the critique of the Enlightenment tradition and the Cartesian focus on individual intelligence as constituting the human being. The French philosopher Maurice Merleau-Ponty (died 1961) was one of many pursuing an anti-Cartesian project arguing that the dichotomy between body and mind is false. Instead he bases his understanding of human nature in an ontology that stresses unity and interconnectedness.

He sees body and mind as necessary dimensions of each other. A subject is a unity that cannot become a person without a social world of language, meaning and work. In reaction to the Cartesian emphasis on the mind, he argues that truth does not "inhabit" only the "inner man". He claims that "there is no inner man, man is in the world, and only in the world does he know himself". He finds not a "source of intrinsic truth, but a subject destined to the world".[4]

Hence being a social subject is something you learn by acquiring the ability to practise oneself as one's life world. Knowledge is acquired through bodily existence in and with an already existing world. A subjectivity like this, focusing on the *intermode* between the subject and other subjects and things might be an opening where Europe could transcend its previous, secular emphasis of the individual as a mind. This might create a new understanding of Asian traditions focusing on the collective, community and people living in interaction. Yet, also here there might be tensions, even clashes in relation to Asian dichotomies of mind-body as well as in relation to the strong emphasis on the given, i.e. on static positions of the individual. This tension is something I will return to in my concluding remarks.

Emergence of Secular Human Rights in Europe and America

So-called Western ideas focusing on autonomy, personal integrity and rights of the individual in relation to authorities are closely connected to the Enlightenment era. A new understanding of the relationship between the individual and the state transformed the role of the individual from being a subject under a divine king to being a citizen with rights to choose whom to be governed by. Contract ethics connected with philosophers such as Rousseau, Hobbes and

---

[4] M. Merleau-Ponty (1962), *Phenomenology of Perception*, New York: Routledge, p. xi.

Locke are basic in the emergence of liberal democracies as they developed in Europe. Needless to say, the individual citizen, described as born free and equal in the American Declaration of Independence from 1776 was a white, property-owning man. Citizenship at that time was not supposed to be for black people or for women, who are still not mentioned in the American Constitution except in the amendments. The Western universality of the rights of citizens obviously was not as universal as it has been said to be. Yet, it has been an ideal inspiring the citizen's rights movement led by Martin Luther King in the 1960s as well as for many women and liberation movements in various parts of the world.

An understanding of personal dignity and autonomy also influenced the relationship to religious authorities. Christian Reformation movements connected with Martin Luther in Germany and John Calvin in Switzerland in the 16th century gave religious underpinnings to what was later developed as Enlightenment philosophy. For Martin Luther, the personal capacity to read and to interpret the Bible led to an understanding that everybody was able to relate to God without mediators such as the clergy or the Church as an institution. Under the banner "*Sola Scriptura*" he challenged the Pope and the Roman Catholic authority to excommunicate those searching salvation outside of its religious "jurisdiction", i.e. the Roman Catholic Church and its clergy.

From the 16th century the Lutheran churches in Scandinavia had become the established churches. Every Swedish, Norwegian, Finish and Danish citizen was supposed to be Lutheran and active in the state church. Other denominations emerging as Calvinist, reformed religious movements in the 17th and 18th century, started to make claims that they wanted to express their Christian faith in their own way. Under the banner of individual rights they pursued group rights for their new congregations. Hence, the rights to freedom of expression and of association were crucial to these reformed, revitalist religious movements that were often inspired from the UK and the USA. In Europe and the United States there is, therefore, a close link between such religious claims for pluralism and the freedoms expressed in the Universal Declaration of Human Rights from 1948, as "the right to freedom of thought, conscience and religion; this right includes freedom to change his religion or belief; and freedom, either alone or in community with others in public or private to manifest his religion or belief in teaching, practice, worship and

observance" (UDHR, 1948, Art. 18). Article 19 expressing the right
to "freedom of opinion and expression", the right to "hold opinions
without interferences and to seek, receive and impart information
and ideas through any media and regardless of frontiers" as well as
article 20 affirming the "right to freedom of peaceful assembly and
association" are often labeled the first generation of human rights.

The International Covenant on Civil and Political Rights, (ICCPR,
1966) that express these rights in a covenant, was actually the second of the two covenants that emerged out of the declaration of
1948. ICCPR and The International Covenant on Economic, Social
and Cultural Rights, (ICESCR, 1966) were both concluded at New
York, 16 December, 1966. The ICCPR was, however, the first to
enter into force on 3 January, 1976 while the ICCPR was postponed
until 23 March, 1976.[5] This legal curiosa knowledge is, however, of
minor importance. More significant is the debate in relation to these
two covenants. The United States immediately launched an understanding of civil and political rights as being basic human rights.
People in Asia, Africa and Latin America, on the other hand, pointed
out that economic, social and cultural rights were the crucial ones.
From 1966, these two covenants became part of the political struggle between the Soviet Union and the United States during the Cold
War. While the US never ratified the Covenant on Economic, Social
and Cultural Rights, the Soviet Union did not ratify the Covenant
on Civil and Political Rights. Both sides accused the other of vio-
lating human rights. Many governments from Africa and Asia sided
with the Soviet Union to claim that economic, social and cultural
rights should have priority. "What is the point with freedom of
expression and the right to vote if you don't have food and shelter?" was one of many questions asked during this period. European
welfare states that themselves pursued economic and social rights for
their citizens often took a middle position in this struggle, trying to
accommodate the two covenants as well as the two sides.

It is often pointed out that even the Covenant on Economic, Social
and Cultural Rights has the individual person at its centre. Except
for the opening part, Article 1 on people's right to self-determination, which is the same in the two covenants, the rights expressed

---

[5] Covenants are legally binding. See Burns H. Weston & Richard A. Falk &
Anthony D'Amato, *1990 Basic Documents in International Law and World Order*, Minn.:
West Publishing Co. St. Paul.

relate to state responsibilities in relation to the individual, not in relation to groups or peoples. Furthermore, this first paragraph, which was formulated as a gracious gesture in relation to demands from the South, has never been legally invoked in the UN system. Independently of the covenant's formulations, there seems to be a different emphasis in the human rights discourse between various cultures. As Bas De Gay Fortman points out:

> It is noteworthy that while in their Western historical context human rights developed as a protective concept—to defend the autonomy of individual citizens against particular threats from sovereign (states) that wished to extend their power into the citizen's own realm—in the cultural context of Africa, Asia, South and Central America the idea of human rights is of a much more *emancipatory* character: a struggle for rights of the have-nots[6] (Fortman, 1995).

One of the more serious arguments against how the human rights discourse is being used, not only by Euro-American, liberal democracies but also by social movements in the West, is the accusation that they overemphasize the right of the individual at the expense of the collective and shared. This often results in focusing only on civil and political rights while neglecting social, cultural and economic rights, thus leading to double standards as civil and political rights have had a longer life in Europe and the US. Even more important, however, is that the greatest challenge for the future has to do with caring for what is shared, locally and globally. Bas de Gay Fortman points out:

> it is exactly those cultures in which possessive individualism has strong roots—and that includes the global village as such—that experience great difficulty with economic and social rights, already at the stage of standard-setting. While individualism may offer a sufficient moral foundation for respecting everyone's freedom, it is inadequate as a basis for accepting other people's needs as grounds for justified claims. Economic, social and cultural rights presuppose not just free individuals but a community that accepts responsibility for the fulfillment of everybody's basic needs[7] (Fortman, 1996).

---

[6] Bas De Gay Fortman, (1995), "The Problem of Cultural Receptivity" in Abdullah A. An-Nai'im, Jerald D. Gort, Henry Jamsen, Hendrik M. Vroom (eds.), *Human Rights and Religious Values*, Michigan, Grand Rapids, p. 75.

[7] Bas de Gay Fortman, "Religion and Human Rights: Mutually Exclusive or Supportive?" in *Studies in Interreligious Dialogue*, 6/1996.

To accept responsibilities requires more than just a legal basis. To ratify conventions, to establish courts for human rights and to develop the jurisprudence of human rights is not enough. The moral foundation for responsible living needs to be nurtured by a worldview.[8]

From a European perspective, the Cold War is over and we live in a world often described as being in a new phase of globalization. The accusations against Europe and the United States for universalizing their concerns and enforcing them upon other cultures and regions in the world are, however, very much part of the globalization debate. Which values are really universal? Is the Euro-American concern for personal autonomy and rights really being shared globally? Or are these proclamations just another version of hegemony and global imperialism where social, cultural and economic rights are being neglected?

The relationship between states and citizens has been the focus for legal developments of human rights. Now there is a growing interest in the kind of responsibility other actors have for implementing the international human rights regime. The legal International Law framework of the United Nations is challenged by strong transnational actors who operate above and beyond state legislation. The pursuit of human rights is, therefore, taking other routes as well. As a consequence of globalization, non-governmental organizations work increasingly within transnational networks. Sometimes together with states, they address transnational corporations pushing them to pursue human rights.[9] In this development, values and norms get more attention. Cultural values are often invoked by governments to explain different emphases or to excuse lack of implementation of human rights. The reality is, however, filled with complex and intriguing relationships between power structures and references to deep cultural or religious values. My analysis here of some religious and cultural value hierarchies involved in the discussion aims to point out that religious values may be invoked in many directions. Clashes or convergence do not necessarily follow only geographical or cultural regions. They are associated with time and context and political interests as well.

---

[8] See for instance Mary Grey (1996), "Empowered by a Vulnerable God: The Roots and Wings of Relational Theology", unpublished paper.

[9] The UN initiative to form Global Compact is an interesting example to pursue civil human rights, ILO rights, environmental concern and to ban corruption.

Clashes and Tensions

Individual vs Collective

This paper will discuss religious diversity in relation to human rights on the understanding that cultures are permeated by religious thoughts and practices that influence ways of life and how to understand the position of the human being.[10] Existence is interpreted by various religious concepts of humanity, where the individual person has a given place and position within a larger context. Depending on the religions, this can be the tribe, the Jewish people, the Kingdom of God, the Umma, dharma, rita, karma and the chain of causality. The understanding of the person is related to "a view of reality as it really is". This includes ontological and metaphysical statements as well as anthropology and instructions on how to live. Henrik M. Vroom claims:

> Insofar a concept of humanity is present, it is an anthropology that is universally valid, an anthropology that consequently, holds true for all people[11] (Vroom, 1995).

Vroom points out that Hindus who believe in reincarnation do not exclude Christians from being reborn. Muslims believing in a final judgment after death also expect non-Muslims to be judged as well. Jews who observe the Halakah hold that non-Jews are also created in the image of God and that they must observe the Noahitic prohibitions. "Each ideological tradition makes universal claims about personal human existence, society and morality".[12] What is of interest here is how these diverse universal claims relate to human rights.

The discourse on human rights is in many aspects a heritage from the Enlightenment and therefore a part of the modern project. All major world religions on the other hand emerged during pre-modern times. Traditional religion has often been connected to agrarian epochs in which God's demands are understood in a vertical, authoritarian, exclusive, hierarchical system with religious leaders on the top, followed by political leaders, men, and finally women. Modernity,

---

[10] I am not discussing the relationship between religion and culture which in itself is an intriguing relationship.

[11] Vroom (1995), "Religious Ways of Life and Human Rights" in An-Nai'im, Gort, Jansen, Vroom, (eds.), *Human Rights and Religious Values*, Amsterdam: Eerdmans Publishing Company, p. 31.

[12] Vroom (1995), p. 32.

on the other hand, brought a mechanical faith in reason and secularism, which was often just as absolute. The pre-modern and the
industrial, modern cosmology have in common their conviction that
there is only one Truth. While the agrarian worldview was enchanted
and spiritual and life had a meaning in which everything had its
proper place and purpose in a context given by God, modernity
meant that the world was despiritualized as part of secularization
and faith in rationality.

Another important feature of modern anthropology is to see the
human being as an independent actor, somebody entitled to make
choices about how he, and gradually also she, would like to live.
Change, movement and transition are charged with positive value
within modernity. If there are tensions between the individual and
the group, the individual, according to this understanding, has a
right to personal choice of group belonging, even to descent from a
religion.[13] In most pre-modern worldviews, this is seen as dubious
not only in relation to the collective, be it family, tribe or nation,
but also in relation to a divine cosmic order.

Autonomy vs Theonomy

One crucial tension between the idea of human rights and many
religious traditions has had to do with an understanding of life that
sees the role and the position of the individual as given and static.
The idea of autonomy is at odds with the idea of theonomy, i.e. a
faith that God is supposed to control and decide everything in life
without human consent.[14] For Hindu thought, everything is based
on the cosmic order. The caste or the lineage determines each person's place in the hierarchy.[15] In contrast, the Jewish and the Christian
traditions base the value of the individual on creation where every
human being is created in the image of God.[16] Islam shares this
understanding of the human being as being created with duties and

---

[13] In the UDHR (1948), the right to "change" religion or belief was pointed out
in Art. 18. This has never been repeated, neither in the Covenants from 1966 nor
in the Declaration on the Elimination of all Forms of Intolerance and of Discrimination
based on Religion or Belief, UN Doc. (A/36/684(1981) due to resistance from especially Muslim countries.

[14] Hendrik M. Vroom (1995).

[15] M. Biardau (1992), *Hinduism: The Anthropology of a Civilization*, Tr. R. Nice, Dehli:
Oxford University Press, p. 12.

[16] Genesis 1:27.

responsibilities first and foremost in relation to God but also in relation to the community. The Qur'anic vision of human destiny is embodied in the classic proclamation: "Towards Allah is thy limit."[17] Many of the clashes between the Muslim Shari'ah law and human rights have to do with what is experienced or described as a tension between autonomy and theonomy.[18] Vroom claims:

> Thus, each religious tradition determines the values of the human person within the whole of a view of human beings and the world. It still makes a difference whether one holds than one lives only ones, has a special place in the whole of creation and furthers the cause of righteousness in the world or whether one views humans from the perspective of their karmic connection to the cosmic order, or from a humanistic understanding of human beings. If the basic idea is that the task of the human is determined by the *rita*, than his own perspective and preference is secondary in comparison with the insight into *dharma* that is transmitted by the religious spokesman[19] (Vroom, 1995).

It does make a difference if the human is understood as somebody that may be reincarnated as a plant, animal, human or divinity or if the human is understood as sharply distinguished from other non-human beings. From such a perspective, the emphasis on the individual as a bearer of rights seems closer to Western cosmologies. Here as well, however, duties and obligations rather than freedom and rights have been the focus of religious authorities.

David Novak, professor in modern Jewish studies at the Virginia University in the United States bases the idea of human rights in the relationships between, on the one hand, the commandments, "*misvot*" and the obligations "*hovat*", and on the other side, what is permitted "*reshut*". He claims that classic Hebrew actually lacks an equivalent to the notion "rights", although there is a word for "right" both in biblical literature and prayers in Hebrew namely "*zechut*", *zechiot* in plural.

Novak argues that Hebrew certainly has notions and terms corresponding to the concept of "obligations". Closest to our term "right" is "permission". Thus, he holds that what is allowed in practice becomes everything that the law does not mention, requisites that

---

[17] Surah 53; An-Na'im: 42.
[18] For a discussion of three different Muslim hermeneutical positions in relation to the Quran and Shari'ah, see Jonas Svensson (2000), *Women's Human Rights and Islam, A Study of Three Attempts at Accommodation*, Lund Studies in History of Religion.
[19] Vroom (1995), p. 33ff.

are left for the individual choice. Yet, as a duty is something one owes somebody else, in practice, it becomes a right for the other. Duties imply rights. Novak points out that the whole Jewish system of duties is understood in the context of God's absolute right as the Creator. This, individual freedom has traditionally been understood within a framework of God as the absolute who sets the limits.[20]

Hierarchical Social Ordering vs Democratic Ideals

One obvious clash between human rights and some components of religious traditions has to do with accepting hierarchies as something divine or given by nature or implicit within natural law.

Traditional Lutheranism for centuries had an almost feudal understanding of life. Martin Luther's anti-authoritarianism, democratic understanding of the right to read and interpret the bible and of the individual person with direct access to God without mediator was channelled as critique of the clergy in the Roman Catholic Church. However, it was not applied in relation to hierarchies in society or in the family. Official Roman Catholic interpretations of natural law still hold on to various hierarchies as divine or natural.

The Confucian tradition in its early phase first emphasized the relations between father and son, minister and ruler. Later the five relationships (*wu-lun*) between parent and child, husband and wife, elder and younger siblings, ruler and minister, friend and friend were developed.[21] Virtues in this tradition have to do with fulfilling one's social role, a precondition for good government. Harmony, balance and complementarity are important notions.

Hence, democratic ideas that emphasize personal autonomy and pursuit of individual happiness have been met with suspicion in all these traditions. One of the most visible tensions in contemporary international debate occurs in relation to family values. Claims for

---

[20] Novak mentions seven different relationships with obligations and, implicitly rights; (1) God to person (2) persons to God (3) God to community (4) community to God (5) persons to persons (6) persons to community (7) community to person. David Novak (1996), "Religious Human Rights in the Judaic Tradition" in John Witte, Jr. and Johan D. van der Vyer (eds.), *Religious Human Rights in Global Perspective: Religious Perspectives*, 1–16, Martinus Nijhoff Publishers.

[21] Irene Blom (1996), "Confucian Perspectives on Individual and Collectivity" in Blom, Martin, Proudfoot (eds.), *Religious Diversity and Human Rights*, New York: Columbia University Press, p. 117.

democratization, equality and mutuality within the family are often rejected by referring to nature, cosmic order, biology or divine laws.

Male-female hierarchy

While hierarchical structures in the West have been challenged for a long time within public space there is more complicity about such structures within private spheres. This has also influenced the human rights debate. There is a tendency to describe issues such as justice, democracy and equality as belonging to the public sphere of justice while the private life has to do with diverse expressions of the good life. Most traditional political philosophers have, therefore refrained from discussing such issues in relation to families and in relation to women.[22] Through the private-public distinction women who socially and historically have been associated with the private domains have been expected to accept gender hierarchies within the family. The ethical challenge to democracy and justice that is taken seriously in public affairs has often been neglected in family relations.

Further, family law has often become a symbol of the right to diversity in the interpretation of the good life by religions. Issues concerning the "good life" are not supposed to be discussed. They have been situated outside of the domain of justice also in most inter-faith dialogues. Hence, there are many alliances, for instance in the United Nations, between the Vatican, conservative Muslim countries and right wing Protestant groups.[23]

In a critical analysis of John Paul II's encyclica *Centigesimus Annus*, Vrooms points out that the idea of human rights is accepted by the Roman Catholic Church, but not without qualification. In the first half of the 19th century, the Roman Catholic Church, RCC, rejected freedom of conscience. In *Rerum Novarum* this was changed. Freedom of association as well as the right to a just wage was acknowledged. In the *Centigesimus Annus*, there is a "prioritizing and interpretation of human rights" that brings the understanding in line with the Catholic concept of humanity:

---

[22] This is, for instance, pointed out by Seyla Benhabib (1992), *Situating the Self, Gender, Community and Postmodernism in Contemporary Ethics*, New York: Routledge, s. 109.

[23] See e.g. Elisabeth Gerle (2003), "Participatory Democracy and Human Rights for Women in Globalization—New Possibilities and Challenges" in Diana Amnéus & Göran Gunner (eds.), *Mänskliga Rättigheter, sedd från forskningens frontlinje* (Human Rights—From the Frontier of Research), Stockholm: Iustus.

Thus the emphasis is on the unborn, young children, and the family as an institution, over against both a view of the rights of women that implies that they can terminate their pregnancies and the freedom of married couples to end their marriage. (Cf. Congregation of the Doctrine of the Faith, 36). Another caveat is that the encyclical recognizes the responsibility of the state to guard the exercise of human rights in the economic sector but at the same time limits this role—in line with the principle of subsidiarity—through giving primary responsibility to individuals and different social groups rather than to the state[24] (CA, 39).

This is, according to Vroom, an example of the Roman Catholic Church's ambivalent view on human rights when they are formulated by other institutions. The Church claims to know the truth and out of this understanding it "constructs a hierarchy of human rights and a specific interpretation of them."[25] Vroom points to the contraception debate as an example of discrimination against women. In my view, the rejection of women as autonomous subjects and moral agents runs much deeper. The procreation debate is just the tip of an iceberg. It can be seen as a contemporary example of a discussion about whether the woman is really created in the image of God or as the second human in a social order that since creation has given man the first position in a hierarchy next to God. This discussion has taken place within Christianity since the early Christian period. Some Church fathers argued in favour of hierarchy and complementarity while others as Augustine (died 430) argued in favour of original equality based on the first chapter of the Bible.[26]

Clashes between human rights for women as formulated in the Convention on the Elimination of all Forms of Discrimination Against Women, CEDAW, 1979, and in the Universal Declaration on Human Rights, UDHR, 1948, regularly occur in relation to traditional Muslim interpretations of Sharia's emphasis on women and men as complementary rather than equal. The notion equity instead of equality was pursued by many Muslim states at the UN Women Conference in Beijing 1995. The alliance between the Vatican and conservative Muslim states was also active there. Further, Julia Kristeva among others has pointed out that the Confucian appreciation of right rela-

---

[24] Vroom (1995), p. 36.
[25] Vroom (1995), p. 36.
[26] For an analysis on gender and exegesis in the Latin Fathers see Kari, Elisabeth Borressen (2003), *From Patristics to Matristics*; Herder, Rom (2000), *Augustinianum, Periodicum semestre Instituti Patristici*" Augustinianum.

tions has had its focus on various male relationships.[27] Complementarity between women and men are interpreted within cosmologies that assume male hierarchy.

During the preparation process of the UN Conference on Human Rights in Vienna 1993, many Asian countries pursued somewhat of a relativistic agenda while affirming the universality of human rights. In a regional meeting for Asia of the World Conference on Human Rights governments stressed:

> the interdependence and indivisibility of economic, social, cultural, civil and political, and the inherent interrelationship between development, democracy, universal enjoyment of all human rights, and social justice, which must be addressed in an integrated and balanced manner;[28] (Bangkok Declaration, 1995)

In the same document, called the Bangkok Declaration, 1993, they expressed that although

> human rights are universal in nature, they must be considered in the context of a dynamic and evolving process of international norm setting, bearing in mind the significance of national and regional *particularities* and various, historical, cultural and religious backgrounds;[29] (Bangkok Declaration, 1995)

Other non-governmental voices in the Asian-European dialogue express a concern about possible misuse of references to religious or ethnic particularity. The Bangkok NGO Declaration on Human Rights from a meeting of 110 NGOs from Asia and the Pacific 1993 states:

> In the Asia-Pacific region women's rights are violated by increasingly militant assertions of religious and ethnic identity[30] (Alfredsson and Tomasevski, 1995).

The declaration states that universal human rights are rooted in many cultures. While advocating cultural pluralism such cultural practices

---

[27] Julia Kristeva (1977), *About Chinese Women*, London: Marion Boyars Publishers.
[28] Bangkok Declaration, Regional Meeting for Asia of the World Conferences on Human Rights, (United Nations, 1993) (1995), in Gudmundur Alfredsson & Katarina Tomasevski, *A Thematic Guide to Documents on the Human Rights of Women*, Raul Wallenberg Institute Human Rights Guides, Vol. 1, p. 48.
[29] Ibid. p. 48. Emphasis added.
[30] Gudmundur Alfredsson & Katarina Tomasevski (1995), *A Thematic Guide to Documents on the Human Rights of Women*, Raul Wallenberg Institute Human Rights Guides, Vol. 1, s. 49.

that derogate from universally accepted human rights, including women's rights, must not be tolerated. The formulations are sharp:

> Patriarchy which operates "though gender, class, caste and ethnicity, is integral to the problems facing women. Patriarchy is a form of slavery and must be eradicated. Women's rights must be addressed in both the public and private spheres of society, in particular in the family. To provide women with a life in dignity and self-determination, it is important that women have inalienable, equal economic rights (e.g. right to agricultural land, housing and other resources, and property)[31] (Alfredsson and Tomasevski, 1995).

There is a growing movement in Asia as well as in Europe arguing that a notion such as complementarity is being used to disguise a gender hierarchy where men are able to choose, women are not. The American philosopher Martha Nussbaum argues that women in much of the world today are less well nourished than men, less healthy, and more vulnerable to physical violence and sexual abuse. She argues that international political and economic thought must be sensitive to gender difference as a problem of justice. A capability approach shows that many more men that women in the world are able to choose their lives, within certain limits.[32]

Politics of Semantics

Hierarchical relationships be they European or Asian in origin all have some implicit tensions with ideals of participatory democracy and representative rights.[33] It is easy to find examples of accepted or prescribed hierarchies from pre-modern time within all religious traditions. However, it is often neglected that these tensions are reappearing in new forms in late or post-modernity. The position of the individual understood as determined by divine, cosmic laws may be invoked against democratic participation not only in feudal times but

---

[31] Ibid. p. 49.

[32] Martha Nussbaum (2000), *Women and Human Development, The Capabilities Approach*, Cambridge: Cambridge University Press. A gendered dichotomy and hierarchy is, however, not the only one at work. Other hierarchies created around class and ethnicity are relevant as well.

[33] For a deeper analysis of the concept of justice understood both as freedom of oppression and as a procedurial concept that includes rights and possibilities of participating in political work and decision making, see Iris Marion Young (1990), *Justice and the Politics of Difference*, Princeton, N.J.: Princeton University Press, p. 33ff.

also in the present phase of globalization. An important issue to raise in these very different contexts is, therefore, the question of power conceived as relations between individuals and between groups and regions in the world. Various cosmologies and philosophies are often used in such intricate power relationships.

Afro-American ethicists within a "womanist" tradition have pointed out that economic interests and power relations behind colonialism and slavery went hand in hand with ethical theories emphasizing care. Colonialism was interpreted as being in the interest of the colonized, it was the burden of the white man to care for the colonized. A paternalistic ethics of care is, therefore, met with great suspicion today. Hence, religious-cultural arguments in the service of political interests are also being scrutinized in contemporary Euro-Asian dialogues.

The human rights advocate Chandra Muzaffar in Malaysia holds that notions such as democracy and human rights may be used as "a mandate to intervene".[34] He argues that human rights are part of a power game where the United States and the West are talking of human rights as a way of maintaining their dominant power in Asia. Muzaffar himself, however, still does not argue in favour of giving development precedence over democracy. He does not read Asian economic successes as an outcome of dictatorship and repression of labour. Rather he credits "parliamentary democracy":

> It is this system of governance which legitimates both multi-party competition and political dissent that is partly responsible for social stability—which in turn has facilitated continuous economic growth and progress. The ability of the national leadership to balance the diverse, sometimes conflicting interests of the different communities . . . should also be given due weight[35] (Muzaffar, 1994).

To interpret tensions between Europe and Asia as a clash between human rights and authoritarianism may often be misleading. Tensions between secular and more spiritual forms of life, between commitment to community versus individualist consumer greed and materialism are not mainly tensions between Europe and Asia but are

---

[34] Chandra Muzaffar (1994), "High Commission for Human Rights", in *Just Commentary* (Penang) no. 7, 3 January.

[35] Chandra Muzaffar (1994), "From Human Rights to Human Dignity" address to the International Conference on Rethinking Human Rights, 6–7 December, 1994, p. 3, unpublished paper. A somewhat revised version is published in Peter van Ness (ed.) (1999), *Debating Human Rights*, New York: Routledge.

part of internal struggles within most societies, regions and cultures. In these rhetorical set-ups, communities are always described as more unselfish, negating also that communities may be greedy. Attempts to pursue more flexible and just gender relations are a challenge worldwide when many of the ideals of the traditional family from pre-modernity do not suit a modern society any longer. According to an analysis of Edward Friedman, the notion of Western democracy as well as Asian authoritarianism are rhetorical categories rather than analytical ones:

> The usual contrast between a so-called "West" and a so-called "East" such that the West allegedly privileges the individual over the group while the East privileges the group over the individual forgets that all nation-states put the national whole first[36] (Friedman, 1999).

Friedman argues that the standard Anglo-American description of democracy as built on individualism and clashing interests is as much a mystification as the rhetorical references to soft Asian authoritarianism. A deeper look into one's own history might help reveal such mystifications. Non-conforming Protestants had to flee England in pursuit of religious freedom for their communities and English Protestants oppressed the community of Irish Catholics. The conventional self-understanding of democracy emerging out of a democratic culture of Protestant individualism is misleading and dangerous. Leaders of Asian democratic countries do not consider Asian cultures as "singularly anti-democratic".[37] From Korea, one of the world's most Confucian societies, President Kim Dae Jung points to the Asian "rich heritage of democracy-oriented philosophies and traditions" that were developed long before Europeans did.[38] He points to the democratic elements in Mencius' political philosophy that argues that "the people are the most elevated". After the people come the state and then the sovereign. Chinese despots therefore saw Mencian philosophy as too democratic by putting the people first and by giving legitimization to the overthrow of tyrannical rulers.[39]

---

[36] Edward Friedman (1999), "Asia as a Fount of Universal Human Rights," p. 64, in Peter Van Ness (ed.), *Debating Human Rights*, London, New York: Routledge.
[37] Friedman (1999), p. 57.
[38] Kim Dae Jung (1994), "A Response to Lee Kuan Yew" in *Foreign Affairs*, November–December, pp. 199, 192.
[39] Friedman (1999), p. 77.

Chandra Muzaffar has increasingly been criticizing, not human rights as such, but the selective use and the Euro-American bias to describe human rights exclusively as individual, civil rights. The dominance of strong Western states within international financial institutions such as the IMF and the WTO, in the United Nations Security Council and in global media is in itself a lack of democracy.

> This ability to force others to submit to their will is backed by the West's—particularly the United States'—global military dominance. It is a dominance which bestows upon the West effective control over high-grade weapons technology and most weapons of mass destruction. The dominant West also controls global news and information through Reuters, AP, UPI, AFP, and most of all CNN. Likewise Western music, Western films, Western fashions, and Western foods are creating a global culture which is not only Western in character and content, but also incapable of accommodating non-Western cultures on a just and equitable basis. Underlying this Western-dominated global culture and information system is an array of ideas, values, and even worldviews pertaining to a position of the individual, inter-gender relations, inter-generational ties, the family, the community, the environment and the cosmos which have evolved from a particular tradition—namely the Western secular tradition[40] (Muzaffar, 1999).

This long quotation shows a style of argumentation that combines a critique against American hegemony through the military, global media and international financial institutions with defending traditional family structures. It also portrays Asian cultures as less secular and more concerned about societal ties. While this critique against military, economic and cultural hegemony may be relevant, the intriguing relationship between modernization and changing social roles is completely excluded in the analysis. The argument, therefore, becomes part of a "we-them discourse" where the pre-colonial is described as an ideal and the former colonies as the enemy. He, therefore, comes close to what many postcolonial writers have pointed out as nostalgic descriptions of the past. Such idealized memories of a golden past often function as an easy escape from many complexities of life.[41]

---

[40] Chandra Muzaffar (1999), "From Human Rights to Human Dignity" in Peter Van Ness, *Debating Human Rights*, London, New York: Routledge, p. 27.

[41] See e.g. Gayatri Spivak (1999), *A Critique of Postcolonial Reason, Toward a History of the Vanishing Present*, Cambridge: Harvard University Press.

On the other hand, The Third World Network have argued that many human rights campaigns against, for instance, child labour seem to be launched when market and labour in European countries are threatened. The question in this context, therefore, can be raised if this is a new form of colonialism disguised as "paternalistic ethics of care" but less interested in just relations or a free trade that may threaten markets in Europe or the United States. If some Asian governments are using "soft authoritarianism" and nostalgic descriptions of a homogenous, pre-colonial past as a shield against Western infiltration, Western liberal democracies and social movements are using human rights as a rhetorical discourse that may have implicit political interests as well. It seems to be so much easier to expose deficiencies when they are far away and in another context.

For both sides, I think that the challenge for the future is to take democracy and human rights seriously, within the family and the close community as well as in relation to international institutions, business and trade regulations. A private-public dichotomy may not be used to excuse the lack of democracy in one or the other. What is considered private or public and what is understood as culturally Asian or European is constantly renegotiated. Not only social hierarchies but also traditional hierarchies of values are in transition both in Europe and in Asia.

Convergence

There are many historical clashes within all religious traditions between authoritarian interpretations and claims of human rights. At the same time, many of the basic thoughts around human and communal dignity originate from religious traditions as well. As the examples above show, neither clashes nor convergence between traditions and human rights follow geographical or cultural lines. It is, therefore, too simplistic to describe human rights as ethnocentric and connected to Europe or the United States. Some ideas that use to be associated with Europe can also be found elsewhere even though they might be formulated differently. Even for values with a more specific origin, it is important not to conflate validity and genesis. That is a mistake that needs to be avoided.

However, not to emphasize religious motivations regarding human rights widens the gulf between European and Asian theories on rights. Many traditions with their origin in Asia, especially those that have to do with Islam, Hinduism, Buddhism and a variety of traditional religions cannot imagine, and even less accept, a system of rights that excludes religious dimensions since religion is understood as an aspect of the totality of life.[42]

Further, religious worldviews often offer a more profound language as they are based on the transcendent, something that Hans Küng often points out.[43] The challenge to implement human rights therefore may be expressed more strongly. Religious traditions not only offer resistance in relation to greed, the "religion of secular modernism". They also offer inspiration and background for notions such as human dignity as well as for personal and communal responsibility. This inspiration is very important, as implementation is crucial in the context of human rights with so many beautiful words, statements, declarations and conventions. Many of these declarations carry ethical challenges and create visions of a good society. Yet, many of them still remain to be implemented.

Last but not least, most religions have a greater emphasis on community. This emphasis is, however, often limited to one's own ethnic or religious community. The discourse of human rights is, in this context, able to facilitate cohabitation and collaboration between religions. We are far from the faith of liberal theology that world religions would develop ever-greater similarity. Dissimilarities in worldviews and life horizons are here to stay. On the other hand, we as human beings have only one planet and therefore some shared interests to solve problems inspired by the opening words of the UN Charter: "to live together as good neighbors". In the contemporary world, this is a challenge not only for states but even more for civilizations, cultures and religions that often coexist within the same states and regions. Neighbours are not necessarily fond of each other. Yet, respecting differences facilitates cohabitation.

Such a respect, however, ought to be especially focused on the person. Cultures consist of human beings worthy of respect. Cultures

---

[42] Martin E. Marty, "Religious Dimension of Human Rights" in John Witte, Jr. and Johan D. van der Vyer (eds.), *Religious Human Rights in Global Perspective: Religious Perspectives*, 1–16, Martinus Nijhoff Publishers.

[43] Hans Küng & Karl-Joseph Kuschel (1993), *A Global Ethic, The Declaration of the Parliament of the World Religions*, Continuum.

in themselves are not entitled to respect. They consist of liberating as well as oppressive elements that in most cultures are being evaluated and renegotiated by individuals belonging to this very culture. Such evaluations are also undertaken interculturally.

Within communicative ethics as developed by Seyla Benhabib, in the tradition and spirit of Jürgen Habermas, there are two basic conditions which make communication meaningful. One is that we respect the right for each person to participate in moral discussion. The second is the right for each person to raise new issues and to discuss the preconditions of the discussion.

Benhabib calls the first the principle of universal moral respect, the second the principle of egalitarian mutuality.[44] Benhabib claims that the modern project can only be reformed from within through the intellectual, moral and political resources at our disposal and by developing modernity globally:

> Among the legacies of Modernity which today need reconstructing but not wholesale dismantling are moral and political universalism, committed to the now seemingly "old-fashioned" and suspect ideas of universal respect for each person in virtue of their humanity; the moral autonomy of the individual; economic and social justice and equality; democratic participation; the most extensive civil and political liberties compatible with principles of justice; and the formation of solidaristic human associations[45] (Benhabib, 1992).

As modernization is a contemporary global process, the values listed above may be some of the most important ones to gather around from various points of departure.

Towards the Future

Later developments in the discussion on human rights, e.g. the formulations at the UN Conference on Human Rights in Vienna, 1993, express the indivisibility of all human rights. The research of Amarthya Sen has pointed to an intimate relationship between civil and political rights and the right to life. He argues that, for instance, some of the large famines in Asia would have been impossible had people had access to free information and political participation.

---

[44] Seyla Benhabib (1992), *Situating the Self, Gender, Community and Postmodernism in Contemporary Ethics*, Cambridge: Polity Press.
[45] Benhabib (1992), p. 2.

In late modernity, the production of knowledge, politics and spirituality is understood in less polarized terms as either or. Just as human rights are seen as indivisible and interdependent so cultures, religions and regions are interdependent in new ways. People within cultures and religions that are secure enough to respect others and to engage in dialogues with the other are also able to argue for crucial values interculturally. Continuing discussions within cultures and religions on how to understand and interpret values may then be combined with interreligious explorations.

Could we possibly be mature enough today for a new kind of spirituality built on mysticism with greater humility in relation to the inner core, God? Interpretations would then be more open and democracy and human rights become central values. In the post-industrial society where information is replacing industrial production, we are facing a new fundamental transformation that Luyckx describes:

> Analytic logic, which is linear and "modern" has been called into question by the new complexity and non-linearity and by the possibilities of horizontal communication and networking. Although reason is not being discarded, its hegemony (and, in the words of Max Weber, its "disenchanting" function) is on the way out. The quest for meaning is being extended into areas until now reserved for reason. One might therefore be heading towards the "re-enchantment" of the world. The epistemology is actively tolerant. Nobody owns the Truth, but it does exist. Post-industrial cosmology envisages thus a "post-secularised world" in the sense that it is open to the transcendental but opposed to any authoritarian or vertical imposition of religious authority. It acknowledges that it is important for all civilizations to be receptive to that which is alien, whatever form this may take[46] (Luyckx, 1996).

For the future, there is a possibility that the tensions between authoritarian religion and human rights that existed in pre-modernity and that within modernity developed into a kind of rivalry may be replaced by a new creative relationship inspired by the openness of late- or post-modernity.

---

[46] Marc Luyckx (1996), "Paths Toward a Dialogue between Religions", paper presented at the second Euro-Islam conference in Mafraq, Jordan 10–13 June, inititated by the Swedish Ministry for Foreign Affairs.

Human Rights and Postmodern Critiques

The view of human nature as being shaped and constructed in the *intermode* may provide a path for Europe to transcend its previous "over"-emphasis on the individual as an island constituted by independent reason. A growing European interpretation of the human being as shaped in relation to other human beings and other things in the world may be closer to Asian values, stressing harmony and interconnectedness.

It is, therefore, also possible to relate to the postmodern discourse positively in the context of human rights. The critique against the great narrative of Europe and America has helped dismantle monolithic solutions. Euro-American hegemony based on Enlightenment self understanding to be "right" in all its cultural expressions and to have a "right" to force its way of life on others is being challenged. Further, when the great narrative of a victorious West is met with scepticism, the deep asymmetries between people, countries and regions become visible. Many of the disagreements about how to interpret human rights in various contexts have to do with asymmetries between cultures and religions where many people in Africa, Asia and Latin America resist and challenge the Euro-American secularist hegemony that they experience as economic and cultural oppression. To criticize the other by describing them as an alien culture is often used to escape inner tensions. Yet, no cultures are monolithic. European or American ways of life or systems of value are not radically different from those of other civilizations. With Seyla Benhabib I think that it is important to recognize that most cultures are "polyvocal" and "multilayered" rather than holistic and monolithic[47] (Benhabib, 2002).

While most pre-modern societies consider human rights in relation to, and even depending on social positions, age and sex, the modern era argues that human rights ought to be related to each human person, independent of "race, color, sex, language, religion, political or other opinion, national or social origin, property, birth or other status" (UDHR, Art. 2). Equality is seen here as an issue of justice and morality. When post-modernity emphasizes difference,

---

[47] Seyla Benhabib (2002), *The Claims of Culture, Equality and Diversity in the Global Era*, Princeton: Princeton University Press, p. 25.

it is important not to undermine the pursuit of justice and equal value of each person while recognizing various forms of differences. The moral and political ambition of universal equality and justice needs to be pursued within all cultures. To accept an understanding of social positions as something given and static is to allow the powerful to prescribe the value of other persons. Human rights need to be related to the person, not to social position, age, colour or sex.

In my view, we constantly need to pursue basic values such as respect for the individual person. We need to deconstruct American hegemonic use of the human rights discourse to advance its own interests. We also need to deconstruct various rhetorical games that refer to asymmetry, diversity, Asian or European values as a disguise for other interests. However, we also need to develop the constructive sides of postmodern thinking. In this case it might be better to talk about late modern thinking where we combine elements from pre-modern life horizons with the best of modernity in a path forward. We need to nurture positive aspects of the pre-modern including a sense for what is shared as well as recognizing our responsibilities to others, to nature and to generations to come. Here, various religious and spiritual traditions may provide inspiration. Positive features of pre-modern understanding of life need to be combined with a deeper respect for the individual that is a heritage of modernity.

Finally, the postmodern critique may help us develop a more dialogical and humble attitude in relation to other cultures and religions and to understand that the world is multidimensional. Thus, in the discussion about religious diversity and human rights, my conclusion is that religious thought and practice as well as the rights tradition may both be important sources of inspiration in the Asian-European dialogue. Such a perspective may create a new openness for different languages, for religious contributions in terms of old and new symbols, spirituality, transcendence and for mysticism that is able to unite human beings in a shared understanding that neither God, cosmos nor human beings may be fully portrayed by words.

CONTINENTS AND REGIONS OF THE WORLD

EUROPE AND ASIAS:
IN THE GLOBAL POLITICAL ECONOMY
AND IN THE WORLD AS A CULTURAL SYSTEM

Göran Therborn
Swedish Collegium for Advanced Study in the Social Sciences
and Cambridge University

What is the world that we should try to locate and compare Asia and Europe in? The world economy? Yes, but is that all? The global system of power? Yes, but what does that mean? Capital plus "weapons of mass destruction"? Does not power have a cultural dimension too, involving patterns of identity, of beliefs, convictions, and doubts, of knowledge and ignorance, of desires and aspirations, and so forth?

We all have some idea of the global political economy, including of Europe as its modern centre and of East Asia as its current pole of growth. But what do we know about the cultural system of the world? There is a need for a conceptual apparatus to capture the world, not only as "the modern world system" of capitalist economics (Wallerstein, 1974–), as a "world society" of planetary communication (Luhmann, 1997) or of worldwide membership (Bornschier, 2002), and not just as a "world culture" of common global models of social arrangement (Meyer, 2000). There is a need for a framework to grasp the world—systematically, and not just as a set of trans-continental anecdotes—as a complex, multidimensional configuration, particularly now that the "globalization" travelogues have lost most of their thrill of exotic discovery, and now that high-level armed combat and profound cultural clashes are demonstrating that the world has a topography. It is not reducible to a chessboard of corporate strategies, nor to frictionless communication or cultural diffusion. Nor is the number of bombs and missiles, although deadly important, the only thing that counts. Winning a war is not the same as winning peace.

The World as a Cultural System

Among other perspectives, complementary rather than rival, the world should be seen and analysed as a cultural system, that is, as a worldwide configuration of patterns and processes of identity, cognition, values, and symbolic forms. This global cultural system provides meanings of the world, meanings of oneself in the world, as well as the meaning of others in it. Such a configuration is obviously imbricated with world economics and world power politics, but those complex interrelations will have to be largely left out here, in this first, provisional spelling out of the world as a cultural system. We shall, however, try to locate the parts of the huge Eurasian continent in the global political economy, as well as in the world cultural system.

The task will be approached, not from a comprehensive global conceptualization downwards, but from some comparative reflections on the locations of Europe and Asia in such a cultural system. However, no inductive generalization is intended. This work builds upon earlier theoretical work, by my illustrious forerunners of global analysis, among whom I have been particularly impressed by Immanuel Wallerstein and John Meyer, but also on my own grappling with general social theory and its application to contemporary European history (Therborn, 1995) and to global processes (Therborn, 2000, 2002a, 2003, 2004, and 2006). In some sense, it also means turning a previous concern with European identity and European location in the world (Therborn, 2002b) into questions such as: What is the world like that Europe and Asia have their places in? But while I might pass as a Europeanist, I can claim no expertise as an Asian scholar. Does that necessarily mean Eurocentric myopia? I hope not, counting on the global perspective to provide a discipline of critical self-reflection.

World outcomes, whatever they are, from divisions of labour to institutional norms, from income distributions to cultural configurations, had better be analysed and explained as following from global or globally pertinent social processes of various kinds. These processes should include at least some specifications of historical time and socio-geographic, socially defined, space. From analyses of world inequality (Therborn 2003, 2006), I have found the following simple model, with their causal arrows, helpful.

The basic ideas of the model are the following. There is an enduring legacy of layers of historical processes larger and wider than any currently existing polity, bearing upon all the current divisions and connections of the globe. Power divisions of planetary space, into states or, more generally and more vaguely, polities, are crucial, if

Figure 1. A General Model of Global Social Dynamics

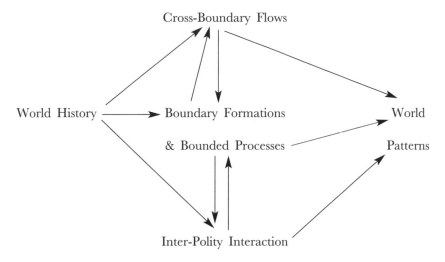

not exclusive, units of global analysis. (Cf. the various non-state polity concepts developed with respect to Southeast Asia, the *mandala* (Wolters), the *Negara* or "theatre state" (Geertz), and the "galactic polity" (Tambiah), (Acharya 2000:20ff). From their centrality, two kinds of contemporary language, but not historically, could be called transnational processes. This means flows across the divisions of power, and interpolity relations, of conflicts, alliances, and entanglements.

How the world cultural system should be summed up and presented is much more complicated than world inequality which is not without fundamental controversies. As a preliminary layout, I would suggest the following.

Cornerstones and Patterning of the World Cultural System

A. *Cornerstones*
1. The architecture of identities: self- and other identifications in the world by major social groups, e.g., continents, regions, nations, classes, beliefs and other cultural life-moulds
2. The production and diffusion of knowledge
3. The shape and distribution of large-scale value systems, and of normative patterns
4. The production and diffusion of symbolic forms, of art, entertainment, sports, brands of consumption

Figure 2. Current Global Socio-Cultural Dynamics

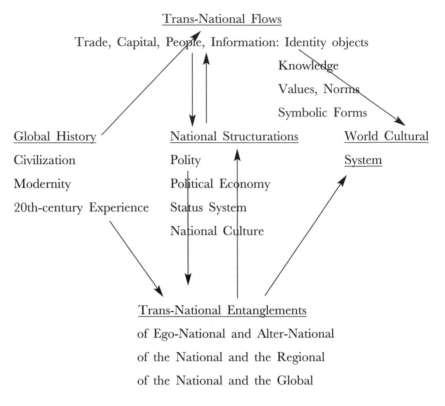

B. *Configuration variables*
1. Horizontal: Socio-spatial divisions. Mechanisms and processes of transmission (not dealt with in this paper)
2. Vertical: Hegemony, dependence, resistance, alternatives

The explanatory schema then has to be filled out with key variables. Figure 2 spells them out with respect to the world cultural system.

Civilizations, Modernities, and History

To get a handle on "world history" in the model, we have to transform it into a small set of variables. "Civilization" has been defined in several different ways and has been used for many different purposes. In spite of its controversial context, it nevertheless seems to be the most convenient way for highlighting an important dimension of pre-modern history (cf. Arnason, 2003). Here "civilization" is being used to denote a large, trans-ethnic pre-modern culture area with some enduring impact on contemporary culture, providing the latter with what Wang Gung-wu (this volume) has called its "deep structure". This might be more similar to Samuel Huntington's (1996) view, if not applying it in the same way, than Felipe Fernández-Arnesto's (2000) thick historical descriptions.

Because of the unique longevity of religions, civilizations tend to have a strong religious loading, but they also include canons of "classicism", of classical art, literature, philosophy, and, at a more popular level, oral treasures of tradition and aspects of ancient habitus, often deriving from the ecological context of the culture. (Here I am linking up with Fernández-Arnesto.) In this particular context, the aim is not an analysis of civilization, but serves only to distinguish a few Asian and European civilizations.

"Modernity" is another useful as well as often misused word. Here, and elsewhere, I have found it most fruitful, and least prejudging, a priori judgmental, perhaps, to stay very closely to the literal temporal meaning of the word. Modernity is then considered as a culture, an epoch, a society, a social sphere having a particular *time orientation*, that is, a time conception looking forward to a this-worldly future, open, novel, reachable or constructible, a conception seeing the present as a possible preparation for a future, and the past either as something to leave behind or as a heap of ruins, pieces of which might be used for building a new future. Modernity in this sense does not designate *per se* a particular chronological period or any particular institutional forms. In principle, different periods of modernity, followed by de-modernization or re-traditionalization, are conceivable. It means a culture, an epoch turning its back to the past and seeing a novel future in front it.

This break with the past may take different forms, the most important of which make up a rather small historical set.

Major Modern Past-Future Contrasts

The Past Was	/	*The Future Will Be*
Heteronomy, oppression		**Emancipation**, liberation
Poverty, ignorance, stagnation		**Progress**, evolution, growth
Different in its preconditions		**Victory**, successful survival
Old, passé, sclerotic		**Vitality**, full of life, creative, a new community

Roughly and very approximately, we might say "emancipation" was the call of the modernist left—from the French Revolution, the labour movement, nationalism and anti-colonialism to women's liberation. "Progress" was the aim of the Liberal centre, and "victory" the sombre worldview of Social Darwinism, of military modernism and Fascism. "Vitalism" was above all an artistic and intellectual vision of modernity, which might be combined with both left and right politics.

More pertinent to our Euro-Asian concerns here, however, is another crucial distinction, that is between different historical routes to and through modernity. The most economical as well as the most systematic way of identifying these roads is to define them by the conflicts surrounding the rise of modernity. Everywhere, modernism and modernity meant a rupture with what had been, and this rupture was naturally conflictual. But the forces for and against a modernist break differed fundamentally from one part of the world to another. (I first hit upon this when studying the history of the right to vote in different parts of the world, Therborn, 1992).

Roads to/through Modernity by the Location of Forces and Cultures For and Against

Pre/Anti-Modernity   **Pro-Modernity**

	Internal	*External*	
Internal	Europe	*Imported & Learnt*	*Forces*
		Reactive Modernization	Colonial Zone
External	New Worlds		

Note: Countries of Reactive, or externally induced, Modernization, e.g., Japan, China, Ottoman Empire/Turkey, Iran, Siam/Thailand.

The new future orientation of the last centuries first emerged in Europe, not as a natural emanation of European civilization, but out of conflicts internal to Europe, to north-western Europe primarily. In other words, the European route was one of civil war, which pitted the forces of reason, enlightenment, nation/people, innovation, and change against those of the eternal truths of the Church, of the sublime wisdom and beauty of Ancient philosophy and art, of the divine rights of kings, of the ancient privileges of aristocracy, and of the customs of fathers and grandfathers.

In the New Worlds of European settlement, anti-modernity was, in the first rise of modern currents, perceived as mainly external, in the conservative metropolis, in Britain to North America, in Spain and Portugal to Latin America, *and*, increasingly, in the local Others of the settler societies, the natives, the slaves, and the ex-slaves. Independence got rid of the external metropolis, but what to do with the local Others was to haunt the moderns of the New Worlds for a very long time. It still does.

To the Colonial Zone, from north-western Africa to Southeast Asia, modernity arrived literally out of the barrel of guns, with the colonial conquest, subduing the internal forces of tradition. Modernity was not carried further by settlers, but by new generations of natives, of *"évolués"* who turned what they had learnt from their conquerors against the latter. After Independence, the ex-Colonial Zone carried a complex legacy of nationalism, a colonial elite culture—of language, habitus, and, e.g., exotic sports interests (like cricket in South Asia and the Anglo-Caribbean)—and colonial-turned-excolonial state-society bifurcation.

The countries of Reactive Modernization were challenged and threatened by colonial domination, and in the face of these threats a part of the internal elite started to import innovation from the outside. Meiji Japan is the most successful and clear-cut example, but several pre-modern empires embarked upon it, late Qing and Republican China, rather unsuccessfully, Siam very cautiously, Iran and the Ottoman empire/Turkey hesitantly and belatedly, but finally with a strong push from above.

At another level of comparative generalization, we should take note of the fact that the great modern tasks, of emancipation, progress, or survival looked differently along these roads to and through modernity. Different modernities have had different Others as obstacles or as categories of reference.

Locations of Modernist Tasks

The Past was/	*The Future will be*	
	In our (r)evolution	In catching up with others
In our society till now	Europe	Colonial Zone
Under external rule	Dep. New Worlds	Ex-Colonial Zone
Under native rule	Indep. New Worlds	
Our military/ economic decay	Successful RM	Early RM countries

Note: RM: Countries of Reactive Modernization

Among the self-centred modernizers one might further distinguish between those cultures which have a universalistic self-conception, seeing themselves as the best model for others, and those with a particularistic conviction of their own uniqueness and essential difference to all others. The European Enlightenment and its North American off-shoot, American Liberalism, have this universalistic self-conception to a very pronounced extent, and it has been a general part of European colonialism and American imperialism. Japanese modernity, by contrast, has been more particularistic, although till 1945 with a regional colonial slant.

For all their worth, civilizations and modernities are not sufficient to grasp the historical moulding of contemporary cultures and polities. Traumatic and/or euphoric experiences of 20th century events are also crucial. Such events are hardly classifiable *a priori*, but the analyst had better pay good attention to wars, political transformations, and the economic record.

With the help of the analytical scaffolding sketched above, we might venture into a comparative look at Europe and Asia.

One Europe, Several Asias

There is a sense, in which we may talk about one Europe, and not primarily because of the enlargement of the European Union. which took place in 2004. In terms of world history, Europe is basically

one civilization, with a common Antiquity or Classicism—of philosophy, art, and architecture—derived from the city states and empires
of Greece and Rome 2,500 to 1,500 years ago, and a common
Christian religion, although it has been deeply divided for a thousand years.

It is sometimes argued, that Eastern Europe falls outside this civilization, for not having had the resurgence of this Antiquity in what
in Europe is called the Renaissance of the 15th–16th centuries.
However, this was the time, after the fall of Constantinople to the
Muslim Ottomans in 1453, that the religious and political authorities of Muscovy, began to refer to Moscow as the "Third Rome",
and Greek architecture became from the 18th century part of Russian
imperial Classicism. (Most of the showpieces of the new capital of
Saint Petersburg were built by Italian architects.) Germanic as well
as Slavic Europe were outside the Roman empire, and Sweden did
not even exist on the maps of Ancient geographers, but later on an
Ancient legacy was learnt and claimed all over European high culture.

There is a basically common European road to modernity, beginning in the British 17th century, with its scientific breakthroughs and
its political civil wars, and winning the centre stage through the 18th-
century Enlightenment and the French Revolution, but then having
to fight its way all through the long 19th century, and only becoming victorious with the outcome of World War I. Dynasties—with
the brief 18th-century qualification of "Enlightened Absolutism",
stretching from Lisbon to St Petersburg, including aristocracies, all
established churches, Catholic, Orthodox, and Protestant—were against
a rupture with traditional sources of authority. However, burghers,
artisans, secular intellectuals, dissident aristocrats, and, increasingly,
the big city populace, the new industrial workers, and nationalisti-
cally aroused peasants were in favour of questioning traditional authority. Modernity in Europe was endogenous, its conflicts civil wars,
and from the French Revolution to the Russian Revolution increasingly reflected class conflict. To this day, the democratic party systems of Europe have a class-rooted left-right cleavage pattern.

Europe also has a common, traumatic 20th century history, being
the main theatre of the two World Wars and of the global Cold
War—all three originating and decided in Europe. This traumatic
war experience has had two important consequences in particular.
One is the drive for overcoming the violent divisions of the past,
first of the Franco-German wars, which led to the creation of what

is now the European Union, then of the Cold War division of Germany into German Reunification, and thirdly of the Cold War "Iron Curtain", to be overcome in part (if not fully) by the "Eastern enlargement" of the EU in 2004. (Left out after 2004 are Bulgaria and Romania, which have clear prospects of later membership; the remaining states of former Yugoslavia, Albania, Belarus, Russia, and the Ukraine, whose European future is still uncertain, and, in the cases of Ukraine, Russia, and Belarus still controversial. Upon strong American pressure, the EU has agreed to give priority to negotiations with Turkey, another very controversial candidate.)

Secondly, pioneered by post-World War II Germany, 20th century history has taught Europe guilt. European culture has become significantly preoccupied with digging up, commemorating, and redeeming its crimes of the past, mainly, but by no means exclusively, the Nazi genocide and the collaboration or collusion with it, and also the dictatorship of Communism, the dirty Cold War by the West, and the crimes of colonialism.

The loss of its colonies and of its Big Powers have been remarkably less traumatic than expected, although they do provide a very relevant background to the Rome Treaty of 1957, which launched the European Economic Community. Those losses, and in particular the former, were overshadowed by the unprecedented boom of the European economies after the war, which had made the European continent a magnet of immigration in the early 1960s, reversing an almost 500-year-old tradition of out-migration.

European civilization as well as European modernity has a strong universalistic, missionary streak. Christianity is a world religion of salvation, and European explorers, traders, and conquerors were usually from the very beginning accompanied by Christian missionaries, who ventured into Sub-Saharan Africa, South America, and East Asia by the 16th century. The European scientism and the rationalism of the 17th and 18th centuries were also explicitly universalistic, which did not exclude a high respect and admiration for some non-European cultures, the Chinese in particular, revered by some of the greatest minds of the European Enlightenment, like Leibniz and Voltaire. But universalism is inherently self-righteous. In the 20th century, European Communism, Social Democracy, and Liberalism have all continued this universalistic Europeanness.

This common European legacy of civilization, modernity, and 20th century traumata has always been full of conflict, contrary interpretations, and exclusivist claims. The commonality of Europe is by no means a cultural emanation, but a commonality of conflict, of war, as well as of bargaining, truces, and compromise.

There is no Asia in the same sense. Not even the wonderful pan-Asian journal *Inter-Asia Cultural Studies* has a fully pan-Asia basis, restricting itself to the huge area from India to Japan (inclusive). The range of the grand Singaporean millennium conference, "We Asians" (Kwok Kian-Woon *et al.*, 2000) is the same, repeating the stretch a century earlier, by Okakura Tenshin and a couple of other Japanese artists going to Calcutta and linking up with Bengali culture for a pan-Asian effort. When Okakura (1903) opened his *Ideals of the East* by saying "Asia is one", he was proclaiming a new Japanese intellectual programme, against the anti-Asianness of the early Meiji modernizers, who with Fukuzawa Yukichi called for a dissociation with Asia, "*datsu-A ron*", but he was thinking primarily of the Sinic and the Indic civilizations (cf. Karatani, 1993). The Japanese concept of "the East", *toyo*, which was established as topic of historiography on par with "the West" from the 1890s, did formally include Eurasia east of Europe, while excluding what is now seen as Southeast Asia, and was in fact centred on Sino-Japanese relations (Tanaka, 1993).

But more mainstream Asianness has been expressed by Tommy Koh (2000:12), Singapore's shrewd and worldwise Ambassador at Large. When asked to speak about Asia and the Western world, he defined Asia as "Pacific or East Asia". In Chinese, the name of the continent is derived from European languages, the rendering of which in Chinese characters has a peculiar literal meaning, "Inferior Continent" (*Yaxiya*) (Korhonen, 2002).

How many Asias there are more or less equivalent to "Europe" is a question hardly raised before, and one that is unlikely to have a non-controversial answer. There are at least three, and sometimes, in analyses of patriarchy, family, and gender relations, it is most meaningful to talk about four (Therborn, 2004a), but the number might easily be extended.

West Asia is one, with an Arab-Turkic civilization, glued together by Islam and a culture of nomads and merchants, enriched and enlarged by Persian culture. This is a part of Asia significantly turned to the Mediterranean, largely continuing on the latter's southern, African shores, and for a thousand years was importantly shaped by its conflicts, and occasional alliances, with European powers. Its road to modernity was that of Reactive Modernization, against the encroachments of European imperialism. The second half of the 20th century in West Asia has been shaped by having to redeem the (Nazi) European genocide by accommodating the state of Israel thrust upon it.

Sparsely populated Central Asia may in a panoramic overview be regarded as a frontier zone of West Asia, historically moulded by the same or a similar Turkic and Iranian Islamic culture and its encounters with Chinese and Mongols along the Silk Road. True, its path to modernity has been significantly different, through Russian annexation and Soviet *khudzum* ([modernist] storm).

At the other end is East Asia, the realm of the Sinic civilization, from Korea to Vietnam, with the Middle Kingdom at its centre. Its contacts with Europe have mostly been limited, and when Europe was rising, this region and its polities—in particular those of Japan and Korea—, tried to seal themselves off. Later, and largely through trans-Pacific challenges from the US,, this Asia became, in the shape of Japan, the first and the most successful example of Reactive Modernization. East Asia had a common 20th-century history though each country could be in opposing camps in the World Wars and in the Cold War. The Sino-Japanese conflicts became, in their own way, linked with the German-Franco/British wars. After World War II, North and South Korea became Asian mirrors of East and West Germany.

Between those two wings of Asia—briefly connected before modernity by the Mongols, thereafter falling apart—, there is Indic civilization, the core of current South Asia. Although it includes an important West Asian input, of Islamic religion and the Persian high culture of the Mughal empire, and although it once exported Buddhism to the East and mathematics to the West, in all its multiformity it is a culture very different from the West and from East of Asia, in religion, life philosophy, and symbolic forms. It has a classical canon of its own.

The South Asian road to modernity went through British colonialism and later anti-colonialist nationalism. Colonialism and nationalism were also their specific experiences of 20th-century history, alongside bloody communal conflicts. And South Asia has kept an imprint of the British *Raj*, English as the actual state language, the parliamentary and the judicial protocol, even cricket as a favourite sport.

The case for Southeast Asia as a fourth Asia would be based on the region's interstitial character, between the Indic and the Sinic civilizations, and at the crossroads of Buddhism, Islam, Christianity, Confucianism, and Hinduism, upon a receptive and mellowing Malay culture. In my work on the family in the world (Therborn, 2004a), I have found it useful to treat the area from Sri Lanka—originally invited to and then rejected by ASEAN—to the Philippines as a cultural region of its own, different from the harsh patriarchies of the rest of Asia. Although Siam was never colonized and gradually embarked on a Reactive Modernization, regional modernization was marked by a multiplicity of colonialisms—Dutch, British, French, Spanish, American, even Portuguese—and by national liberation from them.

In spite of anti-colonial and civil wars, and the monstrous massacres in Indonesia in 1965, the currently predominant interpretation of late 20th-century history seems to be one of epochal economic development. And the record is indeed impressive. Today Singapore has a national income per capita (in purchasing power parities) on par with Britain (or Sweden). Singapore and even richer Hong Kong are the only non-settler colonies which in modern history have ever caught up with their former masters. Malaysia has a GDP per capita which today is higher than the 2004 members of the EU, Latvia and Lithuania (World Bank, 2003: Table 1.)

Culturally, Malaysia may be seen as the pivot of all Asia. Alongside its Southeast Asian Malay majority, it has very sizeable Chinese and Indian minorities. Through its increasingly emphasized (majority) Muslim character, it is also connected to West Asia, and to the latter's holy places of Islam. In the wake of West Asian withdrawal from an increasingly unreliable and hostile America and Europe, Malaysia is also wooing West Asian capital. However, in spite of the flair of its leadership, Malaysia is too small, by Asian standards, to carry a pan-Asian project.

Positions in the Current Political Economy of Flows and Entanglements

The world as a cultural system should not be seen in isolation from the multidimensional flows and entanglements which make up global processes. The point here is not culturalism—that "culture matters"—

but the multidimensionality of global processes. Through the key cultural processes of identity construction and perception, above all but not only, positions in the political economy are highly pertinent to cultural formation. So, before we go into their location in the world cultural system, we had better try to make a brief summary of the most salient features of Europe and the Asias in the global political economy. We shall then find some important clues as to how different peoples see and talk about their place in the world.

Europe: The World's Trader and the World's Lawyer

Europe has acquired a special position as the world's foremost trader and as the world's first lawyer (see further Therborn, 2002b). True, without the 2004 "Eastern Enlargement" of the EU, one would have had to restrict "Europe" to Western Europe in this context but from 2004, East-Central Europe, west of Ukraine, will be part of the characterization.

In the international flows of trade and capital, Western Europe is still *the* centre of the world, even if less so than just before World War I. and Europe's 20th-century serious attempts at self-destruction. In 1913, one-third of world trade was intra-European, and trade between Europe and the rest of the world made up a good half of all international trade.

In 2000, a good fourth of all global foreign trade, 27 per cent, took place within Western Europe, almost a third (29 per cent) within all Europe, and 40 per cent of world exports originate in the countries of Western Europe. US exports, including commercial services, amount to 14 per cent of the world total, and Japanese to 7 per cent. Intra-EU trade is twice the size of intra-NAFTA trade (WTO, 2001: tables III.1, III.3, III.5, and I.9, respectively). If Japan alone is much smaller economically than the US and the EU, East Asia as a region carries much weight. It has become the world's second export region, holding a fourth of global export market shares. Among the twenty largest export economies, ten are in Western Europe, seven in East Asia (the four largest in the north, the three smallest in the south), and three in North America (including Mexico with its assembly exports to the US) (UNCTAD, 2002a: figure VI.1).

In 2000, Western Europe owned more than half of the world's stock of foreign direct investment, 57 per cent, while the US owned a fifth, and Japanese investors barely five per cent (4.7 per cent).

Western Europe is also the largest host of foreign investment, holding almost 40 per cent of the world stock in 2000, while the US
harbours 20 per cent, and Japan less than 1 per cent. In flow terms,
the EU countries of Western Europe sent out more than 60 per cent
of global foreign direct investment in 2001 (70 per cent in the acqui-
sitions bonanza in 2000) and received a good 60 per cent of it.
United States sent out a fifth of world outflows and received a fifth
of inflows. Japanese outgoing direct investment was about a tenth of
that of the EU, and Japan was marginal as a receiver. China has
become an important receiver of foreign investment, but in comparison with Europe, it is still modest, less than 10 per cent of the
global total, and slightly less than UK, France, Belgium-Luxemburg,
and Netherlands individually (UNCTAD, 2002a:6ff):

In sum, while no longer the richest part of the earth and no longer
the prime economic model of the world, Europe is still the central
node of global flows of trade and of capital. While the US has
become the prime producer and the prime owner of global wealth,
Europe is still the main mover of economic flows, something often
forgotten in national pictures of globalization. Regional characteristics and regional positions are important because economic globalization is strongly regional.

Generally speaking, and contrary to what might seem implied in
the word "globalization", there was in the last third of the 20th century a tendency towards a greater regionalization of trade, not dramatic but nevertheless significant. Europe has been a forerunner in
this respect, but it is by no means a unique achievement, and the
formal, institutional integration of Europe has played at most a secondary or tertiary role in this.

In Western Europe (including non-members of the EU), intra-
regional (merchandise) trade was 64 per cent of all exports in 1963
and 68 per cent in 2000. Intra-regional import shares grew from 56
to 65 per cent. In North America, intra-NAFTA exports rose from
28 to 50 per cent, while intra-regional imports remained at its old
level. The difference is due to a surge of Asian imports, and the US
import surplus. Japanese trade in the same period became more
Asian-oriented. Chinese trade is also primarily Asian, in spite of its
large export surplus to the US. (WTO, 2001: tables II.4, II.3, and
II.5, respectively)

However globalized, some parts of the globe are much closer to
each other than others. In the case of trade flows, that tendency of

spatial distance dependency has rather been strengthened recently, not weakened.

Trade and markets always presuppose some kind of normative framework. But in Europe, trans-national law and trans-national norms have acquired a special importance. Law has been a crucial part of the post-World War II process of European integration, and in the contemporary world Europe, again primarily Western Europe, is the main protagonist of international law. It is in the normative framework of the UN, and in the WTO—and its "constitutional-ization" of international trade, that Europe is playing a key part in the global institutional entanglement of states. Europe is pushing the UN Human Rights Conventions, the Kyoto Protocol on the reduc-tion of pollution, and the International Criminal Court. In all these respects, the US is the main counter-player, fearful of being bound by international rules.

Transnational (or, less anachronistically, trans-polity) law has an old, pre-modern background in Europe. Owing to the Roman empire, law, as a formal system differentiated from general social normativ-ity, was an important part of European civilization, carried into the Middle Ages by the Christian Church. From early modernity a spe-cial international law developed, largely to deal with intercolonialist rivalries among European states.

Europe became the world's lawyer in the 19th century. The newly independent Latin American states adopted Napoleonic legal codes, still weighing upon the Hemisphere, not the least in family law. Imperialist expansion brought European extra-territoriality to the threatened and bullied pre-modern polities of Asia, from the Ottoman empire to Japan. In 1865, the British set up in Shanghai "Her British Majesty's Supreme Court for China and Japan". Colonial conquest introduced European law into Africa Asia, and created a new dual legal system, with domestic customary law, a duality of law persist-ing till this day in family matters. Meiji Japan imported a legal sys-tem from Europe, from France and, above all, from Germany, a legal change then inspiring Chinese attempts at law reform. Post-Ottoman Turkey later adopted a derivative of the Swiss Code. The Paris-based Institute of International Law in 1874 graciously accorded the theoretical equality of all nations, non-Christian as well as Christian, thereby proclaiming a universality principle of international law (Cf. Mommsen and De Moor, 1992).

The weakened power of Europe has diminished the current global significance of European law and regulation. The dynamic of US capitalism, and business education, has also meant that international business law is informally gravitating to American conceptions. However, Europe has become the main force of international public law and of global normative governance.

Where the European commitment to transnational law and transnational normativity is most clearly manifested in the current world is within Europe itself. Europe is the world's high-density area of transnational legal and normative entanglements of cross-national jurisdiction.

The Council of Europe adopted in 1950 the first international, legally binding convention on human rights, enforced by a commission, a committee of ministers with a majority voting system, and a court. It was concerned with civil and political rights only, and it took more than a decade for its supranationality to be fully recognized by all member states, but it did take effect. In 1961, an extensive European Social Charter was adopted, formulated as obligations accepted by the member states, with a supranational monitoring and complaint system, in the last instance issuing into recommendations of the Ministerial Committee with two-thirds majority (Steiner ad Alston, 1996; ch. 10.B).

Postwar Western Europe was, then, a normative area before it became a Common Market, the goal of the Rome Treaty of 1957, and a Single Market, the achievement of 1992. It is noteworthy, that of the various forms of European integration projects after World War II, it was the trading one, which was most successful and far-reaching. On the world arena, it is also first of all in trading contexts that EU actually operates as one body, in the WTO, for example. But it is also to be noticed, that law and legal regulation has played a crucial part in this economic unification.

The European judiciary, the European Court of Justice with support from the national judiciaries of the EEC/EU member states, has constituted a major supranational force in the construction of a new Europe. In a couple of early landmark decisions the Court established the principles of *direct effect* of Community law, and of its *supremacy* over national law, including, within its area of jurisdiction, over national constitutional law. In the last-mentioned case, the Court stated, that "the validity of a Community measure ... cannot be affected by allegations that it runs counter to . . . fundamental rights as formulated by the constitution of that state . . ." (Wouters, 2000:46–47).

In more personal statements, leading European judges called these judicial rulings to "take Community law out of the hands of the politicians and bureaucrats and give it to the people" (thus Judge Federico Mancini, here quoted from Schepel and Blankenburg, 2001:11). Furthermore, there soon developed the practice, that national courts petitioned the European Court on how the founding Treaty and subsequent European legislation should be interpreted.

The European Court has established its powers gradually and cautiously, as well as with impressive transnational firmness, effectiveness and legitimacy. The latter has recently been partly contested in some cases, true, but in a world of states, the regional entanglement of European and national law and jurisdiction, the possibility of individuals and organizations to bring their state governments to an international court in a broad range of civic cases, is a historical change of national sovereignty, not to be found anywhere else in the world, although in looser forms inspiring attempts at regional integration on all the other continents.

While officially inspiring the new African Union launched in 2003, this European conception of transnational law has no equivalent in Asia. It is almost the direct opposite of "the ASEAN way", of non-interference in other states' affairs, of consensus and non-binding plans, and on national institutions and actions, in other words of informal, discrete, top-level diplomacy behind closed doors (Tay and Estanislao, 2000; Gates 1999; Funston, 2000; Surin Pitsuwan, 2001). However, it may be noticed, that the ASEAN diplomats nowadays have to pay some attention to the peoples they are representing. In 2000, an ASEAN People's Assembly met in Batam, Indonesia, a carefully orchestrated affair of respectable organizations of "civil society".

Heavy-Weight Masters of Globalization, and Other Players

There is no necessary symmetry of the Asian and the European positions in the world economy. To assume otherwise would amount to either a Eurocentric or an Asiacentric view of the world. Outstanding Asian features will have to be searched for on their own terms, like the European ones were.

Most remarkable here, I think, is East Asian—North as well as South—discourse and stance on globalization. Whereas in Europe and in the Americas—even in the US—globalization is almost always seen as an external force you have to submit to, alternatively should resist. In East Asian elite discourse, globalization is an option, chosen, managed, mastered. To "globalize" is an active verb. A centrally located Indonesian analyst has put it this way, referring to the ASEAN countries: ". . . the ASEAN economies of Indonesia, the Philippines, Thailand, and Vietnam began to globalize only in the 1980s . . ." Globalization is regarded as something a nation-state can initiate: "In Vietnam, as in the other ASEAN economies, globalization was initiated by the government" (Soesastro, 1998:27–28). In 1994, the Thai Royal Academy officially endorsed *lokapiwat* as the proper Thai translation of "globalization", rejecting the first used word *lokanuwat*. The discarded translation meant "act according to the world", but the endorsed one meant roughly "expanding globally" or "conquering the world" (Chantana Banpasirichote, 1998:259).

Similar perspectives can be found in Northeast Asia. A major Korean work deals with globalization in a possessive form, as "Korea's Globalization" (Kim, 2000). While there are many different Japanese treatments of globalization, including one of the extreme postnational argumentations (Ohmae, 1990), it is, I would suggest, symptomatic, that a set of distinguished Japanese scholars can put out a book on Japanese globalization, in the sense of Japan as one of the creators, one of the centres of globalization (Befu and Guichard-Anguis, 2001; cf. Iwabuchi, 2002). While there has been varied Chinese discussion on globalization (see Yu Keping in this volume), the main tendency is one of choice and self-management. A Chinese scholar has summed up the phenomenon very well, from a cultural anthropological angle: "The Chinese case demonstrates a new type of cultural globalization: a managed process in which the state plays a leading role, and the elite and the populace work together to claim ownership of the emerging global culture." (Yunxiang Yan, 2002:44).

This East Asian conception of globalization as one's own option, as one's own property is not a fantasy, but an interpretation of a dramatic economic experience of the last four to five decades. That experience has three components, which together provide a strong material basis for the type of discourse mentioned. First, there has been a spectacularly successful economic performance, in terms of national income growth. It began in Japan in the 1950s, followed by Korea and Taiwan in the 1960s, the ASEAN region in the 1970s, and China in the 1980s. Secondly, in all cases exports have played a crucial role, raising seven countries of the region to the twenty largest exporters of the world. Thirdly, this outward, globalizing orientation has been successfully combined with various forms of skilful national protection, a (so far) successful deselection of several external global forces. Korea and Japan have kept inward foreign investment at bay, and have also shielded their agrarian and retail sectors from foreign competition. China, by contrast has welcomed foreign investment, but has kept not only its Communist party-state but also its currency inconvertible.

Malaysia, a smaller market dependent on foreign investment has managed to attract capital enough for half of its manufacturing exports (in 1995) which were provided by foreign affiliates (UNCTAD, 2002a: table 8). At the same time, it has pursued an active Malay empowerment policy, not the least in the economy. Although starting with a tiny industrial base, Malaysia has, better than, say, Mexico, managed to link up with foreign investment, increasingly producing value added in the country, rather than mainly importing components to assemble (UNCTAD, 2002b: chart 3.7). Singapore is the most open economy of the region, but the government is closely monitoring information flow into the nation, and sometimes stop unwanted items from entering.

This East Asian globalizing nationalism has taken some blows recently, with the financial crisis of 1997–1998 and with the current Japanese stagnation. But is has bounced back rather well. Malaysia refused to go along with the IMF policies in the Asian financial crisis of 1997–1998, introducing capital controls instead, and got away with it. In early August 2003, Thailand proudly paid back its IMF loan ahead of due time, with the Prime Minister ceremonially promising that the country would never let itself fall into the claws of IMF again. (An American commentator called the gesture a "turning point for globalization", Philip Bowring in the *International Herald Tribune*, 7 August 2003, p. 6, and the London *Financial Times* signalled its importance in an editorial on 11 August.). Korea and Taiwan are again on the high growth track, and China was never derailed from it.

East Asia is the master of globalization. (North) East Asia is also the demographic heavyweight of the world, housing about a fourth of world population.

South Asia—with Indian software production and call centres as exceptional counter-examples—has still a peripheral position in the world economy, providing 1 per cent of world (merchandise) exports and barely 2 per cent of world production (at current exchange rates, 7 per cent in purchasing power parities; World Bank 2003: tables 2 and 3.). Its recent growth record, of India in particular, is already raising expectations of a global economic breakthrough in the near future, though. In any case, South Asia is the world's second demographic heavyweight, with a good fifth of global population. To the extent that human rights and planetary human interconnection have any significance, the large number of humans in East and South Asia should matter, increasingly.

Pro-active globalization has come more easily to non-colonized countries. None of the key countries in the East Asian promotion of globalization was properly colonized by European or American powers. Korea and Taiwan were subjected to Japanese rule, more effectively developmentalist than European colonizers, although very much resented in Korea. Singapore was a (Chinese) settlement (under British rule), more comparable to North America than to South Asia. The Malayan principalities, which were to form the core of Malaysia, remained protectorates of the British Empire, rather than colonies. Significantly, the Malay princes and aristocrats preserved their continuity to provide the first Prime Ministers of independent Malaysia. Reactive Modernization in East Asia led on to the very specific pro-active globalization.

West Asia owes its world economy significance to the oil deposits of the Gulf sub-region, which have made the area the 20th to 21st-century *rentier* of the world, with its poor dependents (Yemenis, Egyptians), its struggling less endowed outliers, like Turkey and (North African) Morocco, and its imported labourers. The economic role of the oil sheikh is similar to that of the pre-modern landowning pashas, so the successful reproduction of archaic polities in the Gulf should not surprise. Turkey, an early Reactive Modernizer, was significantly formed in the era of inward-looking development before World War II. The Gulf sheikhdoms, on the other hand, entered the modern world only recently, in the post-industrial world of finance, tourism, shopping, and media, and a few of them, like Dubai, may be on the road from a rentier fiefdom to a second- or third-rate "global city".

The World Cultural System: Some Provisional Indications

The Architecture of Identities

From a global vantage point, the first, decisive question about Europe is: Does it exist? Or is it just a part of "the West"?

Huntington (1996), like many American writers, subsumed Western Europe under—an America-led—"West". In the era of European supremacy and imperialism, "West" and "Western" were often European self-designations. But in the second half of the 20th century, with European decline, American ascendancy and the Cold War division of the world, "the West" became the US, its allies and its dependents.

With the end of the Cold War, and with the consolidation of the EU, there is in Europe an assertion of Europeanness, and a corresponding decline of Westernness. But the relation of "Europe" to "the West" remains a contested question, above all on the elite level, as the different views among European political leaders of their necessary loyalty with the US showed. The relative weight in Africa and Asia of perceiving Europe as Europe or as (part of) the West, seems to be unknown.

Europe was the cradle of nationalism, but the traumata of 20th-century history have made Europe, in particular Western Europe, and Germany above all, a relatively limited nationalist culture. Little more than a half of Western Germans said in the mid-1990s that they felt (any) national pride, and only a half or less were prepared to fight for their country. Outside Europe, there is a certain parallel in the response pattern of the Japanese, the other key loser of World War II. In other parts of Asia, from China to Turkey, nationalist identities are much stronger (Klingemann, 1999:42ff; cf. Therborn, 1995:280; Pettersson, 2003:220). Continental allegiance was not spectacular in Europe of the 1990s, similar to Latin America, but less than Africa. However, Asian identity was particularly low, as tapped in China and Japan (Therborn, 1995:250).

While its resilience to sharp national or continental issues has not been tested, it is clear, that Europe, and again Western much more than Eastern, contains a strong global commitment. It was manifested recently in the enormous demonstrations against a war against Iraq in February–March 2003. In Rome, Madrid, and Barcelona, about a million people or more were in the streets protesting against the subservience of their government to the US war plans, and in London at least hundreds of thousands. In Spain and Italy, these were more or less the largest demonstrations in national history, and in Oslo of Norway, the anti-war demonstration was larger than any political manifestation before, national day celebrations excepted. Nowhere else in the world, was there anything of similar size, not even in the Arab world. Movements and demonstrations against neoliberal globalization—Attac and "Genua", respectively—have a larger resonance in Western Europe than elsewhere. Although it is true, that a great deal has been done in the Americas, from the Seattle demonstration against the WTO in 1999 to the World Social Forum in Porto Alegre, Brazil, that forum is moving to India in 2004, but so far the Asian manifestations of popular globalism have been much more modest. In brief, to the extent that Europe exists in the global architecture of identities, it is secular, significantly global, partly continental, delimitedly, though still quite significantly national.

Religious identities are clearly much more important in West and South Asia, probably also in most parts of Southeast Asia. South Asia was partitioned along religious lines in 1947, and the recent and rather arbitrary and accidental Arab polities of West Asia do not seem to have generated strong national identities. But that is only part of the picture. West and South Asia have also important secular nationalist currents, and West Asian and South Asian identity structures seem to be hung up on a bifurcation between religious and national-secular identities, with the former recently being strengthened at the expense of the latter. Arab Nasserism was crushed by the Israelis in 1967, the Baath party became only an instrument of dictatorial rule in Syria and Iraq, and before its recent toppling by the Americans, Iraqi Baath under Saddam Hussein had abandoned its original secularism. Turkish Kemalism was recently electorally defeated by Islamic Democracy, whereas the Indian Congress party remains in the doldrums.

In East Asia, a very strong, secular nationalist identity seems to prevail, although accompanied in Japan by considerable unofficial national modesty. In contrast to Germany, no historical culture of self-criticism has been built in postwar Japan (Buruma, 1994). On the contrary,, recurrent officious wartime apologetics has again and again created serious friction with Korea and China. In spite of increasing regional economic entanglements and cooperation, no grand regional identity project, of a Sino-Japanese commonality similar to the Franco-German in Europe, is in sight. Nor is there any equivalent of the universalistic globalism of European culture. While East Asian countries are increasingly important players in the global economy, East Asian identities and cultural outlooks are likely to remain overwhelmingly national for the foreseeable future.

Cognition, Science, and Information

Knowledge is formulated variably in different parts of the world, which complicates cultural diffusion and translation. Only within the modern North Atlantic context, a German sociologist has distinguished some characteristic national forms of "formulating knowledge": the British "enquiry", the American "paper", the German "work", and the French "essay" (Münch, 1986). If such variation may be expressed on a regional level as well remains to be seen.

But we do have good evidence from experimental psychology that the very process of cognition itself is culturally different in the contemporary world, deriving from ancient civilizational roots. Most of this evidence, assembled by the American psychologist Richard Nisbet (2003), refers to East Asia and North America/Western Europe, and is based on experiments with students of different regional backgrounds. Occasionally (pp. 114–15), an experiment with (Asian) Indians and Euro-Americans is also referred to. East Asians tend to perceive the world more in contextual, relational, contradictory, and spatial terms than Euro-Americans, who focus more on actors' dispositions, on objects and their categorization, on abstract rules, and on an excluding logic of either/or. In spite of these and related studies, an unravelling and a mapping global knowledge patterns are still only in their beginning. Anyway, a grasp of the characteristic cognitive skills of both East Asians and of Europeans would be a significant enrichment of the world cultural system.

While there is much more to "knowledge" than science, science is the main component of a world system of cognition. The configuration of the production of scientific knowledge is a very important part of the contemporary cultural system, at a time when a "knowledge-based economy" has become a major slogan of political economy, officially endorsed by the EU, for instance. From a forthcoming study by the distinguished German sociologist of science Peter Weingart (2004: figure 11), we may borrow some very indicative data and tabulate them.

Table 1. Shares of International Science Citations 1996–2000.
(Percentage of World Totals)

USA	39
EU	39
of which	
UK	10
Germany	7.5
France	5
East Asia	8
of which	
Japan	6
China	1
Russia	1
India	0.6

Source: P. Weingart, "Knowledge and Inequality", in G. Therborn (ed.), *Inequalities of the World*, London: Verso, 2004, figure 11.

Put together, the current EU15 fare surprisingly well in comparison with the United States. The tie with the US tells us something about the broad scientific base of Western Europe, while East Asia comes out as a poor third. Nevertheless, the overwhelming picture is the high geographic concentration of the world science system, a concentration which is probably exaggerated by the selection of journals scanned. And at the top level, the US dominance is striking. Out of 371 Nobel Laureates in science and economics for 1946–2000, 218 or 59 per cent were based at US institutions, 139 or 37 per cent at Western European ones. Four per cent is then left to the rest of world (Nobel e-Museum).

News are still produced and diffused mainly by national and local media, but there is also an increasingly important transnational production and distribution. By using national languages, it is not only reaching small elite audiences. The major global players are all Anglo-Saxon, the American CNN, the BBC, and Australian-American Rupert Murdoch's Star in Asia, Sky in Europe, and Fox in the US. Regional networks of importance include the European Euronews, and the two independent-minded Arab broadcasters—a thorn in the flesh both of the US government, which repeatedly has tried to silence them, and to Arab autocracies—Al-Jazeera in Qatar and the very recent Al-Arabiyya in Dubai.

Religious and Secular Values

Northeast Asia, perhaps with a reservation for South Korea, constitutes together with the bulk of Europe the most irreligious, secularized part of the world. On a 0–10 scale of the importance of God in one's life, the Japanese score about 5, the rest of the Sinic civilization area 5.4, and the bulk of Europe between 5 and 5.5, with some Catholic (Poland, Ireland, Lithuania), Orthodox (Romania), and secularized (Scandinavia) outliers. The Indian value is 7.6, the US 8.5. Most religious people are to be found in the Islamic area of West Asia/North Africa with Pakistan and Indonesia, score 9.45, in Sub-Saharan Africa (9.4) and Latin America (9.1). Southeast Asian Philippines is one of the most religious countries of the world, scoring 9.6 in the World Value Survey 1995–2000.

The Atlantic divide between American religiosity—with 70 per cent of the population believing in religious miracles (as opposed to a third in Britain, France, and Germany, Talavera, 2002:278), and a largely secular Europe is a noteworthy point against the notion of one "West". Interestingly enough, Western Europe includes a value scepticism with respect to science as well (Therborn, 1995:276).

In contrast to Christianity, Islam, and Buddhism, Hinduism is not a universalistic religion, but Indian mystical philosophy and life-views have made a significant contribution to global "New Age" culture. Peter Berger (2002:13–14) has argued that this, together with Buddhist inputs, has been "the most important cultural influence coming from Asia into the West".

The reach of "Asian values" is probably limited, a discourse brought forward mainly from the small Southeast Asian countries of Singapore and Malaysia. Even in the Southeast Asian region their existence is controversial. The former Thai Foreign Minister and ASEAN chairman Surin Pitsuwan (2001:9) said bluntly: "The European Union certainly has common values, and simply we don't", referring to ASEAN. However, the argument about "Asian values" is noteworthy and interesting.

A succinct formulation of these [East] Asian Values has been made by the senior Singaporean diplomat Tommy Koh (1993), listing the values which have "enabled East Asia to achieve economic prosperity, progress, harmonious relations between citizens, and law and order". The ten may be grouped into three clusters. One refers to family: "East Asians believe in strong families"; and not in "extreme forms of individualism"; and they "want their governments to maintain a morally whole environment in which to bring up their children". Another cluster refers to personal behaviour: "East Asians revere education"; "consider hard work a virtue"; and "believe in the virtues of saving and frugality". A third cluster comprises state-citizens relations: "There is an Asian version of a social contract between the people and the state. Governments have an obligation to treat their people with fairness and humanity. Citizens are expected to be law-abiding, respect those in authority, work hard, save and motivate their children to learn and be self-reliant"; "national team-work" of "government, business and employees". Two more values of this third cluster are more specific, referring to only parts of the region: "Good governments in Asia want a free press", but "the press must act responsibly"; "In some Asian countries, governments have sought to make every citizen a stakeholder in the country."

Few Europeans who have thought about values would find that list unfamiliar. But they would probably locate them in 19th rather than 20th/21th-century Europe. To Britons, Koh's Asian values are likely to sound Victorian, in France they might remind of Moderate Republicanism, but perhaps they most of all resemble the hegemonic values of late 19th century Germany.

But 20th century experiences, traumatic as well as positive, have led to new mutations of European values. We may compare Koh's list with a recent formulation of European values by two distinguished European social philosophers, Jacques Derrida and Jürgen Habermas (2003), Habermas being the main author. The two value sets are not formulated in the same manner, that by Habermas and Derrida is more discursive, and does not quite make up a list, and it is presented as "candidate" "key words" to the European "postwar mentality". Nevertheless a juxtaposition may be worth while.

The state is religiously neutral and within civil society, religion has "a non-political position".

Politics is a positive value in Europe, deriving from the French Revolution, and includes a confidence in the "civilizing formative power of a state", as a correction of "market failures".

The European party system is an "ideological competition", between conservative, liberal, and socialist interpretations of the world.

"Collective action" is held necessary in order to achieve more social justice.

A "self-critical confrontation" with its own horrible past, first of all the Nazi genocide of European Jewry, and the widespread collusion in it, has led to a high "sensibility against violations of personal and bodily integrity".

Their imperial past and even more their loss of imperial power have given European powers an opportunity to keep a "reflexive distance to themselves".

Contemporary East Asians and the secularists of South and Western Asia would probably have little difficulty in subscribing to the first two, more general "keywords". Competitive electoral Asian polities tend to have different cleavages than European ones, and the ideological profiles of Asian parties may sometimes be more vague as compared to those in Europe, but there seems to be no continental divide in this respect. Collective action is part of Asian Socialist, Communist, and socially concerned religious traditions, like in Europe.

What is distinctively European in the Habermas-Derrida enumeration seems to be the European lessons of World War II and its loss of colonial rule, that is, values derived from recent, specific experiences, although it is true that Japan seems to have learnt less from its loss of empire. Rather than from Asia, what Habermas and Derrida imply, deliberately or not, is a European distance from "the West".

Symbolic Forms: Art, Entertainment, Styles, and Brand Icons

In their manifestations in art, architecture, and etiquette, symbolic forms have roots in the pre-modern cultures of civilizations as well as in national and local modern cultures. But since the advent of modernism, in the heyday of European imperialism, in the decades around 1900, there is increasingly a world system of art and all kinds of aesthetic symbolic forms, with its centres, models, and hierarchies. This is even more the case with the more cent symbolic manifestations of mass culture, of film and television programmes, popular music, sports, and stylish consumption. High culture, in the form of spectacular architecture and top-quality institutions for performing arts, has become a major instrument of global urban competition for prestige attraction and tourist money.

High culture is largely multipolar, and is probably less centralized than in the first three-fourths of the 20th century. Paris has lost much of previous centrality, although remaining an art centre of the world, in literature (Casanova, 1999) as well as in painting and sculpture. London is a more important centre of publishing. An amateur impression is that New York, which in the 1940s succeeded Paris as the first centre of painting, is no longer that outstanding, although clearly still a major pole of the art world. Mid-century Euro-American "International Style" of architecture has been followed by a more varied architectural elite taste and production, in which Asian architects have a very high profile, while the International Style always had an important competitor in Latin American Modernism, Brazilian in particular.

Film is a good illustrator of the multipolarity of high culture and the heavy concentration of mass culture. Art film of world acclaim has always been produced in a number of countries, from Sweden and Denmark to Japan, from India to Brazil. For more than a decade, the world elite have been applauding the rise of Chinese cinema, of Zhang Yimou, Chen Kaige, and others. On the other hand, the world has only three net exporters of film, the US, India, and China, and while Indian and Chinese export markets are concentrated in parts of Asia and Africa, American films are dominating globally. The global blockbusters are virtually all Hollywood productions.

The world music industry is concentrated in a handful of corporations, but with different geographical origins, Western European EMI, Universal, BMG, Japanese Sony Music, and American Time-Warner (cf. Ferreira Moura Mendonca, 2002).

However, alongside global mass culture, there are also significant regional variants, with regional centres, like Britain in Europe, Egypt in West Asia, India in South Asia. In East Asia there is Japan—although Korea and Taiwan both tried to prohibit the entry of Japanese culture until recently—but the region also produces non-Japanese transnational stars, for instance Korean into Vietnam or Taiwanese into mainland China (Aoki, 2002; Hsiao, 2002; Thomas, 2002). Among the world's 100 most valued commercial brands, 62 are American—eight of the top ten of which include the first five Coca Cola, Microsoft, IBM, GE, and Intel. Regionally speaking,

63 brands are North American (including ex-Cuban Bacardi in Bermuda, no Canadian), 29 are Western European, and 8 are Northeast Asian. No other region of the world has managed to launch any world brand of comparable value. The ranking by *Business Week* (4 August 2003) is based on estimates of sales value, and include some brands which make global sense mainly to business culture, like GE or Citibank, but most are consumer brands.

Hegemony—and Its Constraints

The power structure of the world cultural system may be summed up in two words, hegemony and multi-polarity.

Economic development or growth, with its increasingly expected and estimated discretionary mass consumption, seem to be the predominant human aspirations by far. That is an old modernist striving, which at least on a global scale does not seem to have been weakened by "post-materialism" or "post-modernism". On the contrary, it now stands out more clearly, as it is for the time being little bothered by rival projects of development. World market-oriented capitalism, or "market economy", has no longer any serious competitor. The success of this strategy in East Asia, the final failure of Communist economics—in Asia as well as in Europe—, and the exhaustion of inward-oriented capitalism in South Asia and Latin America settled the issue, for the time being.

Economic wealth and consumption style then naturally become central elements of cultural hegemony in the world. The location of this hegemony is well known—in the United States. The US is the world's wealthiest nation, which neither Western Europe nor Japan have managed to approximate after their impressive post-World War II recovery. US capitalism pioneered consumerism as a mass culture, and the great majority of the world's best known brands of consumer goods are American as we noticed above. Nokia and Mercedes are the only non-American among the world's top ten brands. World popular entertainment is US-centred—in film, TV, music. The attempt of Japanese capital to buy itself into American cultural production failed (Jameson, 1998:67), though it is keeping an edge in electronic games.

The hegemonic language of the world cultural system is English, after World War II and the surge of American power, definitely superseding French as the main language of international diplomacy and information. However, it is important to take notice of the limitations of this hegemony. US cultural domination is in no way comparable to its military might. The world cultural system is in fact rather multipolar, even though the American pole is far bigger, with a much stronger radiance than the others.

There are two significant counter-hegemonic forces which place limits on hegemonic influence. Militant Islamism is one, concerned with *shari'a* and the community of believers rather than with economic development. Secular humanism is the other producing protagonists of sustainable development instead of accumulation and consumerism, militants of peace and human rights. Both are important worldwide forces, although with heavy regional accents—Islamism of Western Asia, from Pakistan westwards into north-western Africa and secular humanism of Western Europe. Neither has a project of political and economic institutions concrete enough to be credible. As they appeal to very different social milieux, they are hardly competitors, but their lack of institutionality also precludes tactical anti-hegemonic alliances.

More constraints and limitations of US hegemony come from what we may call "regional reservations". These cultures of regional reservations do not openly confront the hegemon. The latter's global dominance is accepted with varying mélanges of respect and resignation. But a regional culture affirms itself in its own region. This holds for cultures of political economy as well as for mass cultures of entertainment. Among the continental countries of the EU, for instance, it is a mainstream—if by no means unanimous—opinion that the European "social market economy" or welfare state capitalism is preferable to the American variant of capitalism. Similar views, with respect to Asian socio-economic arrangements, are very widespread and respectable in Asia, not the least in the most successful Northeast and Southeast Asian countries. The American, big money-driven form of democracy has probably more critics than admirers in the world.

Mass culture and entertainment have strong regional centres, such as Japan, Hong Kong and Taiwan in East Asia, Indian Bollywood in South Asia (although challenged within India by southern Telugu and Tamil productions) and parts of Africa; Egypt in West Asia; Britain in Western Europe; Brazil and Mexico in Latin America. The Gulf emirates of Qatar and Dubai have become the unlikely bases of alternative serious TV news journalism, through the Al-Jazeera and Al-Arabiyya broadcasters, which the US government has tried several times to silence, but so far in vain.

In sports, practitioner as well as spectator, there is hardly any US hegemony at all. What the most popular sports are varies widely among countries and regions. US athletes dominate some, and are at best secondary in others. Football, or soccer, for example, has its centres in Europe and in Latin America, with a quite modest US interest and participation. Baseball, on the other hand, is a big American sport, which arouses limited interest outside the country.

High culture is not under American hegemony, neither in the arts nor in elite fashion. *Haute couture* still has its centre in Paris, with Milan being an important location as well. The brands of luxury consumption are more likely to be European than American, like Mercedes and BMW, Louis Vuitton, Gucci or Rolex. Painting may no longer have one centre at all, which means that New York as well as Paris has lost its previous pre-eminence. Contemporary literary taste seems to be governed more from Paris and London than any US location, with Stockholm having a special niche importance as the allocator of the Nobel prizes (Casanova, 1999).

Science, on the other hand, has most of its centres in the US, although the last decades have seen a remarkable bouncing back of European social science and social thought. Something similar may very well happen rather soon in other regions, first perhaps in East and South Asia.

The world cultural system differs from the economic and politico-military systems of the world. Like culture in comparison with wealth or might, the cultural system is more complex and multi-faceted. Easily more fascinating intellectually, culture should not be taken as a veil hiding the stark features of the contemporary world, the power and privilege, the violence and the exploitation. But culture adds a third dimension to the flat field of political economy.

References

Acharya Amitav (2000) *The Quest for Identity. International Relations of Southeast Asia.* Oxford and Singapore: Oxford University Press.

Aoki, Tamotsu (2002) "Aspects of Globalization in Contemporary Japan." In Peter Berger and Samuel Huntington (eds.), *Many Globalizations*, Oxford New York: Oxford University Press.

Arnason, Johann (2003) *Civilizations in Dispute.* Leiden: Brill.

Befu, Harumi and Guichard-Anguis, Sylvie (eds.) (2001) *Globalizing Japan*. London and New York: Routledge Curzon.
Berger, Peter L. (2002) "The Cultural Dynamics of Globalization." In Peter Berger and Samuel Huntington (eds.), *Many Globalizations*, Oxford New York: Oxford University Press.
Bornschier, Volker (2002) *Weltgesellschaft*. Zürich: Loreto.
Buruma, Ian (1994) *The Wages of Guilt. Memories of War in Germany and Jaoan*. New York: Farrar, Straus & Giroux.
Business Week (2003) "The Best Global Brands." 4 August.
Casanova, Pascale (1999) *La république mondiale des letters*. Paris: Seuil.
Chantana Banpasirichote (1998) "Thailand." In Charles Morrison and Hadi Soesastro (eds.), *Domestic Adjustments to Globalization*. Tokyo: JCIE.
Chen, Kuan-Hsing (2002) "Why is 'great reconciliation' im/possible? De-Cold War/de-colonization, or modernity and its tears." I–II. *Inter-Asia Cultural Studies* 3(1) and 3(2):235–52.
Derrida, Jacques and Habermas, Jürgen (2003) *"Unsere Erneuerung. Nach dem Krieg: die Wiedergeburt Europas." Frankfurter Allgemeine Zeitung*, 31 May.
Diez-Nicolás, Juan (2003) "Two Contradictory Hypotheses on Globalization: Societal Convergence or Civilization Differentiation and Clash." In Ronald Inglehart (ed.), *Human Values and Social Change*. Leiden-Boston: Brill.
Fernández-Arnesto, Felipe (2000) *Civilizations*. London: Macmillan.
Funston, John (2000) "ASEAN and the Principle of Non-Intervention—Practice and Prospects." Working paper. Singapore: Institute of Southeast Asian Studics.
Gates, Carolyn (1999) "ASEAN's Foreign Economic Relations: An Evolutionary and Neo-Institutional Analysis." Working paper. Singapore: Institute of Southeast Asian Studics.
Hsiao, H.-H. Michael (2002) "Cultural Globalization and Localization in Contemporary Taiwan." In Peter Berger and Samuel Huntington (eds.), *Many Globalizations*. Oxford New York: Oxford University Press.
Huntington, Samuel P. (1996) *The Clash of Civilizations and the Remaking of World Order*. New York: Simon & Schuster.
Iwabuchi, Koichi (2002) *Recentering Globalization. Popular Culture and Japanese Transnationalism*. Durham NC and London: Duke University Press.
Jameson, Frederic (1998) "Notes on Globalization as a Philosophical Issue." In Frederic Jameson and Masao Miyoshi (eds.), *The Cultures of Globalization*. Durham and London: Duke University Press.
Karatani, Kojin (1993) "The Discursive Space of Modern Japan." In M. Miyoshi and H.D. Harootunian (cds.), *Japan in the World*. Durham and London: Duke University Press.
Kim, Samuel (ed.) (2000) *Korea's Globalization*. Cambridge: Cambridge University Press.
Klingemann, Hans-Dieter (1999) "Mapping Political Support in the 1990s: A Global Analysis." In Pippa Norris (ed.), *Critical Citizens. Global Support for Democratic Government*. Oxford and New York: Oxford University Press.
Koh, Tommy (1993) "The 10 Values that Undergird East Asian Strength and Success." *International Herald Tribune*. 11–12 December.
—— (2000) *Asia and Europe. Essays and Speeches by Tommy Koh*. Singapore: World Scientific Publishing.
Korhonen, Pekka (2002) "Asia's Chinese Name." *Inter-Asia Cultural Studies*, 3(2):253–70.
Kwok Kian-Woon *et al.* (eds.) (2000) *We Asians*. Singapore: Singapore Heritage Society.
Luhmann, Niklas (1997) *Die Gesellschaft der Gessellschaft*. 2 vols. Frankfurt: Suhrkamp.

Meyer, John W. (2000) "Globalization. Sources and Effects on National Societies." *International Sociology* 15(2):233–48.

Mommsen, Wolfgang J., and De Moor, J.A. (1992) *European Expansion and Law.* Oxford and New York: Berg.

Moura, Mendonca Luciana Ferreira (2002) "The Local and the Global in Popular Music *The Brazilian Music Industry, Local Culture, Public Policies.*" In Diana Crane, Nobuko Kawashima, Ken'ichi Kawasaki (eds.), *Global Culture Media, Arts, Policy, and Globalization.* New York and London: Routledge.

Münch, Richard (1986) *Die Kultur der Moderne.* 2 vols. Frankfurt: Suhrkamp.

Nisbett, Richard E. (2003) *The Geography of Thought.* London: Nicholas Brealey.

Ohmae, Kenichi (1990) *The Borderless World.* New York: Harper.

Okakura, K. (T.) (1903) *The Ideals of the East.* London: John Murray.

Pettersson, Thorleif (2003) "Individual Values and Global Governance: A Comparative Analysis of Orientations towards the United Nations." In Ronald Inglehart (ed.), *Human Values and Social Change.* Leiden-Boston: Brill.

Schepel, Harm and Blankenburg, Erhard (2001) "Mobilizing the European Court of Justice." In Gráinne de Búrca and J.H.H. Weiler (eds.), *The European Court of Justice.* Oxford: Oxford University Press.

Soesastro, Hadi (1998) "Domestic Adjustments in Four ASEAN Economies." In Charles Morrison and Hadi Soesastro (eds.), *Domestic Adjustments to Globalization.* Tokyo: JCIE.

Steiner, Henry J. and Alston, Philip (1996) *International Human Rights.* Oxford: Clarendon Press.

Surin Pitsuwan (2001) "Future Directions for ASEAN] Singapore: Institute of Southeast Asian Studies.

Talavera, Arturo Fontaine (2002) "Trends Towards Globalization in Chile." In Peter Berger and Samuel Huntington (eds.), *Many Globalizations.* Oxford New York: Oxford University Press.

Tanaka, S. (1993) *Japan's Orient.* Berkeley: University of California Press.

Tay, Simon S.C. and Estanislao, Jesus (2000) "The Relevance of ASEAN: Crisis and Change." In Simon S.C. Tay, Jesus Estanislao, Hadi Soesasatro (eds.), *A New ASEAN in a New Millennium.* Jakarta: Centre for Strategic and International Studies, and Singapore: Institute of Southeast Asian Studies.

Therborn, Göran (1992) "The Right to Vote and the Four World Routes to/through Modernity." In Rolf Torstendahl (ed.), *State Theory and State History.* London: Sage.

—— (1995) *European Modernity and Beyond. European Societies 1945–2000.* London: Sage.

—— (2000) "Globalizations. Dimensions, Historical Waves, Regional Effects, Normative Governance." *International Sociology,* 15(2):151–79.

—— (2002a) "Asia and Europe in the World: Locations in the Global Dynamics." *Inter-Asia Cultural Studies,* 3(2):287–307.

—— (2002b) "The World's Trader, The World's Lawyer." *European Journal of Social Theory,* 5(4):403–18.

—— (2003) "Dimensions and Processes of Global Inequalities." In Grazyna Skapska, Anna Maria Bukowska (eds.), *The Moral Fabric in Contemporary Societies.* Leiden: Brill.

—— (2004) *Between Sex and Power. Family in the World 1900–2000.* London: Routledge.

—— (ed.) (2006) *Inequalities of the World.* London: Verso.

Thomas, Mandy (2002) "Re-Orientations: East Asian Popular Cultures in Contemporary Vietnam." *Asian Studies Review,* 26(2):233–60.

UNCTAD (2001) *World Investment Report 2001.* New York and Geneva: United Nations.

—— (2002a) *World Investment Report 2002 Overview.* New York and Geneva: United Nations.

—— (2002b) *Trade and Development Report, 2002*. New York and Geneva: United Nations.

Wallerstein, Immanuel (1974–) *The Modern World System*. 3 vols. so far. New York: Academic Press.

Weingart, Peter (2006) "Knowledge and Inequality." In Göran Therborn (ed.), *Inequalities of the World*. London: Verso.

Wouters, J. (2000) "National Consciousness and the European Union." *Legal Issues of European Integration*, 27(1):25–74.

World Bank (2003) *World Development Report 2003*. New York: Oxford University Press.

WTO (2001) *Annual Report 2001*. Geneva: WTO.

Yunxiang Yan (2002) "State Power and Cultural Transition in China." In Peter Berger and Samuel Huntington (eds.), *Many Globalizations*. Oxford New York: Oxford University Press.

INDEX